Stitch by Stitch

Volume 10

TORSTAR BOOKS
NEW YORK · TORONTO

Stitch by Stitch

TORSTAR BOOKS INC.
300 E.42ND STREET
NEW YORK, NY 10017

Knitting and crochet abbreviations

approx = approximately
beg = begin(ning)
ch = chain(s)
cm = centimeter(s)
cont = continue(ing)
dc = double crochet
dec = decrease(e)(ing)
dtr = double triple
foll = follow(ing)
g = gram(s)
grp = group(s)
dc = half double crochet

in = inch(es)
inc = increas(e)(ing)
K = knit
oz = ounce(s)
P = purl
patt = pattern
psso = pass slipped stitch over
rem = remain(ing)
rep = repeat
RS = right side
sc = single crochet
sl = slip

sl st = slip stitch
sp = space(s)
st(s) = stitch(es)
tbl = through back of loop(s)
tog = together
tr = triple crochet
WS = wrong side
wyib = with yarn in back
wyif = with yarn in front
yd = yard(s)
yo = yarn over

A guide to the pattern sizes

		10	12	14	16	18	20
Bust	in	32½	34	36	38	40	42
	cm	83	87	92	97	102	107
Waist	in	25	26½	28	30	32	34
	cm	64	67	71	76	81	87
Hips	in	34½	36	38	40	42	44
	cm	88	92	97	102	107	112

Torstar Books also offers a range of acrylic book stands, designed to keep instructional books such as *Stitch by Stitch* open, flat and upright while leaving the hands free for practical work.

For information write to Torstar Books Inc., 300 E.42nd Street, New York, NY 10017.

Library of Congress Cataloging in Publication Data
Main entry under title:

Stitch by stitch.

Includes index.
1. Needlework. I. Torstar Books (Firm)
TT705.S74 1984   746.4   84-111
ISBN 0-920269-00-1 (set)

98765432

© Marshall Cavendish Limited 1984

Printed in Belgium

ISBN 0–920269–10–9   (Volume 10)

Contents

Crochet / COURSE 42

*Hairpin lace crochet
*Hairpin lace crochet with a single crochet at center
*Linking the strips together
*Alternative method of linking
*Linking edging
*Simple crochet edging
*Patterns for four stoles

Hairpin lace crochet

Hairpin lace crochet is an old craft which was once actually worked on a hairpin. Today hairpin looms or forks can be bought to suit all types of yarns. The resulting work was originally used as edgings and braids for linen, but as you will learn from the following courses, it has many other uses.

Hairpin lace crochet is worked on the prongs of the loom, using a crochet hook to form strips of loops. The loops are removed from the prongs and joined together either by linking the loops through each other or by working crochet panels between the loops.

Hairpin lace crochet with a single crochet at center

The hairpin loom can be used in two ways: by the method we have used here, with the bar held at the bottom, or with the bar held at the top. If the bar is held at the top, the crochet hook will have to be removed each time the loom is turned. For this sample we have used an adjustable hairpin loom set at 2in (50mm), a size F (4.00mm) hook and knitting worsted.

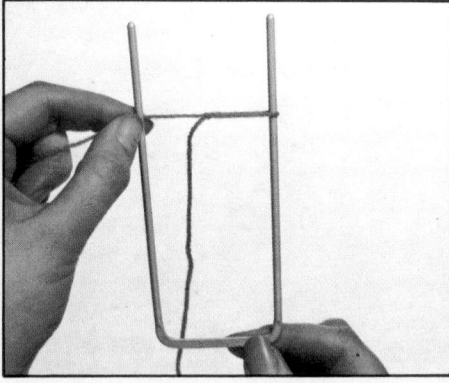

1 Make a slip knot in the yarn and place it on the right-hand prong. Draw the loop out so that the knot is centered between the two prongs and hold the yarn behind the left-hand prong with your left hand.

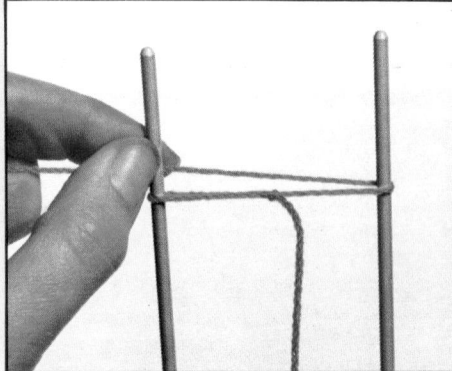

2 Turn the loom from right to left so that the yarn passes around the left-hand prong. Hold the yarn behind the loom as before.

3 Insert the crochet hook through the left-hand loop, take yarn over hook and draw a loop through. Draw yarn through loop on hook. This completes first stitch at center and there is one loop on each bar.

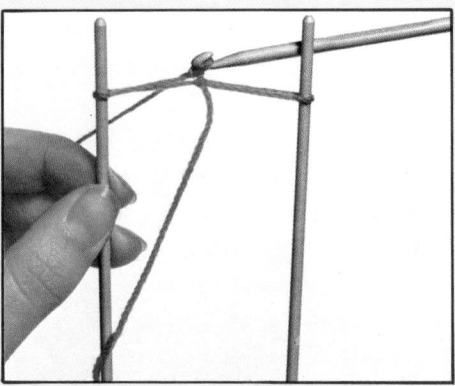

4 Keeping the loop on the hook, lift the crochet hook over the right-hand prong, so that it is behind the loom.

5 Turn the loom from right to left so that yarn passes around the left-hand prong (now at right).

Fred Mancini

4

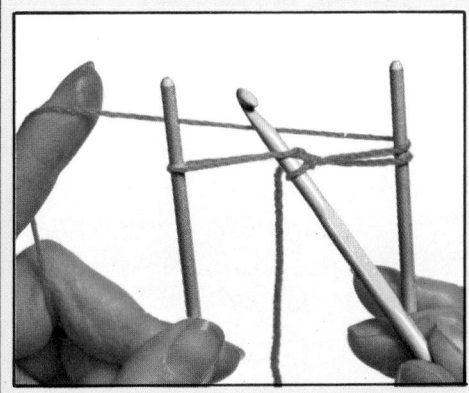

6 Insert the crochet hook into the front of the loop on left-hand prong, from front to back.

7 Take yarn over hook and draw a loop through (two loops on hook), yarn over hook and draw through both loops on hook. This completes a single crochet into loop.

8 Lift the crochet hook over the right-hand prong, then turn the loom from right to left, so that the yarn passes around the left-hand prong (now at right).

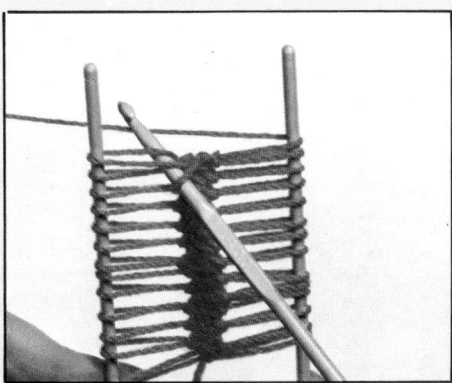

9 Repeat steps 6-8 until the loom is full. Remove the loops from the prongs, then replace the last three loops worked onto the prongs and continue to work loops.

10 When you have worked the number of loops you need, make sure you have an equal number on each prong. Cut off yarn and draw end through loop on hook.

11 An alternative way of working the single crochet at the center is to insert it under both strands of loop instead of through the loop.

Linking the strips together

The strips of loops can be joined in many ways. This is a simple method of joining in which the loops are drawn through each other to give a herringbone effect and no crochet is actually worked.

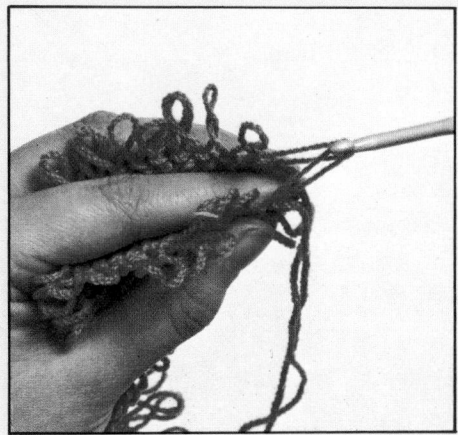

1 Make two strips of hairpin lace crochet each containing 40 loops. Hold the first strip between thumb and first finger and the second strip between second and third fingers of left hand.

2 Insert crochet hook into first loop on second strip, then into first loop on first strip (two loops on hook).

continued

3 Draw the loop of first strip through the loop of second strip to link the loops.

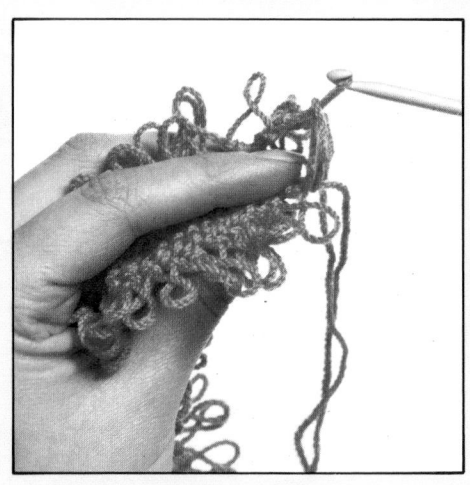

4 Insert crochet hook into next loop on second strip and draw this loop through the loop on hook (the loop of first strip).

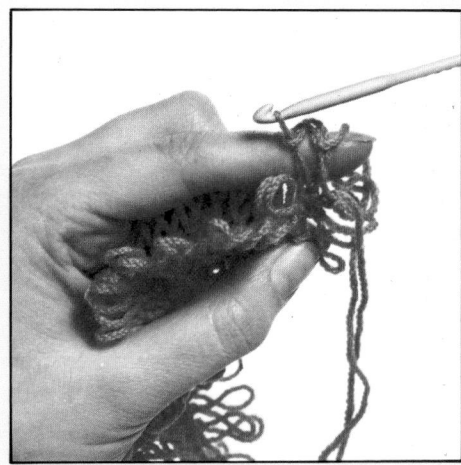

5 Insert hook into next loop of first strip and draw this loop through the loop on hook (the loop of second strip).

6 Continue to link loops this way, taking one loop from second strip, then one loop from first strip each time until all loops have been linked.

7 To anchor the last loop work a single crochet using end at center of first strip. Cut off yarn and draw end through.

8 When the strips are laid flat, you can see the herringbone effect.

9 The number of loops linked together can be varied according to the way you want the finished strip to look. In this sample two loops have been linked each time.

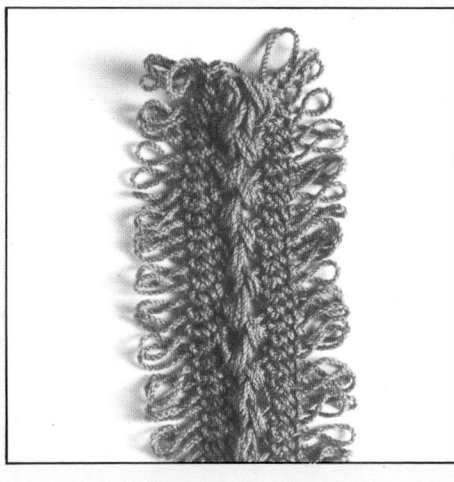

10 In this sample three loops have been linked each time.

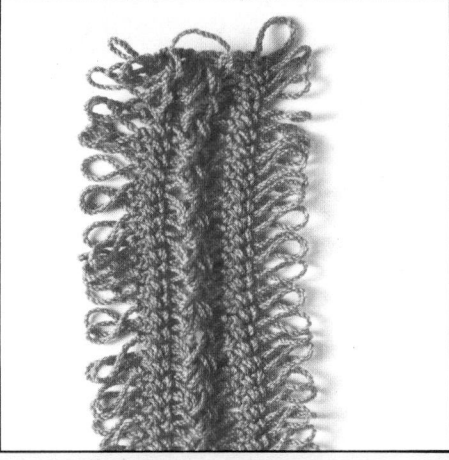

11 In this sample one, then two, loops have been linked each time.

Alternative method of linking

Loops can be linked to give a more open effect by linking from alternate strips and then from the same strip as shown here. We have linked two loops each time, but the number of loops can be varied.

1 Make two strips of hairpin lace crochet each containing 40 loops. Hold first strip between thumb and first finger and second strip between second and third fingers of left hand.

2 Insert crochet hook into first two loops on second strip, then into first two loops on first strip (four loops on hook).

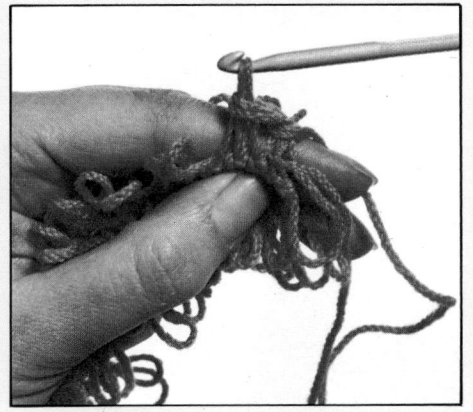

3 Draw the two loops of first strip through the two loops of second strip. Insert hook into the next two loops on first strip. Draw these two loops through first two loops on hook (four loops linked on same strip).

4 Insert crochet hook into next two loops on second strip. Draw these two loops through first two loops on hook.

5 Insert crochet hook into next two loops on second strip. Draw these two loops through first two loops on hook (four loops linked on same strip).

6 Continue linking loops in this way, taking two loops from first strip twice and then two loops from second strip twice until all loops have been linked. Anchor last two loops with a single crochet using end at center of first strip. Cut off yarn and draw end through.

7 The finished sample shows the even spacing, which makes a very attractive seam.

8 Join each additional strip to the previous strip in the same way. Here three strips have been joined together.

Fred Mancini

7

Linked edging

The linking method can be used to finish the outer strips if an edging is needed. Again a varied number of loops can be linked together.

1 Hold strip between thumb and first finger of left hand. Insert crochet hook into first four loops, draw third and fourth loops together through first and second loops.

2 Insert crochet hook into next two loops, draw these two loops through first two loops on hook.
Repeat this step until all loops have been linked. Anchor last two loops as before.

Simple crochet edging

Crochet edgings look very effective. They can be simple, like the one shown here, or more elaborate and decorative, as shown in a later course.

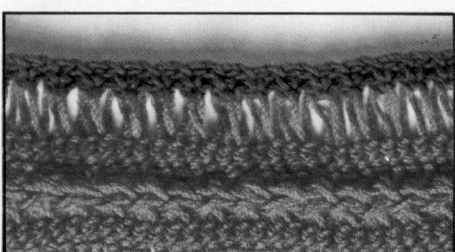

1 Join yarn to first 2 loops with a sc, *1ch, insert hook into next 2 loops and work 1sc, rep from * all along edge. Turn. To work the 2nd row, work 1 sc and 1 ch into each sc. Fasten off.

2 The finished edging produces quite a firm edge and is ideal for finishing off the lower edge of a sweater or a stole as shown on page 10.

Four stoles in hairpin lace crochet

Make these hairpin lace crochet stoles in bulky yarn, knitting worsted, sport yarn and Lurex®-mohair yarn. Ours are in shades of blue, but you could vary the colors to coordinate or contrast with your favorite outfits. Make all four and you'll have a stole for every occasion. There's a sporty stole, a smart one to wear with a suit or jacket, a delicate evening stole and an extra warm version to wear in colder weather.

Bulky-knit

Size
87×18in (220×46cm).

Materials
15oz (400g) of bulky knitting yarn
3in (80mm) hairpin loom
Sizes E and I (3.50 and 6.00mm)
crochet hooks

To make
Following steps on pages 4 and 5 work 9 strips of hairpin lace crochet, with single crochet worked into loop, each strip having 220 loops on a side. Using size I (6.00mm) crochet hook join strips tog using linking method and drawing 2 loops through each time.
Edging
Work linked edging along 2 long edges. Join yarn to outer edge and, using size E (3.50mm) hook, work * 3sc into next loop, 1sc into st at center of strip, 3sc into next loop, rep from * along edge. Fasten off. Finish other edge in same way. Darn in all ends.

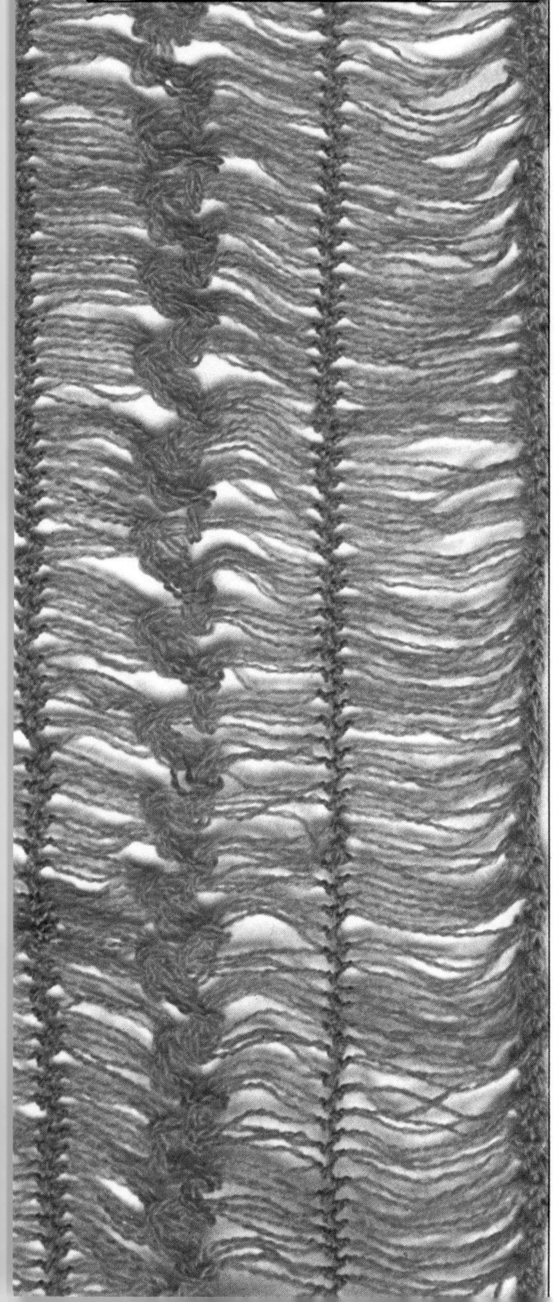

Knitting worsted

Size
87×12in (220×30cm).

Materials
9oz (250g) of a knitting worsted
3in (80mm) hairpin loom
Size E (3.50mm) crochet hook

To make
Following step-by-step guide on pages 4 and 5, work 6 strips of hairpin crochet with single crochet worked into loop, each strip having 356 loops on each side. Using size E (3.50mm) crochet hook join the strips together using the linking method and drawing 2 loops through each time.

Edging
Work linked edging along the 2 long edges. Join yarn to outer edge of one short edge and, using size E (3.50mm) hook, work *3sc into next loop, 1sc into st at center of strip, 3sc into next loop, rep from * along edge. Fasten off. Finish other edge in same way. Darn in all ends on wrong side.

Sport yarn

Size
87×12in (220×30cm).

Materials
3oz (75g) of a sport yarn
3in (80mm) hairpin loom
Size E (3.50mm) crochet hook

To make
Following step-by-step guide on pages 4 and 5 work 5 strips of hairpin lace crochet with single crochet worked into loop, each strip having 496 loops on each side.
Using size E (3.50mm) crochet hook join the strips together using the linking method and drawing 2 loops through each time.

Edging
Using size E (3.50mm) hook, join yarn to first 2 loops on one long edge with a sc, *1ch, insert hook into next 2 loops and work 1sc*, rep from * to * along edge to corner, now work along short edge thus: **6sc into next loop, 1sc into st at center of strip, 6sc into next loop **, rep from ** to ** along this edge, rep from * to * along long edge, then from ** to ** along short edge.
2nd round Work 1sc and 1ch into each sc along each long edge and 1sc into each sc along each short edge.
Fasten off.
Darn in all ends.

Mohair stole

Size
87×18in (220×46cm).

Materials
9oz (250g) of a medium-weight mohair with Lurex®
3in (80mm) hairpin loom
Size E (3.50mm) crochet hook

To make
Following step-by-step guide on pages 4 and 5, work 8 strips of hairpin lace crochet with single crochet worked into loop, each strip having 230 loops on each side. Using size E (3.50mm) crochet hook join the strips together using the linking method and drawing 2 loops through each time.

Edging
Using size E (3.50mm) hook, join yarn to first 2 loops on one long edge with a sc, *1ch, insert hook into next 2 loops and work 1sc*, rep from * to * along edge to corner, now work along short edge thus: **3sc into next loop, 1sc into st at center of strip, 3sc into next loop **, rep from ** to ** along this edge, rep from * to * along long edge, then from ** to ** along short edge.
2nd round Work 1sc and 1ch into each sc along each long edge and 1sc into each sc along each short edge.
Fasten off. Darn in all ends.

Working hairpin lace crochet with half doubles

Hairpin lace crochet can be worked with different stitches at the center of the strips. Single crochet is the stitch most often used (see page 4), but other stitches, such as half doubles and doubles, can also be used.

When half doubles and doubles are worked, the loops will be farther apart because of the height of the stitches.

A 2in (50mm) loom was used for this sample. You could use an adjustable loom set to this measurement instead.

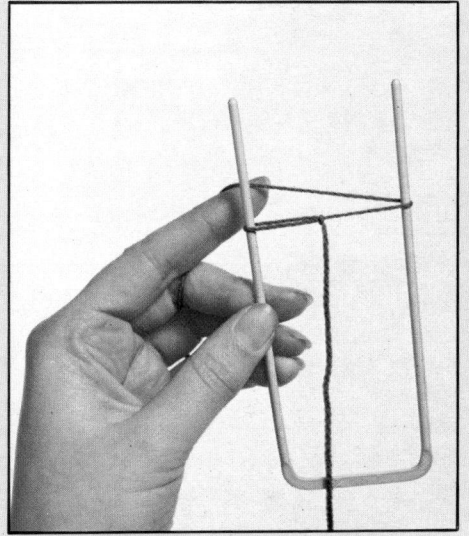

1 For this sample we have used a size F (4.00mm) crochet hook and knitting worsted. Make a slip knot and place it on the right-hand prong. Draw the loop out so the knot is centered between the prongs.

2 Turn the loom from right to left so that the yarn passes around the left-hand prong (now at right, as shown). Insert hook into the loop, yarn over hook, draw loop through and work 1 chain.

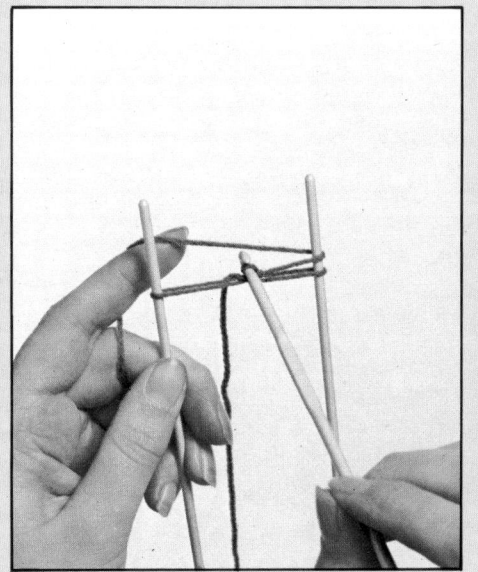

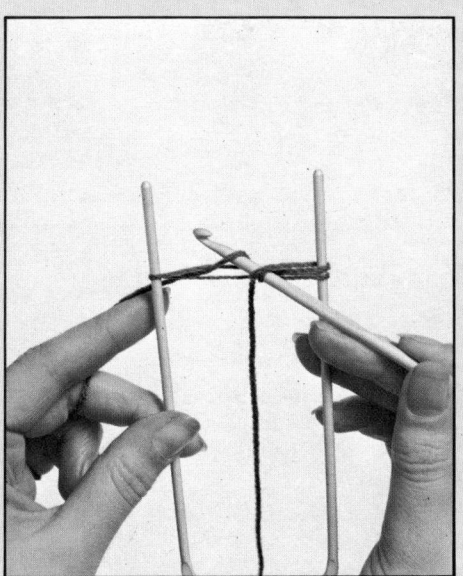

3 Keeping the loop on hook, lift hook over right-hand prong, so the hook is behind loom. Turn loom from right to left so that the yarn passes around the left-hand prong.

4 Take yarn over crochet hook, then insert crochet hook through the loop on left-hand prong.

5 Take yarn over hook and draw a loop through. There are now 3 loops on the hook.

continued

Fred Mancini

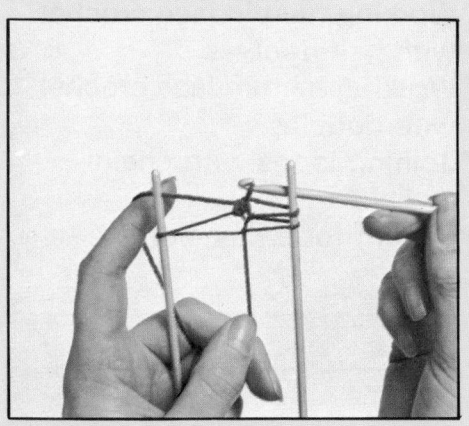

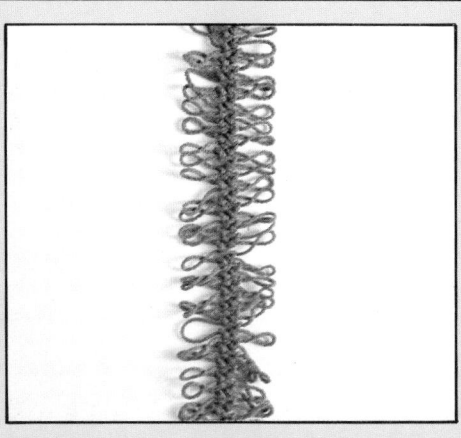

6 Take yarn over hook and draw a loop through all 3 loops on hook, forming 1 half double.

7 Repeat steps 3-6 to make a strip. When you reach the necessary length, cut off yarn, draw end through and fasten off. In the sample above, you will see that the loops are evenly spaced.

8 This sample, worked with a size B (2.50mm) hook and an adjustable hairpin loom set at 1¼in (30mm) in a fine cotton yarn with a half double at center, makes an ideal edging for bed linen.

Working hairpin lace crochet with doubles

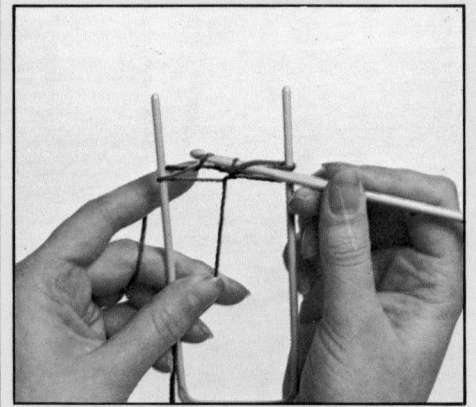

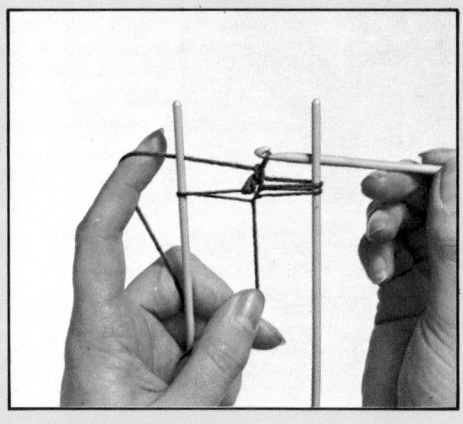

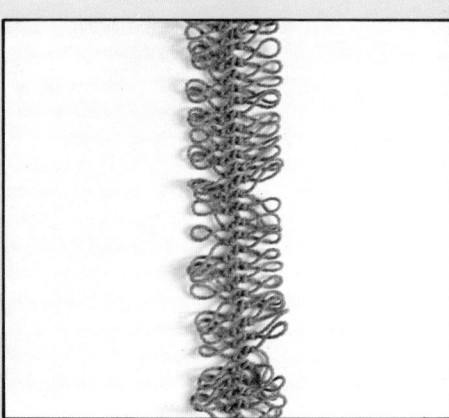

1 Follow steps 1-3 of working half doubles. Take yarn over crochet hook, then insert hook through the loop on left-hand prong. Take yarn over hook and draw a loop through. Three loops on hook.

2 Take yarn over hook and draw a loop through first 2 loops on hook, then take yarn over hook again and draw through remaining 2 loops on hook. This completes 1 double.

3 Continue to work doubles at center until you reach the necessary length. You will see from the sample above that the loops are widely spaced.

Joining loops with chain stitch

This edging forms the loops into groups. Chains are then worked between each group. This decorative method of joining looks very pretty when it is used for mats and covers such as the tray cloth on page 14.

Using a 2in (50mm)-wide hairpin loom, a size F (4.00mm) crochet hook and knitting worsted, make 4 strips of hairpin crochet with half doubles at center, each strip containing 42 loops on each side.

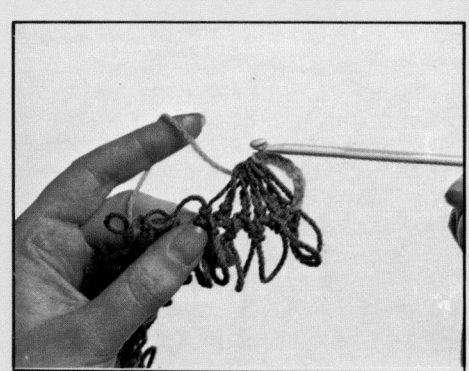

1 Taking the first strip, join yarn to first half double of strip and work 6 ch.

2 Insert hook into first 6 loops of strip, yarn over hook and draw a loop through these 6 loops and loop on hook—a slip stitch worked at top of loops.

3 Work 4 ch, then work 1 double into 6th half double at center of strip.

4 Work 4 ch, insert hook into next 6 loops of strip and work a slip stitch.

5 Now work 4 ch and then 1 double into 6th half double from last double worked.

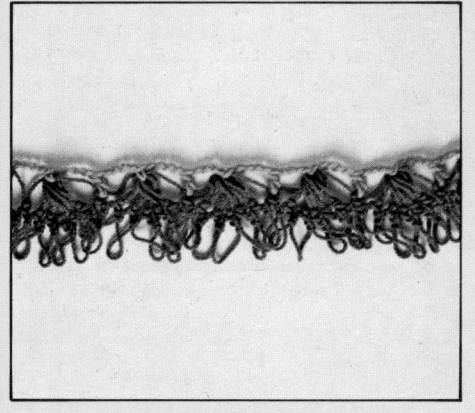

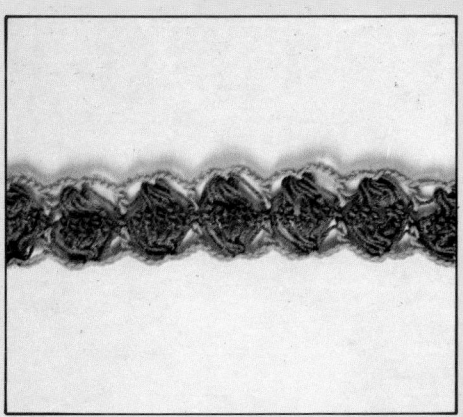

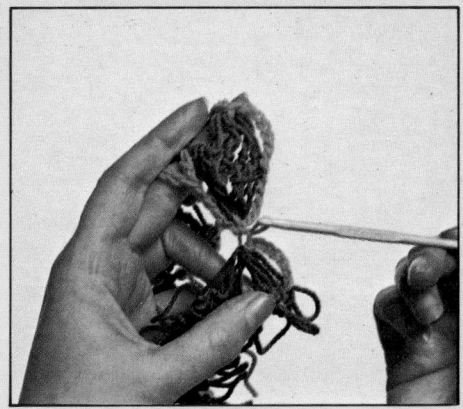

6 Repeat steps 4 and 5 until all loops have been grouped together. 6 ch, slip stitch into last half double at center of strip. This completes the first side.

7 Work along second side in the same way, beginning and ending with 6ch. Slip stitch into half double at center of strip. Fasten off.

8 Taking the second strip, join yarn to first half double of strip and work 6ch. Insert hook into first 6 loops and work a slip stitch. Insert hook into slip stitch of first group on first strip and work a slip stitch to join the groups together.

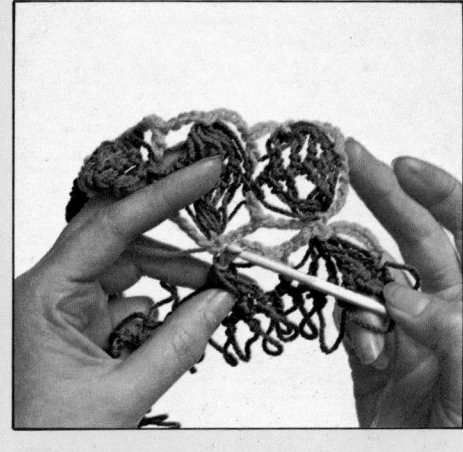

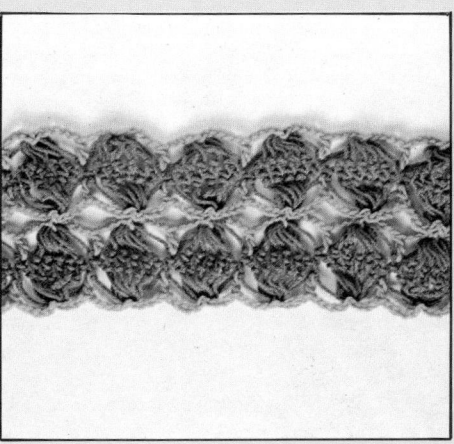

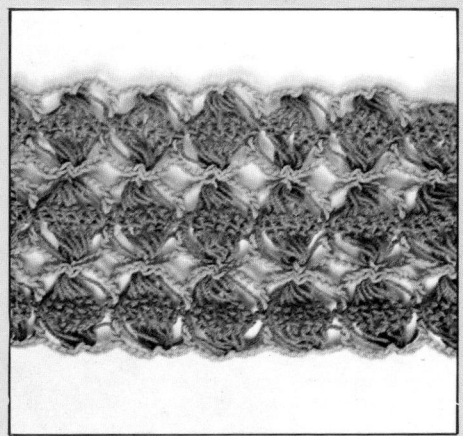

9 Work 4ch, then work 1 double into 6th half double at center of strip. Now work 4ch, insert hook into next 6 loops and work a slip stitch, insert hook into slip stitch of next group on first strip and work a slip stitch to join groups together.

10 Continue to work and join groups in this way until all loops have been joined. 6 ch, slip stitch into half double at center of strip, then continue along other side of strip as for first strip.

11 Join each additional strip in the same way, joining the first side to the previous strip and grouping the loops on the opposite side.

Fred Mancini

Tray cloth

Add a touch of class when you serve drinks or breakfast on this delicate tray cloth.

Size
20½in (52cm) x 15¾in (40cm).

Materials
4oz (100g) of a sport-weight crochet cotton makes one mat
2¼in (60mm) hairpin loom
Size E (3.50mm) crochet hook

Following the step-by-step guide on page 11, work 6 strips of hairpin lace crochet with half doubles worked into loop, each strip having 78 loops on each side. Using a size E (3.50mm) hook join the strips together with chain stitch. Darn in all ends on wrong side.

Edging
Join yarn to first hdc at center of one outside strip and using the crochet hook work *(8ch, sl st into sl st at top of group) 13 times, 8 ch, 1sc into last hdc at center of strip, now work along one short end, working (4ch, 1tr into joining sl st of 2 groups, 4ch, 1sc into hdc at center of next strip) 5 times, rep from * once more.

2nd round *1sc into each of next 3ch, 2sc into each of next 2ch, work 1sc into each st to corner ch, rep from * 3 times more, sl st into first sc.

3rd round *1sc into each of next 4sc, 2sc into each of next 2sc, 1sc into each sc to within corner, rep from * 3 times more, sl st into first sc.

4th round 2ch to count as first hdc, * 2ch, skip next 2sc, 1hdc into next sc, rep from * to end, sl st into first hdc.

5th round *1sc into next hdc, 3ch, insert hook behind sc, yo and draw a loop through both loops on hook, work 2sc into sp, rep from * to end, sl st into first sc. Fasten off.

Kim Sayer

Crochet / COURSE 44

* More joining methods
* Single crochet edging
* Double group edging
* Simple chain joining for single crochet edging
* Simple chain joining for double group edgings
* Patterns for a baby's shawl and a teenager's top

More joining methods

Strips of hairpin lace crochet can be edged before they are joined together, which produces a firmer edge for joining. In this course we show two ways to edge each side of the strips and then two ways of crocheting the strips together. Different combinations of strips, edgings and joining stitches produce a variety of effects.

The single crochet edging and simple chain joining have been used for the baby's shawl on page 18 and the double group edging and simple chain joining have been used on the teenager's top shown on page 19.

Single crochet edging

1 Using a 2in (50mm) hairpin loom (or an adjustable loom), a size F (4.00mm) hook and knitting worsted, make a strip of hairpin lace with 40 loops on each side. To work the edging make a slip knot in the yarn and place it on crochet hook.

2 Insert hook into first 2 loops on one side of strip, yarn over hook and draw a loop through the 2 loops of strip, so having 2 loops on hook.

3 Yarn over hook again and draw through the 2 loops on the hook—1 single crochet worked into the 2 loops.

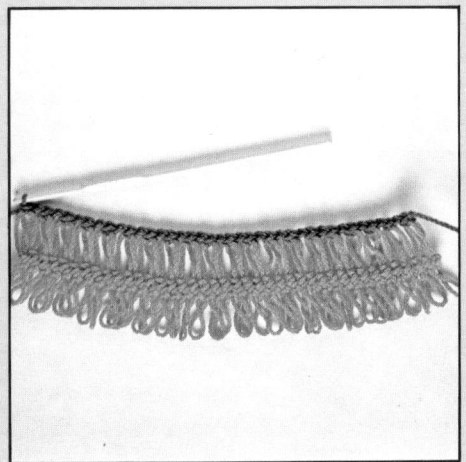

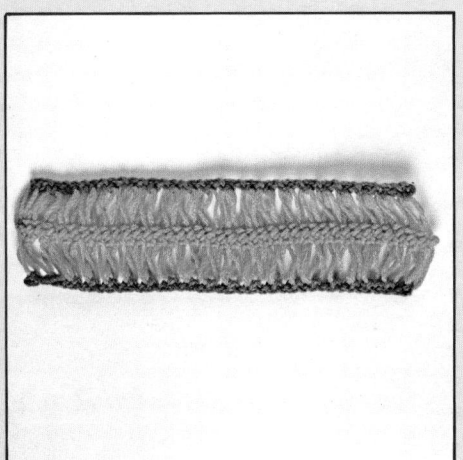

4 Work 1 chain, then insert hook into next 2 loops on strip and work 1 single crochet.

5 Repeat step 4 along first side until all loops have been worked. Cut off yarn and draw end through.

6 Work edging along the other side of strip in the same way.

Fred Mancini

Double group edging

The number of rows worked in the edging can vary according to the type of seam required. A deep edging can be worked so the strips alternate with bands of crochet, or a narrow edging can be worked and then the strips joined by a row of simple crochet, such as chains. Here are instructions for a 2-row edging.

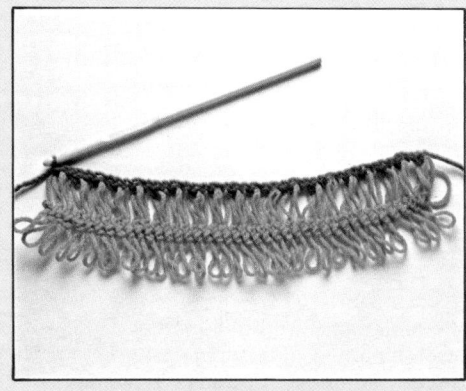

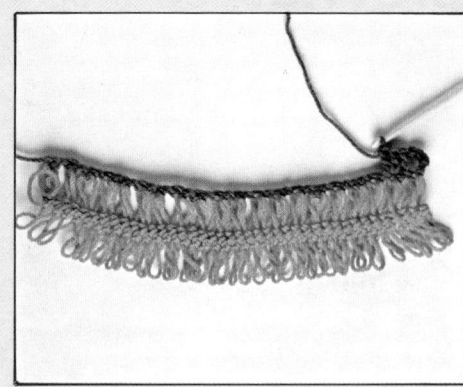

1 Using a 2in (50mm) loom (or an adjustable loom), a size F (4.00mm) hook and knitting worsted, work a strip of hairpin lace with 40 loops on each side. Work a row of single crochet edging along one side of strip; do not fasten off.

2 Turn the strip and work the 2nd row. 4ch, skip first sc, work 3dc into next sc of first row, so forming a 3-dc group.

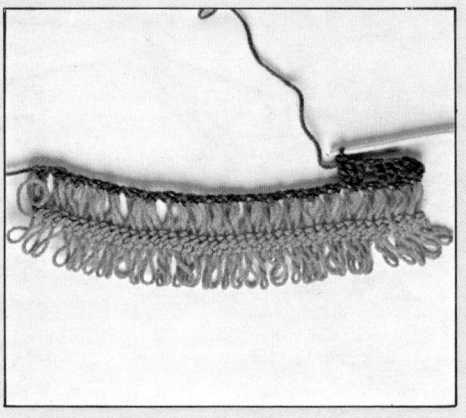

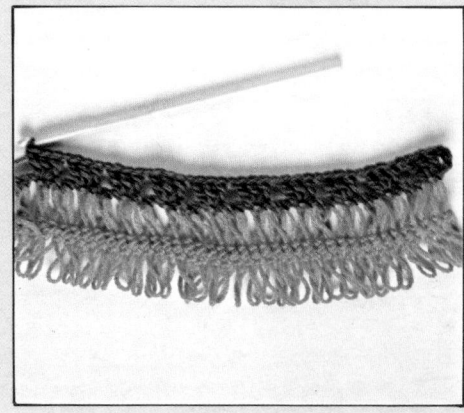

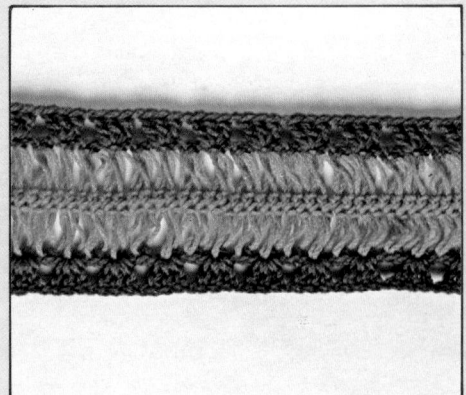

3 1ch, skip the next sc of first row, work 3dc into the next sc, so forming another 3-dc group.

4 Repeat step 3 to within last sc, work 1ch, 1dc into last sc. Cut off yarn and draw end through. First side completed.

5 Edge the remaining side of the strip in the same way.

Simple chain joining for single crochet edging

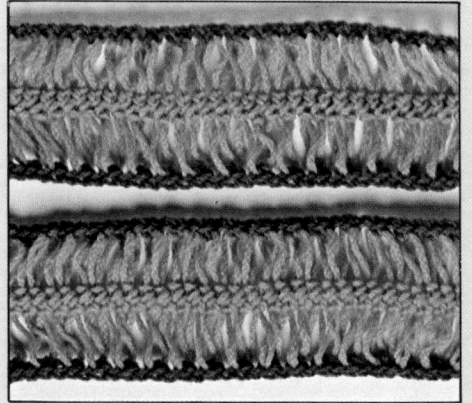

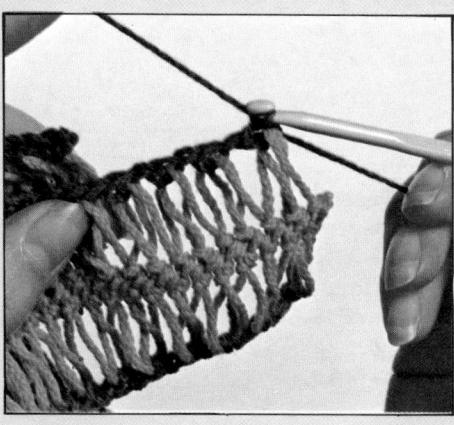

1 Follow steps 1 to 6 of single crochet edging and make 2 strips edged with single crochet.

2 Holding strips in left hand, join yarn to first sc on first strip.

3 Work 5ch, then work 1 single crochet into first single crochet on second strip.

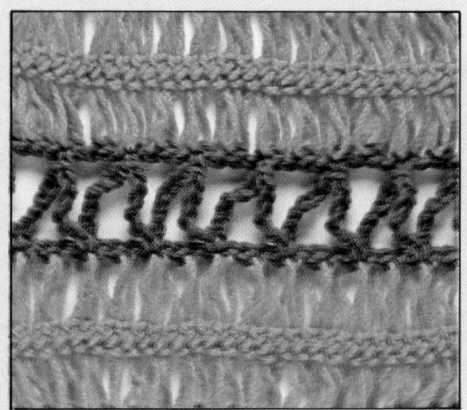

4 Work 5ch, skip next single crochet on first strip, work 1 single crochet into next single crochet on first strip.

5 Work 5ch, skip next single crochet on second strip, work 1 single crochet into next single crochet on second strip.

6 Repeat steps 4 and 5 to end of strips. Cut off yarn and draw end through.

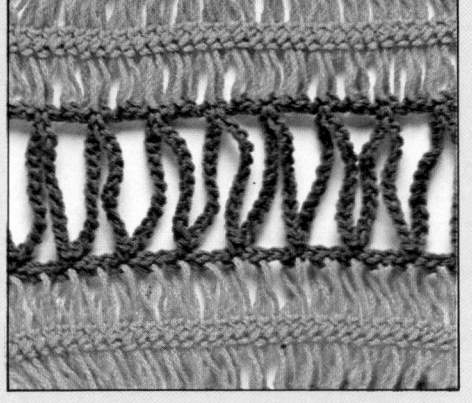

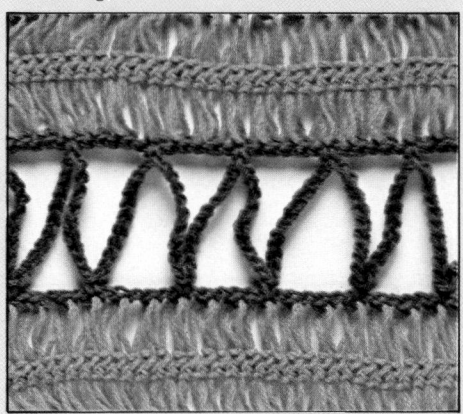

7 The number of chains worked between each strip can be varied depending on how far apart you want the strips to be. Here 10ch have been worked between strips.

8 The chains can be more widely spaced by skipping more sc between the joining chains. Here 10ch have been worked and 2sc have been skipped between each joining.

9 When joining additional strips, all odd-numbered strips begin on an odd strip and all even-numbered strips on an even strip to avoid making a diagonal shape.

Simple chain joining for double group edging

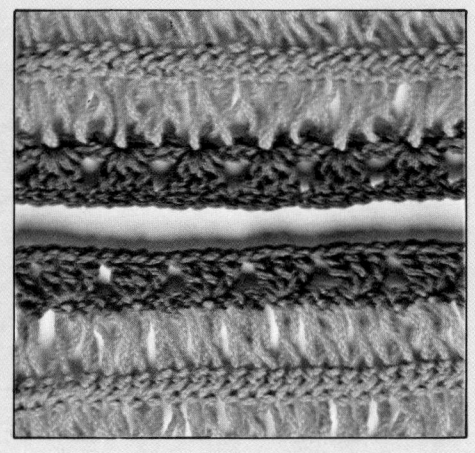

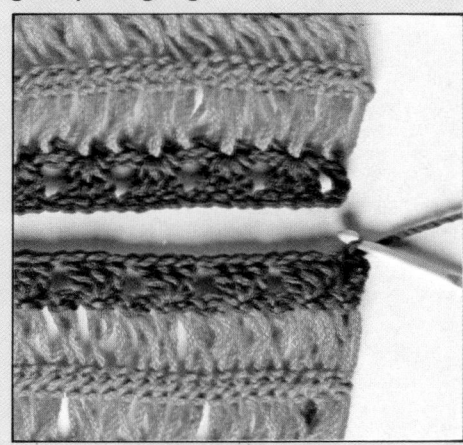

1 Follow steps 1 to 5 of double group edging and make 2 strips edged with single and double crochet.

2 Holding first strip between thumb and first finger and second strip between second and third fingers of left hand, join yarn to 4th ch of first strip with a slip stitch.

3 Work 3ch, then sl st into 1ch space on second strip.

continued

Fred Mancini

4 Work 3ch, then sl st into next 1ch space on first strip (the space between double groups).

5 Work 3ch, then sl st into next 1ch space on second strip.

6 Repeat steps 4 and 5 to end of strips. Cut off yarn and draw end through.

Baby's shawl

Crochet this pure white shawl for a new baby—it will make a welcome gift.

Victor Yuan

Size
Approx 42in (106cm) square.

Materials
13oz (350g) of a sport yarn
1in (25mm) hairpin loom
Size E (3.50mm) crochet hook

To make
Following the step-by-step guide on page 4, work 19 strips of hairpin lace crochet with single crochet worked into loop, each strip having 220 loops on each side.
Edge each side of strip with "single crochet edging," then join the strips together with "simple chain joining for single crochet edging."
Darn in all ends, then press or block according to yarn used.

Shell edging
Using size E (3.50mm) hook, join yarn to first sc, *work 1 sc into sc st, 1 sc into next 1 ch sp*, rep from * to * along first side to corner, 2ch; along second side work **(3sc into loop st) twice, 5sc into 5ch sp **, rep from ** to ** along edge finishing with (3sc into loop sp) twice, 2ch, work 3rd side as for first side and fourth side as for second side, sl st into first sc.
2nd round Work *1sc into each st along side edge to corner, (1sc, 2ch and 1sc) all into 2ch sp at corner*, rep from * to * along remaining 3 side edges, finishing sl st into first sc.
3rd round *Sl st into each of next 3sts, work 3dc into same st at 3rd sl st*, rep from * to * to corner, rep from * to * into 2ch sp at corner, finish remaining 3 side edges in the same way, finishing sl st into first sl st.
Fasten off.

Teenager's top

This lightweight mohair sweater goes well with jeans.

Sizes

To fit 30-32in (76-83cm) bust.
Length, 25½in (64cm).
Sleeve seam, 13½in (36cm).

Materials

13oz (350g) of lightweight mohair
3¼in (80mm) hairpin loom
Size F (4.00mm) crochet hook

Back and front (alike)

Foll step-by-step guide on page 4 work 3 strips of hairpin lace crochet, with single crochet worked into loop, each strip having 66 loops on each side for lower section, then work 2 strips each having 162 loops on each side for sleeve and yoke section. Edge each side of strip with "double group edging," then join the 3 strips of 66 loops together with "simple chain joining for double group edging" and 2 strips of 162 loops tog the same way.

To finish

Mark 13th ch sp from end with colored thread. Join one edge of lower section to yoke between markers, working chain loops as before. Join underarm seams with ch st as before, then join upper sleeve and shoulder seams in same way, leaving 17 sts at center free for neck.

Neck edging

Using size F (4.00mm) hook, join yarn at one side of neck and work 1sc into each st along one side of neck, work 3sc into 3ch sp, then work 1sc into each st along other side of neck, sl st into first sc.
Next round Work 1sc into each sc all around, sl st into first sc. Fasten off.

Cuffs

Using size F (4.00mm) hook, join yarn at underarm and work *2sc into 4ch sp, 2sc into 3ch sp, 2sc into next 4ch sp, 3sc into loop sp, 1sc into center st, 3sc into next loop sp*, rep from * to * around sleeve edge, sl st into first sc. Work 3 more rounds in sc. Fasten off.

Lower edging

Join side seams.
Using size F (4.00mm) hook, join yarn at one side seam and work 1sc into each dc along lower edge, sl st into first sc. Work 3 more rounds in sc. Fasten off.

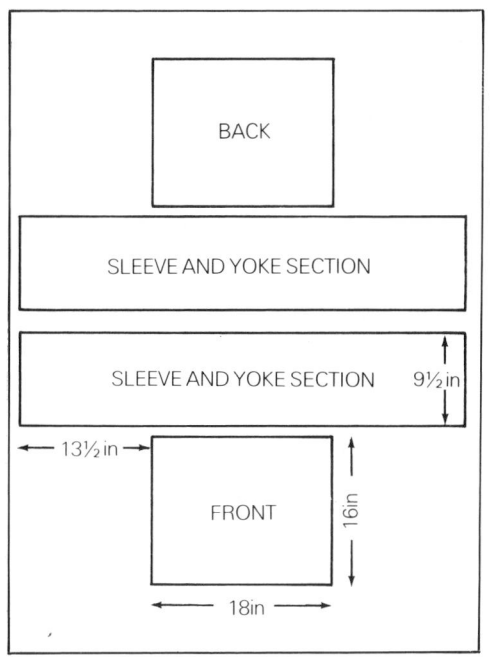

John Hutchinson

BACK

SLEEVE AND YOKE SECTION

SLEEVE AND YOKE SECTION — 9½ in

← 13½ in

FRONT — 16in

← 18in

Crochet / COURSE 45

Edging all around strips

Strips of hairpin lace crochet can be sewn or crocheted together after an edging has been worked into the loops. The edging can be simple or detailed depending on the desired effect.

When the strips are edged and joined together, they are ideal for patchwork designs, such as the child's tunic shown on the right.

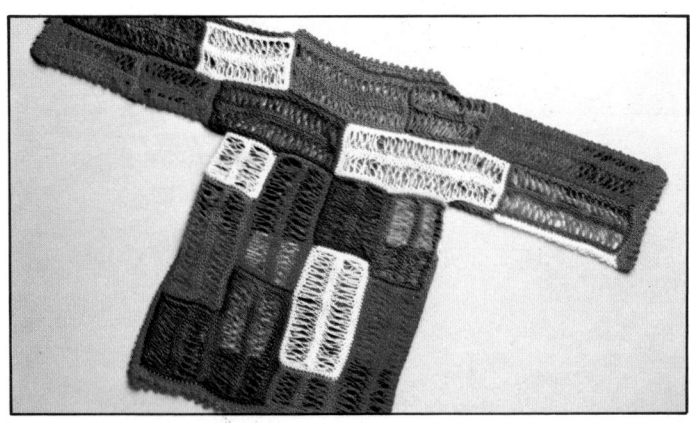

Single crochet and chain edging

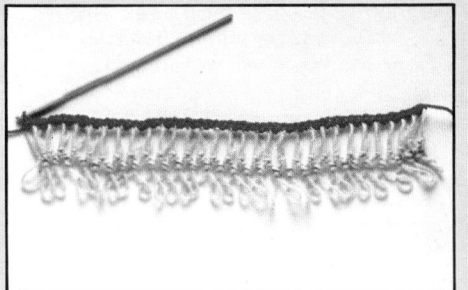
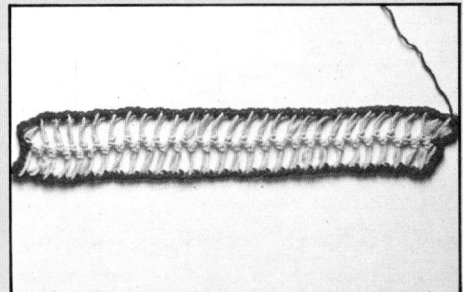
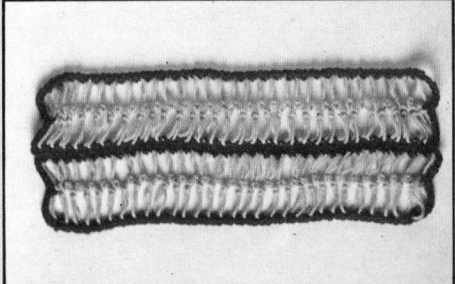

1 Work a strip of hairpin lace crochet with 30 loops on each side. Join yarn to first loop on one side of strip with a sc and work *1 ch, 1 sc into next loop, rep from * to end of strip.

2 Work 6 ch, then work 1 sc into st at center of strip, 6 ch, *1 sc into next loop on other side of strip, 1 ch, rep from * to end of strip, 6 ch, 1 sc into st at center of strip, 6 ch, sl st into first sc. Fasten off.

3 Here two strips of hairpin lace crochet have been edged and then sewn together by overcasting.

Double block edging

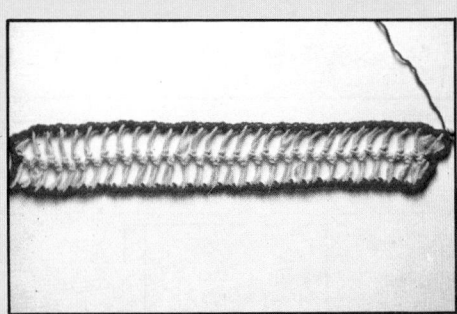
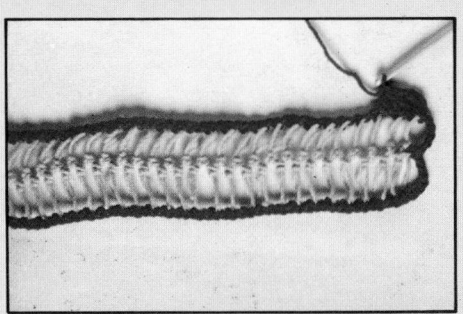
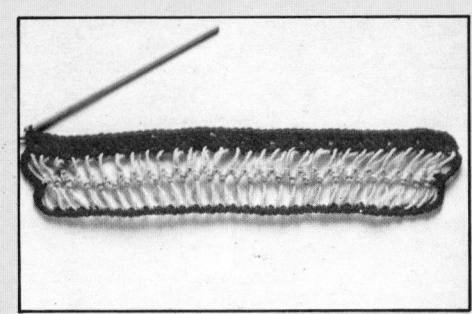

1 Work the first round as for single crochet and chain edging, but do not fasten off.

2 Second round: work 4 ch to count as first dc and 1 ch sp, skip first ch, work 1 dc into each of next 3 sts (1 sp and 1 block formed).

3 *1 ch, skip next ch, 1 dc into each of next 3 sts, rep from * along first side to within last ch and sc, 1 ch, 1 dc into last sc.

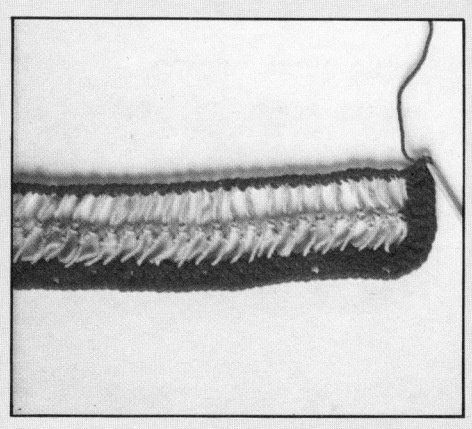

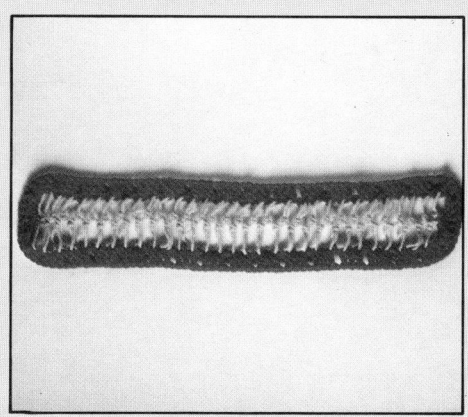

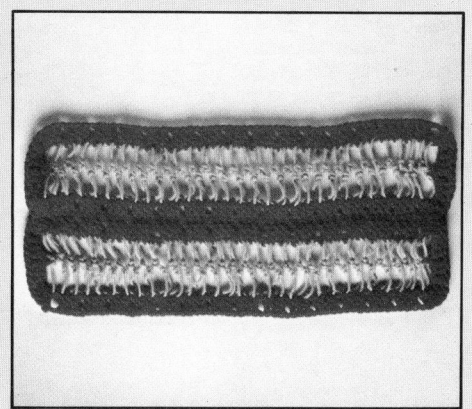

4 Work 1 dc into each of next 2 ch at end of strip, 1 ch, skip next ch, 1 dc into each of next 3 ch, 1 ch, skip next sc, 1 dc into each of next 3 ch, 1 ch, skip next ch, 1 dc into each of next 2 ch.

5 Work 1 dc into first sc on second side, then repeat steps 3 and 4 along remaining sides of strip, sl st into 3rd of the 4 ch. Fasten off.

6 Here two strips of hairpin lace crochet have been edged and then sewn together by overcasting.

Chain group edging

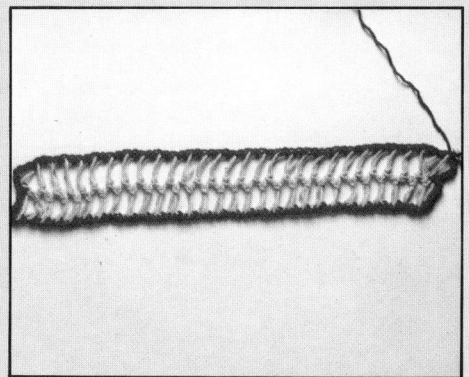

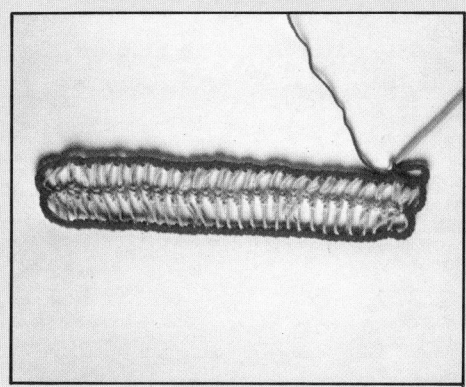

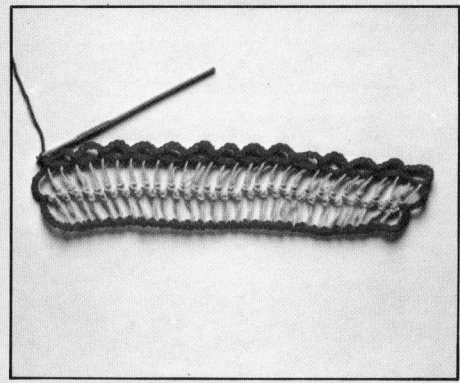

1 Work the first round as for single crochet and chain edging, but do not fasten off.

2 To work the second round, work 7 ch to count as first sc and 5 ch loop, skip next sc, 1 sc into next sc.

3 *5 ch, skip next sc, 1 sc into next sc, rep from * to end of strip.

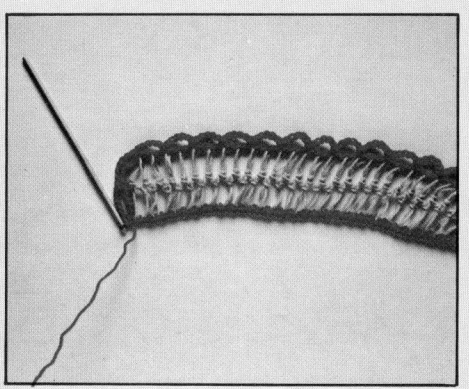

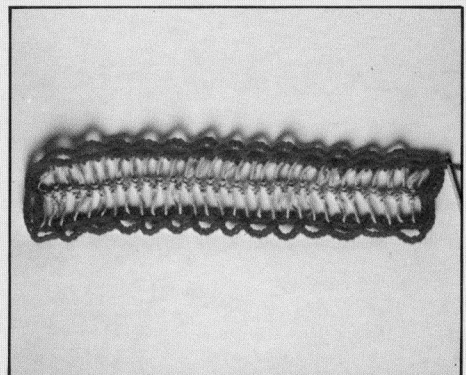

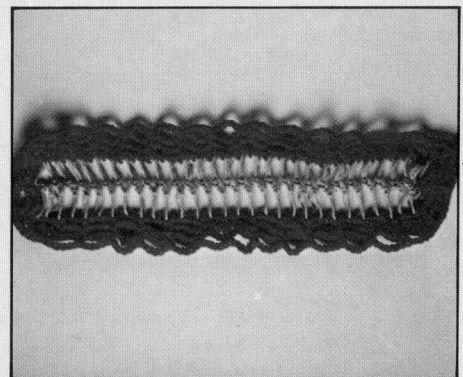

4 5 ch, 1 sc into sc at end of strip, 5 ch, 1 sc into first sc on second side of strip.

5 Now repeat steps 3 and 4 along remaining 2 sides, sl st into 2nd of the 7 ch.

6 To work the next round, work 7 ch to count as first sc and 5 ch loop, 1 sc into next sc, *5 ch, 1 sc into next sc, rep from * all around strip, sl st into 2nd of 7 ch. Repeat this round once more, so that there are now three 5 ch loops in each group.

continued

21

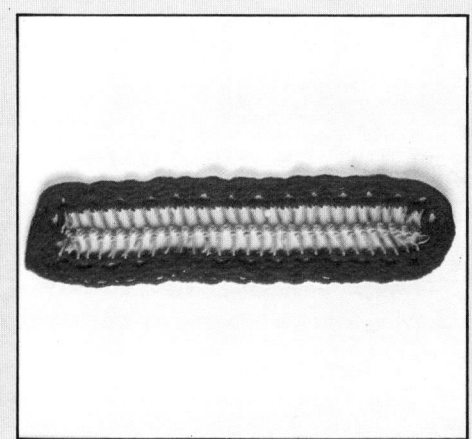

7 On the 5th round the loops are linked together. Work 4ch, yo, insert hook under the first ch loop from front to back and work 1 hdc.

8 Now work 2ch, 1sc into next sc, *2ch, link next 3 loops together with 1hdc as before, 2ch, 1sc into next sc, rep from * all around strip, sl st into 2nd of 4ch. Fasten off.

9 Here two strips of hairpin lace crochet have been edged and then sewn together by overcasting.

Joining the edged strips with crochet

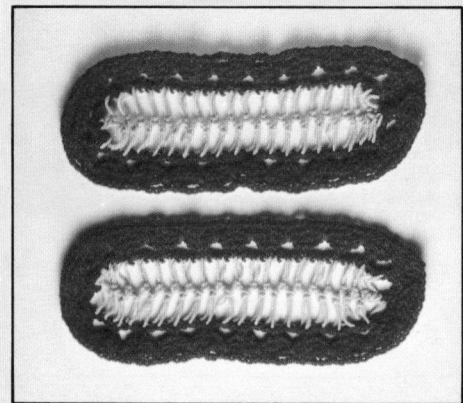

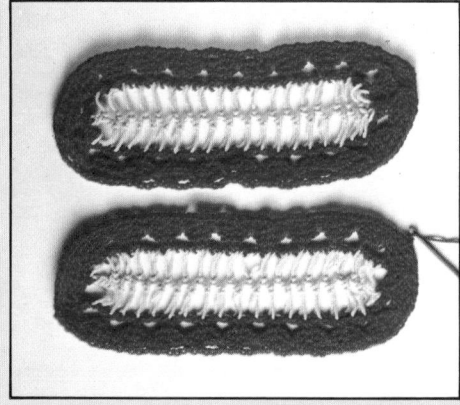

1 Work two strips with chain group edging. When joining the strips, hold both strips in your left hand, keeping the strips apart with your index finger.

2 Using the crochet hook, join yarn to first 1 ch sp on first strip with a slip stitch. 2ch.

3 Work 1sc into first 1 ch sp on second strip, 2ch, then work 1sc into next 1 ch sp on first strip.

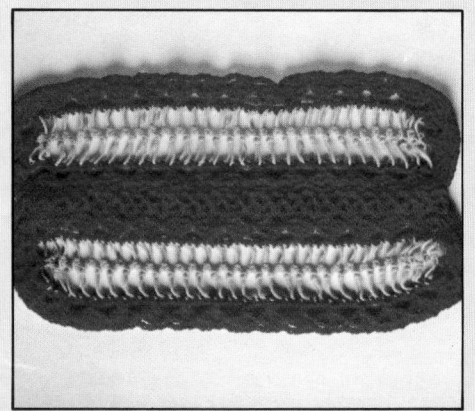

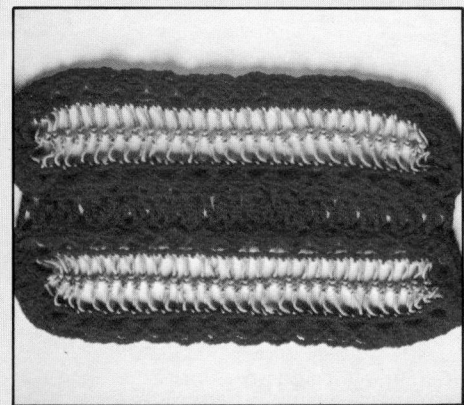

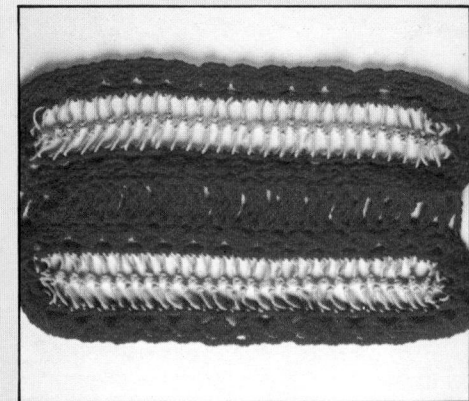

4 Repeat step 3 until all sps have been joined. Fasten off.

5 The more chains worked between the strips the farther apart the strips will become. Here 4ch have been worked.

6 In this sample 6ch have been worked between strips.

Summer tops for children

The versatility of hairpin lace crochet is illustrated by these three children's tops: a casual tunic to wear on the beach, and two lacy vests—one long, one short.

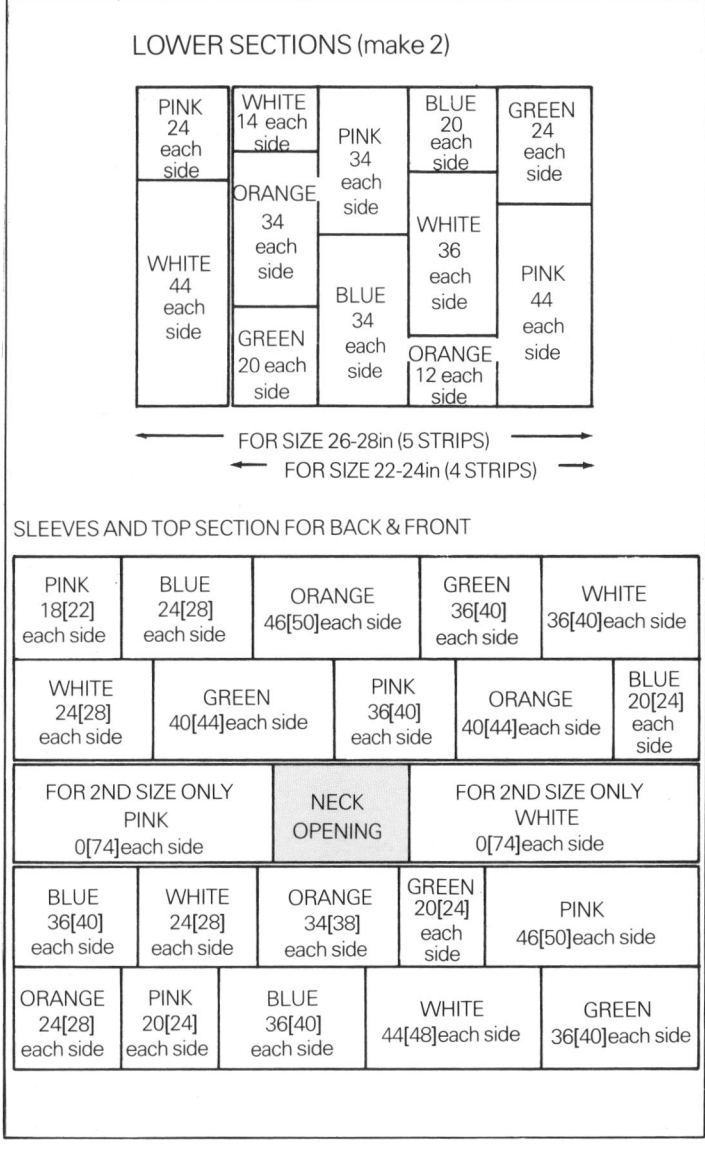

LOWER SECTIONS (make 2)

PINK 24 each side	WHITE 14 each side	PINK 34 each side	BLUE 20 each side	GREEN 24 each side
	ORANGE 34 each side		WHITE 36 each side	
WHITE 44 each side		BLUE 34 each side		PINK 44 each side
	GREEN 20 each side		ORANGE 12 each side	

← FOR SIZE 26-28in (5 STRIPS) →
← FOR SIZE 22-24in (4 STRIPS) →

SLEEVES AND TOP SECTION FOR BACK & FRONT

PINK 18[22] each side	BLUE 24[28] each side	ORANGE 46[50] each side	GREEN 36[40] each side	WHITE 36[40] each side
WHITE 24[28] each side	GREEN 40[44] each side	PINK 36[40] each side	ORANGE 40[44] each side	BLUE 20[24] each side
FOR 2ND SIZE ONLY PINK 0[74] each side		NECK OPENING	FOR 2ND SIZE ONLY WHITE 0[74] each side	
BLUE 36[40] each side	WHITE 24[28] each side	ORANGE 34[38] each side	GREEN 20[24] each side	PINK 46[50] each side
ORANGE 24[28] each side	PINK 20[24] each side	BLUE 36[40] each side	WHITE 44[48] each side	GREEN 36[40] each side

John Hutchinson

Tunic top

Sizes
To fit 22-24[26-28]in (56-61[66-71]cm) chest.
Length, 18[20]in (46[51]cm).
Sleeve seam, 9½[10¼]in (24[26]cm).

Note Directions for larger size are in brackets [], where there is only one set of figures it applies to both sizes.

Materials
2[4]oz (50[100]g) of a medium-weight mercerized crochet cotton in orange
1 ball in each of green, blue, white and pink
2¼in (60mm) hairpin loom
Size E (3.50mm) crochet hook

To make
Following diagram for number of loops required for each strip, work strips of hairpin lace crochet with half doubles at center. Edge each strip with single crochet and chain edging. Sew in all ends, then join strips tog by overcasting, foll positions on diagram. For 1st size only leave 8in (20cm) open at center for neck and for 2nd size only leave square neck opening as shown on diagram.

Edging
Using Size E (3.50mm) hook, join yarn to side seam at lower edge and work 1sc into each st around lower edge.
Next round Work 1sc into each st to end, sl st into first sc.
Next round 1sc into first st, 3ch, insert hook behind sc, yo and draw yarn through and work a sl st, 1sc into each of next 2sts, 3ch, insert hook behind last sc, yo, draw yarn through and work a sl st, cont in this way around lower edge, sl st into first sc. Fasten off.
Finish sleeves and neck edge the same way.

Lacy vests

Short vest

Sizes
To fit 22-24[26-28]in (56-61[66-71]cm) chest.
Length, 12¼[14¼]in (31[36]cm).
Note Directions for the larger size are in brackets []; where there is only one set of figures it applies to both sizes.

Materials
2[4]oz (50[100]g) of a sport yarn
1st size only 2¼in (60mm) hairpin loom
2nd size only 3¼in (80mm) hairpin loom
Size E (3.50mm) crochet hook

To make
Using a 2¼in [3¼in] (60[80]mm) loom and size E (3.50mm) hook work 8 strips of hairpin lace crochet with sc at center having 62[74] loops on each side of strip. Edge each strip with hdc and ch edging, then join 4 strips tog for back and 2 strips tog for each front working crochet as shown in steps on page 22, having 2ch between strips. Join each front to back leaving 4¾[5½]in (12[14]cm) open for armholes.

Shoulders
Join yarn to armhole edge of back, 2ch, (skip next st, 1hdc into next st) 10[11] times. Fasten off. Work front to match but begin at front edge. Crochet shoulder tog as for strips. Work other shoulder the same way.

Lower edge
Join yarn to front at lower edge and work 2ch, (skip next st, 1hdc into next st) all along lower edge. Fasten off.

Neck edge
Join yarn to front at neck edge and work as for lower edge.

Front edge
Join yarn to front edge at lower edge and work (1sc into next 1ch sp, 1 ch) all around outer edge. Fasten off.

Sleeve edges
Join yarn to armhole edge and work as for front edge.

Ties (make 2)
Using size E (3.50mm) hook and yarn double, join yarn to 12th[18th] 1 ch sp from neck on one front and work 40ch. Fasten off.

Long vest

Sizes
To fit 22-24[26-28]in (56-61[66-71]cm) chest.
Length, 18[20]in (46[51]cm).

Note Directions for larger size are in brackets []; where there is only one set of figures it applies to both sizes.

Materials
4oz (100g) of a sport yarn
1st size only 2¼in (60mm) hairpin loom
2nd size only 3¼in (80mm) hairpin loom
Size E (3.50mm) crochet hook

To make
Using a 2¼in [3¼in] (60[80]mm) loom and size E (3.50mm) hook work 8 strips of hairpin lace crochet with sc at center, having 88[100] loops on each side of strip.
Work as for short vest to end.

Crochet / COURSE 46

Shaping in hairpin lace crochet

Most items that are made in hairpin lace crochet are worked with straight strips, making shaping unnecessary. It is easy to shape hairpin lace crochet, either by the linking method or with detailed crochet stitches—both shown in this course. Here we show how to shape at the ends of strips and also how to shape across a row. Shaping across a row makes it possible for circular designs to be worked.

The smock on page 29 has a shaped yoke produced by working various lengths of hairpin lace crochet and then joining them together so that the smaller strip fits around the neck.

Shaping at the ends by linking strips

In this method, decreases are worked only at the ends of the strips, producing diagonal edges while leaving the rows straight.
For this sample we have worked 4 strips of hairpin lace crochet. The first strip has 40 loops on each side, the second strip has 36 loops on each side, the third strip has 32 loops on each side and the fourth strip has 28 loops on each side.

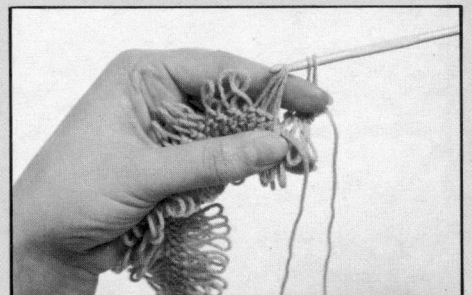

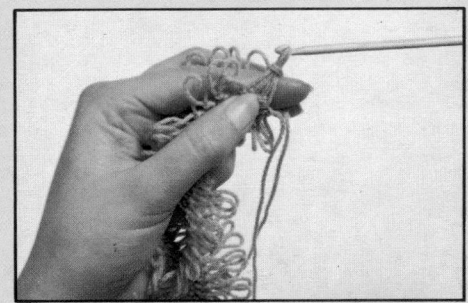

1 Hold the first strip between your thumb and first finger and the second strip between second and third fingers of left hand. Insert crochet hook into first 2 loops on second strip and first 3 loops on first strip.

2 Draw the 3 loops of first strip through the 2 loops of second strip. A decrease has been made.

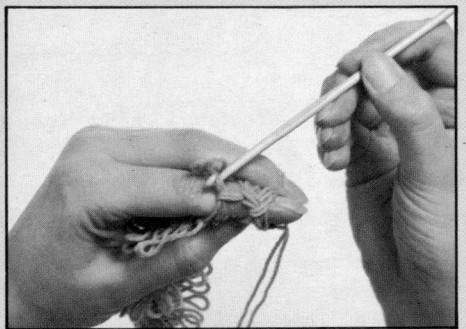

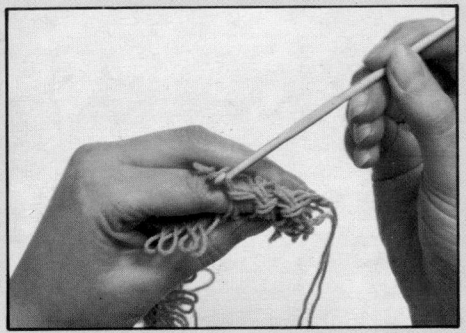

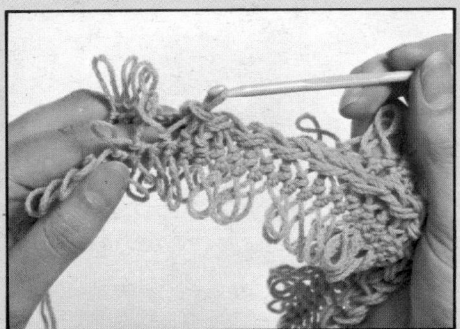

3 Insert crochet hook into next 2 loops on second strip. Draw these 2 loops through the loops on hook. For the second decrease, insert crochet hook into next 3 loops on first strip. Draw these 3 loops through the loops on hook.

4 Now draw next 2 loops on second strip through loops on hook, then draw the next 2 loops on first strip through loops on hook.

5 Repeat step 4 to within last 6 loops on first strip and last 4 loops on second strip.

continued

Fred Mancini

25

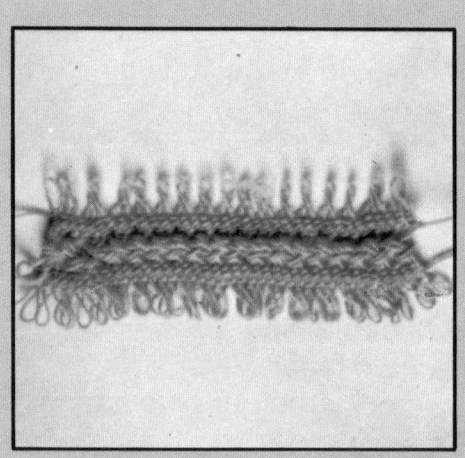

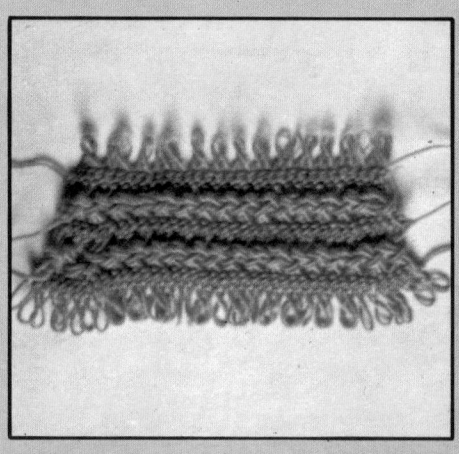

6 Work 2 decreases, as before, over these loops. Fasten off.

7 Join the third strip to the second strip, decreasing loops at each end as before.

8 Join the fourth strip to the third strip, decreasing loops at each end as before.

Shaping across a row with crochet

This method produces a curved shape, unlike the previous method, which leaves the rows straight.

For this sample we have made three strips of hairpin lace crochet. The first strip has 30 loops on each side, the second strip has 20 loops on each side and the third strip has 10 loops on each side.

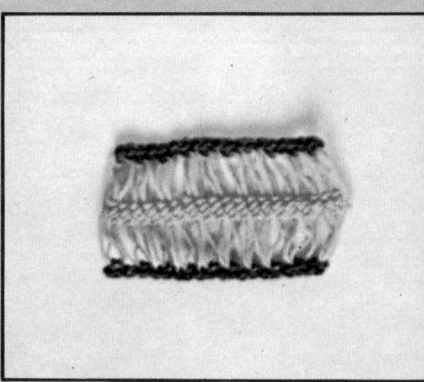

1 To edge first strip, insert crochet hook into first 3 loops, join on yarn and work 1 sc, *2 ch, work 1 sc into next 3 loops, repeat from * to end of strip. Fasten off. Edge other side in same way. Fasten off.

2 To edge the second strip, insert hook into first 2 loops, join on yarn and work 1 sc, *1 ch, 1 sc into next 2 loops, repeat from * to end of strip. Fasten off. Edge other side in same way. Fasten off.

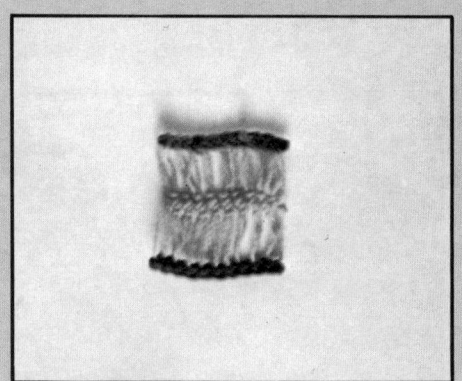

3 To edge the third strip, insert hook into first loop, join on yarn and work 1 sc, then work 1 sc into each sc to end. Fasten off. Edge the other side the same way. Fasten off.

4 Now crochet the first and second strips together: join yarn to first sc on first strip with a sc, 3 ch, 1 sc into first sc on second strip, *3 ch, 1 sc into next sc on first strip, 3 ch, 1 sc into next sc on second strip, repeat from * to end of strips. Fasten off.

5 Now crochet the third strip to the second strip following step 4 and reading third strip for second strip and second strip for first strip.

Shaping across a row by linking strips

This method is similar to the one on the preceeding two pages except that decreases are worked all across a row, producing a curved shape.

For this sample we have worked 2 strips of hairpin lace crochet. The first strip has 39 loops on each side and the second strip has 26 loops on each side.

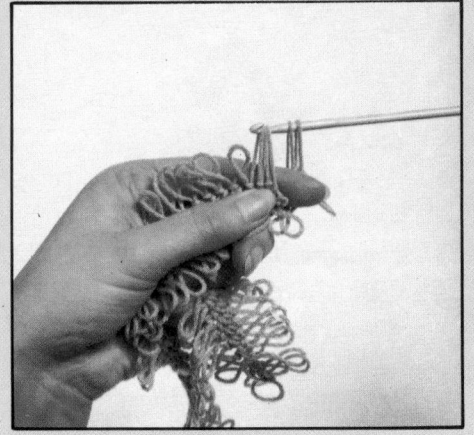

1 Hold the first strip between thumb and first finger and the second strip between second and third fingers of left hand. Insert crochet hook into first 2 loops on second strip and first 3 loops on first strip.

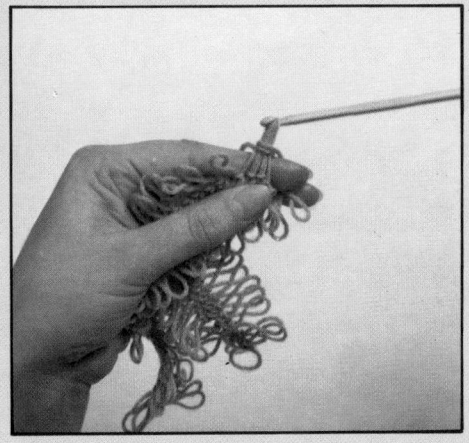

2 Draw the 3 loops of first strip through the 2 loops on second strip. The first decrease has been made.

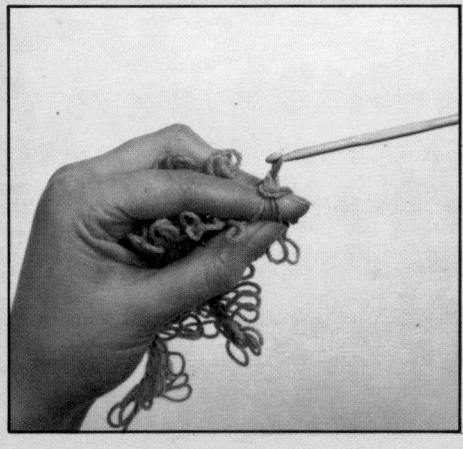

3 Insert crochet hook into next 2 loops on second strip. Draw these 2 loops through the loops on hook.

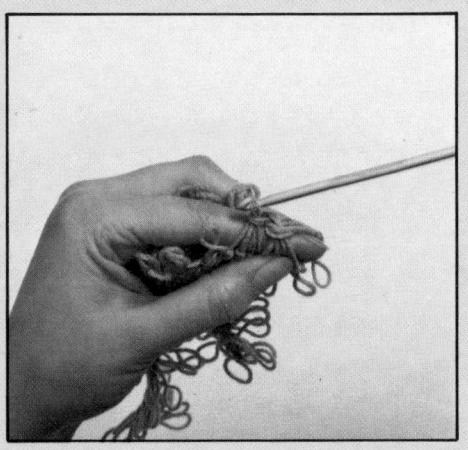

4 Insert crochet hook into next 3 loops on first strip. Draw these 3 loops through the loop on hook.

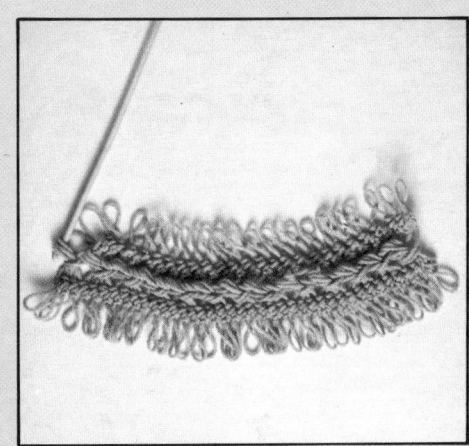

5 Repeat steps 3 and 4 until all loops have been linked, then fasten off.

Fan pattern

1 Insert crochet hook into first 2 loops, join on yarn and work 1sc.

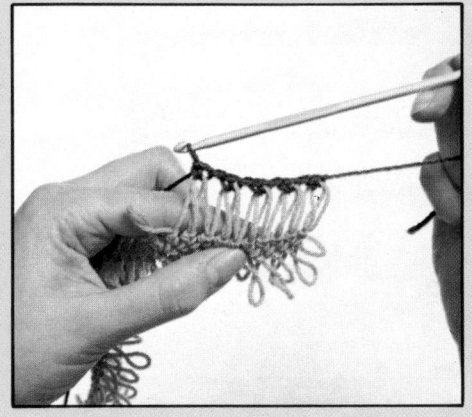

2 *1ch, insert hook into next 2 loops and work 1sc, repeat from * 3 times more.

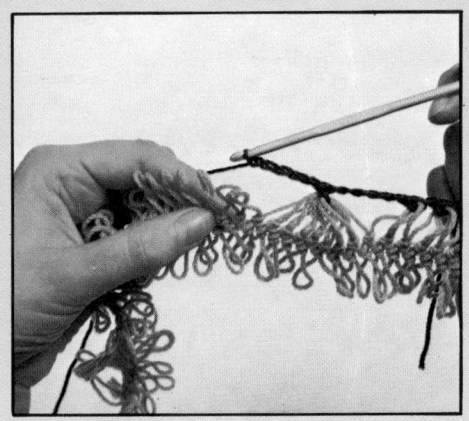

3 5ch, insert hook into next 8 loops and work 1sc, 5ch.

continued

Fred Mancini

27

4 *Insert hook into next 2 loops and work 1 sc, 1 ch, repeat from * twice more, insert hook into next 2 loops and work 1 sc.

5 Repeat steps 3 and 4 along strip, then turn and work the second row. 4 ch, 1 sc into 3rd ch of 1st 5 ch space.

6 4 ch, 1 sc into sc of next 8 loop group, 4 ch, 1 sc into 3rd ch of next 5 ch space.

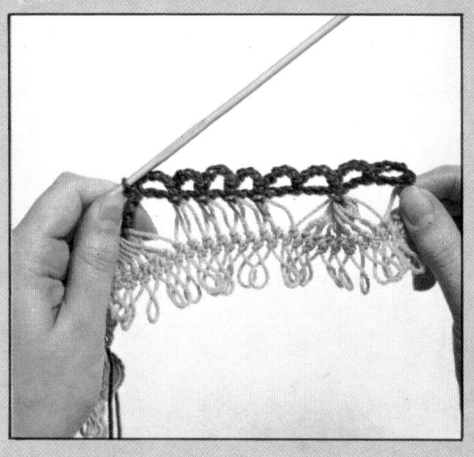

7 *4 ch, 1 sc into sc of next 2 loop group, 1 ch, repeat from * 3 times more, 4 ch, 1 sc into 3rd ch of next 5 ch space.

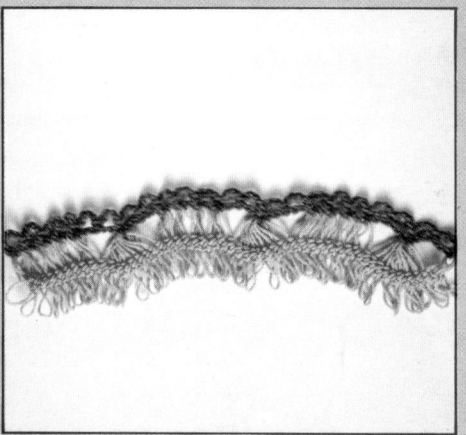

8 Repeat steps 6 and 7 along edge, finishing 4 ch, 1 sc into sc of last 2 loop group. Fasten off.

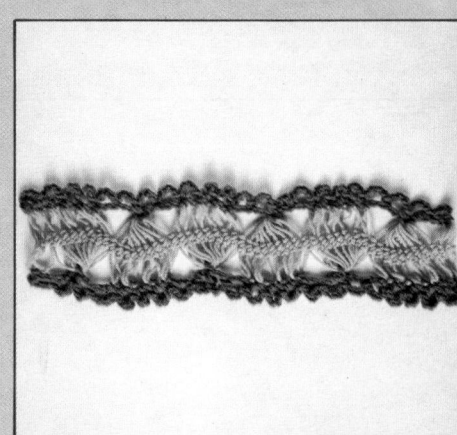

9 Work the other side the same way.

Chain joining for fan pattern

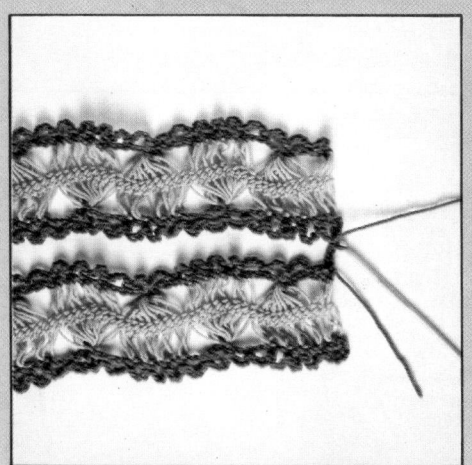

1 Join yarn to center of first 4 ch space of first strip, 2 ch, 1 sc into center of first 4 ch space of second strip.

2 Work 2 ch, 1 sc into next 4 ch space on first strip, 2 ch, 1 sc into next 4 ch space on second strip.

3 Repeat step 2 to end of strips. Fasten off.

Woman's smock

Make this light-as-a-feather smock as a vacation cover-up. You'll also find it useful during cooler weather when you need an extra layer over blouses or sweaters.

Jean-Claude Volpeliere

Sizes
To fit 36-38in (92-97cm) bust.
Length, 31½in (80cm).
Sleeve seam, 17in (43cm).

Materials
11oz (300g) of a lightweight mohair
3¼in (80mm) hairpin loom
Size I (6.00mm) crochet hook

Back
Work 4 strips of hairpin lace crochet with sc at center, having 84 loops on each side.
1st strip Work first row of fan pattern along one edge. Fasten off.
Work the 2 rows of fan pattern along remaining edge.
2nd and 3rd strips Work the 2 rows of fan pattern along one edge.
Fasten off.
Work steps 1 to 3 of fan pattern omitting the 5ch at end of step 3, then work 1ch, *(1sc into next 2 loops) 4 times, 1ch, insert hook into next 8 loops and work 1sc, 1ch*, rep from * to * to within last 18 loops, cont as for fan pattern to end of strip.
Turn.
Work 1 row sc. Fasten off.
Join strips, in correct order, following "Chain joining for fan pattern" on page 28.

Front
Work as for back.

Sleeves
Work 3 strips of hairpin lace crochet with sc at center, having 52 loops on each side.
Edge and join loops as for back.

Cuffs (alike)
Join yarn to lower edge (1st strip) and work 1sc into first sc, *2sc into next 5ch space, 1sc into next sc, 2sc into next 5ch space, (1sc into next sc, skip next 1ch space) 4 times*, rep from * to * along lower edge.
Turn.
Next row Work 1sc into each sc to end.
Turn.
Rep last row 5 times more.
Fasten off.
Join side and sleeve seams. Sew underarm of sleeves to back and front (the section where no decreases were made.)

Yoke
1st strip Work hairpin lace crochet with sc at center, having 76(84) loops on each side.

2nd strip Work hairpin lace crochet with sc at center, having 66 loops on each side.

3rd strip Work hairpin lace crochet with sc at center, having 54 loops on each side.

Joining 1st yoke strip

Join yarn to center sc of front at yoke edge. *Insert hook into next 2 loops and next sc, yo and draw through the sc and 2 loops, yo and draw through the 2 loops on hook, sl st into next sc, rep from * to end of strip. Fasten off.

Joining 2nd strip

Insert hook into first 2 loops on first strip, then into first 2 loops on second strip, draw the 2 loops from second strip through the 2 loops on first strip. **Insert hook into next 3 loops on first strip, draw these 3 loops through the 2 loops on hook. Insert hook into next 2 loops on second strip, draw these 2 loops through the 3 loops of first strip. Insert hook into next 2 loops on first strip, draw these 2 loops through the 2 loops on hook. Insert hook into next 2 loops on second strip, draw these 2 loops through 2 loops on hook.** Rep from ** to ** to end of strips. Fasten off.

Joining 3rd strip

Work as for 2nd but read 2nd strip as 1st strip and 3rd strip as 2nd strip.

Neck edging

Insert hook into first 5 loops on 3rd strip, draw the last 3 loops through the first 2 loops on hook. *Insert hook into next 2 loops and draw through the 2 loops on hook. Insert hook into next 3 loops and draw through the 2 loops on hook, rep from * to end of strip. Fasten off. Join yarn to center front yoke and work 4sc into each loop sp to neck, 1ch, *2sc into next loop sp, 3sc into next loop sp, rep from * along neck, then work 4sc into each loop sp along center front yoke. Turn.

Work 3 rows sc. Fasten off.

Pillow trims

Give plain pillows a touch of class with these hairpin lace crochet trims. Choose from two edgings, a corner and an overall design.

Picot-style edging

Size

To fit 15in (38cm) square pillow cover. Depth, 1½in (4cm).

Materials

2 × 100yd (92m) balls of a medium-weight mercerized crochet cotton
1in (25mm) hairpin loom
Size C (3.00mm) crochet hook

To make

Work 2 strips of hairpin lace crochet with sc at center, having 86 loops on each side. Work 2 strips of hairpin crochet with sc at center, having 100 loops on each side.

Edging for short strips

First side Insert crochet hook into first 2 loops on one strip, yo and draw a loop through, 1ch. Now work *2ch, 1sc into next 2 loops, rep from * to end of strip. Fasten off.

Second side Insert hook into first 2 loops, yo and draw a loop through, 1ch. Now work *4ch, insert hook into next 2 loops, yo and draw through 2 loops on hook, 1ch, 1sc into next 2 loops, rep from * to end of strip. Fasten off.

Edging for long strips

First side Work as for short strip, do not fasten off but work along short edge thus: 4ch, insert hook into 2nd ch, yo and draw through 2 loops on hook, 1ch, 1sc into next 2 loop space, 4ch, insert hook into center st, yo and draw a loop through 2 loops on hook, 1ch, 1sc into next 2 loop space. Fasten off.

Second side Work as for short strip, do not fasten off but work along short edge as for first side. Sew edgings to outer edge of cover.

Overall lace

Size

To fit 15in (38cm) square pillow cover.

Materials

3 × 100yd (92m) balls of a medium-weight mercerized crochet cotton
2¾in (70mm) hairpin loom
Size C (3.00mm) crochet hook

To make

Work 3 strips of hairpin lace crochet with sc at center, having 82 loops on each side.

Edgings

First side Insert crochet hook into first 6 loops and work 1sc, *1ch, (1sc into next 2 loops, 6ch) 4 times, 1sc into next 2 loops, 1ch, 1sc into next 10 loops*,

rep from * to * to end of strip, ending with 1sc into last 6 loops. Turn.

Next row 3ch, (1tr into next sc, 5dc into next 6ch sp) 4 times, *1dc into each of next 3sc, (5dc into next 6ch sp) 4 times* rep from * to * to end, finishing with 1dc into each of last 2sc. Turn.

Next row 5ch, sl st into next dc, *(5ch, skip next 2dc, sl st into next dc) 8 times, 5ch, skip next dc, sl st into next dc*, rep from * to * to end. Fasten off.

Second side Insert crochet hook into first 2 loops and work 1sc, (6ch, 1sc into next 2 loops) twice, *1ch, 1sc into next 10 loops, 1ch, (1sc into next 2 loops, 6ch) 4 times, 1sc into next 2 loops *, rep from * to * to end. Turn.

Next row 3ch, (5dc into next 6ch sp, 1dc into next sc) twice, *1dc into each of next 3sc, (5dc into next 6ch sp, 1dc into next sc) 4 times*, rep from * to * to end. Turn.

Next row (5ch, skip next 2dc, sl st into next dc) 4 times, *5ch, skip next dc, sl st into next dc, (5ch, skip next 2dc, sl st into next dc) 8 times*, rep from * to * to end of row. Fasten off.

Edge remaining 2 strips the same way.

Jean-Claude Volpelière

To join strips

Join yarn to second side of first strip and work 4ch, sl st into first 5ch sp on first side of second strip, *4ch, sl st into next 5ch sp on first strip, 4ch, sl st into next 5ch sp on second strip, rep from * to end of strip. Fasten off. Join third strip to second the same way.

The edging

Join yarn to first 5ch sp on first strip and work (5ch, sl st into next 5ch sp) 8 times, 7ch, skip next 5ch sp, sl st into next 5ch sp, cont in this way along edge to corner, 4ch, sl st into corner sc, *8ch, sl st into center st of strip, 8ch, sl st into next dc, (4ch, sl st into next ch sp) twice, 4ch, sl st into next dc,* rep from * to * along edge. Work remaining 2 sides to correspond. Fasten off. Working along ends of strips, join yarn to corner and work (5ch, sl st into next 8ch sp, 5ch, sl st into same 8ch sp) twice, (5ch, sl st into next 3ch sp) 3 times, cont along edge. Fasten off. Finish opposite edge the same way. Sew to pillow cover.

Loose twisted edging

Size

To fit 15in (38cm) square pillow cover. Depth, 1¼in (3cm).

Materials

2×100yd (92m) balls of a medium-weight mercerized crochet cotton
1in (25mm) hairpin loom
Size C (3.00mm) crochet hook

To make

Work a strip of hairpin lace crochet with sc at center, having 420 loops on each side.

Edging

Insert hook into next 5 loops and work 1sc, (3ch, 1sc into next 2 loops, 3ch, 1sc into next 5 loops) 13 times, 3ch, 1sc into next 9 loops, 3ch, rep from * to * 3 times more. Fasten off.
Turn work, join yarn into first loop of one 9 loop group, *2ch, 1sc into 2nd ch from hook—picot formed—sl st into next loop *, rep from * to * 8 times, **work a picot, 1sc into next 5 loops, work a picot, sl st into next 2 loops * *, rep from * * to * * 12 times more, 1sc into next 5 loops. Cont to work remaining 3 sides and corners the same way. Fasten off. Sew edging around outer edge of cover.

Corner trims

Size

To fit 15in (38cm) square pillow cover.

Materials

3×100yd (92m) balls of a medium-weight mercerized crochet cotton
2¾in (70mm) hairpin loom
Size C (3.00mm) crochet hook

To make (work 4 corner pieces alike).

First strip, work hairpin lace crochet with sc at center, having 16 loops on each side.
Second strip, work hairpin lace crochet with sc at center, having 28 loops on each side.

Third strip, work hairpin lace crochet with sc at center, having 52 loops on each side.

To join strips

Work 1sc into first 2 loops on first strip, 1ch, 1sc into next 12 loops, 1ch, 1sc into next 2 loops. Fasten off.
Join second side of first strip to first side of second strip thus: Holding first strip between thumb and first finger and second strip between second and third fingers of left hand, insert crochet hook through first 2 loops on first strip, then *insert hook into next 2 loops on second strip, draw the 2 loops from second strip through the 2 loops of first strip, insert hook into next 2 loops on second strip and draw these 2 loops through the 2 loops on hook, insert hook into next 2 loops on first strip and draw these 2 loops through the 2 loops on hook, rep from * to end of strips. Fasten off.
Join first side of third strip to second side of second strip the same way.

The edging

Join yarn to center of first side of first strip and work 2sc into same place as joining, *6sc into loop sp, 1sc into center st, 6sc into next loop sp*, rep from * to * to center st of third strip, 6ch, work 1sc into each loop along second side of third strip, 6ch, rep from * to * along side edge to first sc, sl st into first sc.

Next round Sl st into next st, *2ch, sl st into same st, sl st into each of next 2 sts*, rep from * to * all around. Fasten off.
Sew one piece to each corner of cover.

Ray Duns

Shoestring

On key

This pretty key ring is embroidered in cross stitch with a colorful flower motif.

Size
3¼in (8.5cm) in diameter.

Materials
- 4in (10cm) square of evenweave linen, with 22 threads to 1in (2.5cm)
- 3¼in (8.5cm)-diameter circle of clear plastic
- 3¼in (8.5cm)-diameter circle of heavyweight interfacing
- 3¼in (8.5cm)-diameter circle of floral print cotton fabric and a 16 × 1¼in (40 × 3cm) bias strip in the same fabric
- Stranded embroidery floss in light and dark pink, light and dark green, orange, mauve and rust
- Sewing thread to match linen
- Metal key ring

1 Following the chart and the photograph (for color), work the embroidery in the center of the linen. Use three strands of embroidery floss throughout and work in cross stitch (straight stitch for stems at lower corners), working each stitch over two threads of fabric.

2 Press the completed embroidery on the wrong side.

3 Center the clear plastic circle on the right side of the embroidery. Cut away the excess linen from around the plastic circle.

4 Place the plastic-covered embroidery on the circle of interfacing, then place these on the wrong side of the printed fabric circle. Baste around the edges to hold all the pieces together.

5 Place the bias fabric strip right side down on the plastic side of the circle, matching edges. Baste in place. To finish ends, cut off excess strip and stitch short ends together to fit edge of circle. Stitch strip in place, ¼in (5mm) from edge.

6 From excess bias strip make a loop. Fold strip in half lengthwise, right sides together. Pin, baste and stitch down the length, taking a ¼in (5mm) seam. Turn strip right side out.

7 Fold strip in half to form a loop. Stitch loop securely to back of circle at center top, with raw edges matching and loop lying inward.

8 Turn bias strip over edge of circle to wrong side. Turn in ¼in (5mm) on raw edge. Hand-sew in place.

9 Fold loop upward, so that it lies flat against the circle and extends above it. Hand-sew in place.

10 Thread key ring through fabric loop.

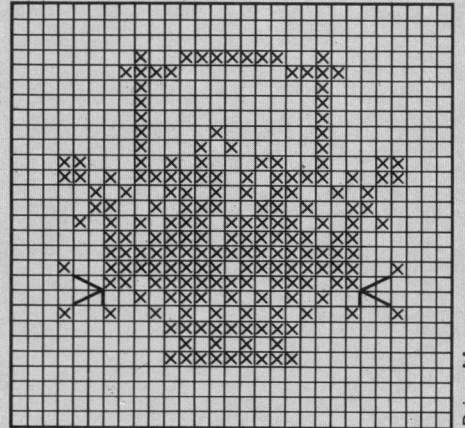

Brian Mayor

Making a picot waistband

A picot waistband is a pretty variation of a widely-used kind in which elastic is enclosed in a knitted casing. The fold-line of the waistband is decorated with eyelet holes which form picot points along the top edge of the finished garment. The waistband is not worked separately, but is a continuation of the main fabric.

An elasticized waist is suitable for most types of full skirts, such as the gathered skirt on page 36. Generally there is enough fabric in the skirt and enough stretch in the elastic to make a side opening skirt unnecessary.

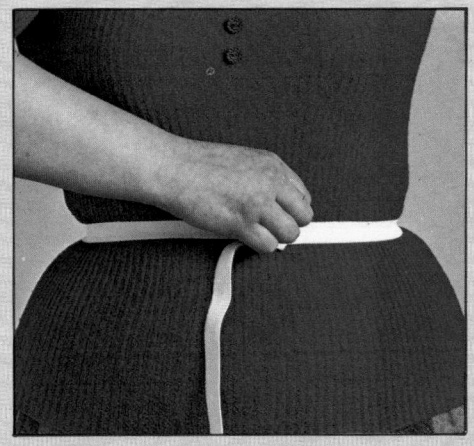

1 You can buy special elastic for a skirt waistband. It is thick, strong and wider than average, usually at least 1 in (2.5cm). Calculate the amount of elastic you need by measuring around your waist, stretching the elastic slightly at the same time. Allow about ½in (1.2cm) overlap at the ends.

2 Patterns give specific details for working a picot waistband. Generally it follows the same principle as working a picot hem (see Volume 5, pages 39-40). Make the front part of the waistband in stockinette stitch deep enough to take the elastic. Mark the foldline with a row of eyelet holes before knitting the back part of the casing, again in stockinette stitch.

3 When the skirt is finished, join the side seams. Fold the waistband hem to the wrong side along the line of eyelet holes; these now form a picot edging. Slip stitch the hem in position using matching yarn (here it is in a contrasting color for clarity). Leave about a 1½in (4cm) opening for inserting the elastic at one side seam.

4 Prepare the elastic to thread through the casing. You need a blunt-ended yarn needle with a large, long eye and a safety pin. Fasten one end of the elastic to the side seam at the opening with the safety pin. Thread the other end (fold it lengthwise if necessary) through the needle. If you prefer, you can use a safety pin instead of a needle.

5 Insert the needle into the casing and draw the elastic through. The elastic is shorter than the knitted casing; when it is fully extended within the casing, stretch the elastic with your right hand and use your left hand to gather the fabric over elastic. Make sure the elastic does not slip out of the eye of the needle.

continued

Fred Mancini

6 Be sure when the elastic is completely threaded through the casing not to let either end slip back. Join the elastic into a circle by overlapping the ends for about ½in (1.2cm). Make sure it isn't twisted within the casing. Overcast the elastic securely along both ends.

7 Now completely enclose the elastic within the casing, making sure that it lies flat. Close the opening by slip stitching it with matching yarn: you will have to stretch the knitting flat to do this.

8 On the right side of the finished waistband the knitting puckers slightly where it gathers over the elastic; when you wear the skirt the elastic stretches and gives a flat waistband.

Other types of knitted waistbands

The waistbands shown here are both knitted casings—one in ribbing and one in stockinette stitch—enclosing the elastic. Thread the elastic through the casing when you have finished the skirt.

Often the band at the waist of a skirt reflects the hem; if the skirt has a ribbed hem, choose a ribbed waistband. Use a picot waistband with a picot hem, and the plain stockinette stitch waistband

with a plain hem. Whichever band you choose, it is important to work as neatly as possible, since any unnecessary bulk will create an unattractive and uncomfortable waistline.

Ribbed waistband

1 Work waistband in K1, P1 ribbing using one size smaller needles than those for the main fabric. The depth must be twice that of the elastic plus a few extra rows.

2 When the skirt is complete, join the side seams. Fold the waistband in half to the wrong side and slip stitch in place, leaving an opening for the elastic.

3 Thread the elastic through as shown in steps 4 to 7 of "Making a picot waistband." This photograph shows the finished band on the right side of the work

Stockinette stitch casing

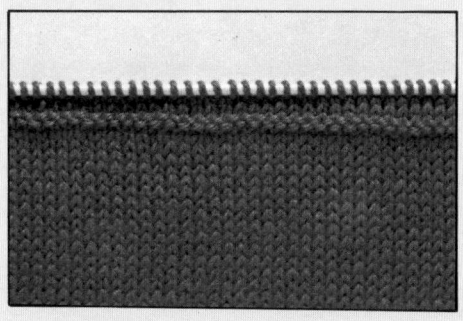

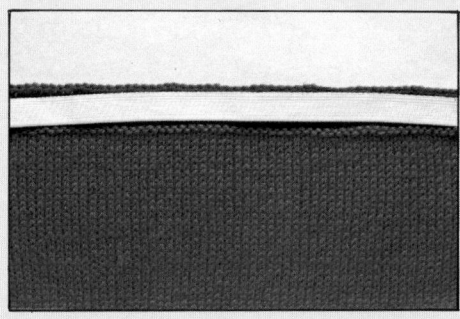

1 This is similar to a sewn-in hem (see Volume 5, page 37). The front part of the casing is a continuation of the main fabric, then a knit row worked on the back of the fabric produces a garter stitch ridge on the right side to emphasize the foldline.

2 Continue to work the underside of the casing; this must be deep enough to cover the width of the elastic plus a few extra rows.

3 When the skirt is finished, turn the casing to the wrong side at the foldline and slip stitch it in place, leaving an opening for elastic. Thread elastic through and complete as shown above. The finished waistband is shown right side out.

Stitch Wise

Eyelet patterns

Groups of eyelet holes may be the simplest form of lace pattern (see the skirt and shawl, overleaf). Technically eyelets must be separated by more than two strands of yarn, while holes in a lace pattern have only one strand (or two strands twisted together) between them. However, the methods of making lace and eyelet patterns are very similar. In general, use needles that are large in proportion to the weight of yarn so that a distinct hole is formed. Patterns must also be blocked and pressed like lace to open out the design and give it its lacy quality.

Eyelet flower pattern

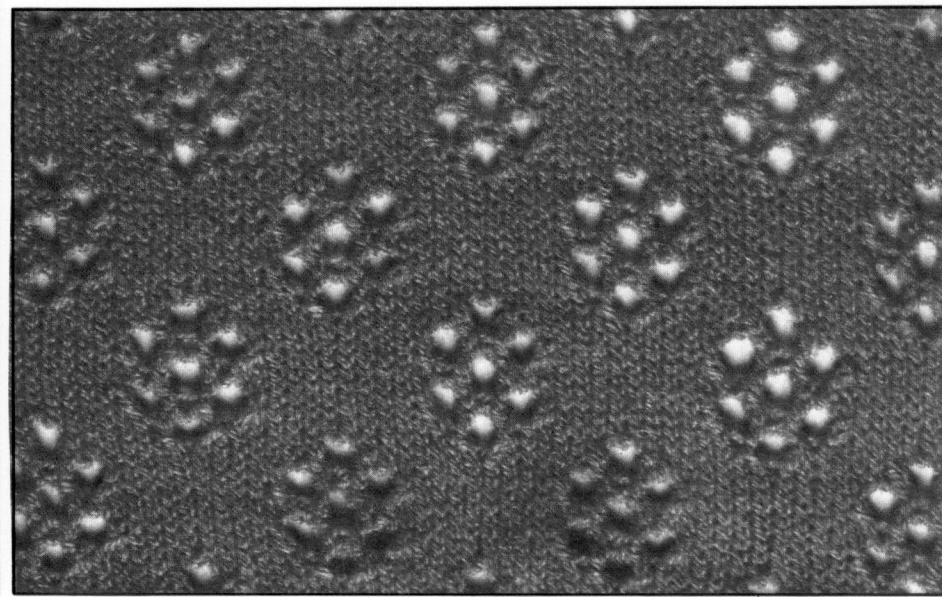

Cast on a multiple of 16 sts plus 8 extra.
1st row (RS) K10, *K2 tog, yo twice, sl 1, K1, psso, K12, rep from * ending last rep with K10.
2nd and all even rows P to end, working (K1, P1) into yo's in previous row.
3rd row K8, *(K2 tog, yo twice, sl 1, K1, psso) twice, K8, rep from * to end.
5th row As 1st.
7th row As 3rd.
9th row As 1st.
11th row K2, *K2 tog, yo twice, sl 1, K1, psso, K12, rep from * ending last rep with K2.
13th row * (K2 tog, yo twice, sl 1, K1, psso) twice, K8, rep from * ending with (K2 tog, yo twice, sl 1, K1, psso) twice.
15th row As 11th.
17th row As 13th.
19th row As 11th.
20th row As 2nd.
Rep these rows to form the patt.

Eyelet leaf pattern

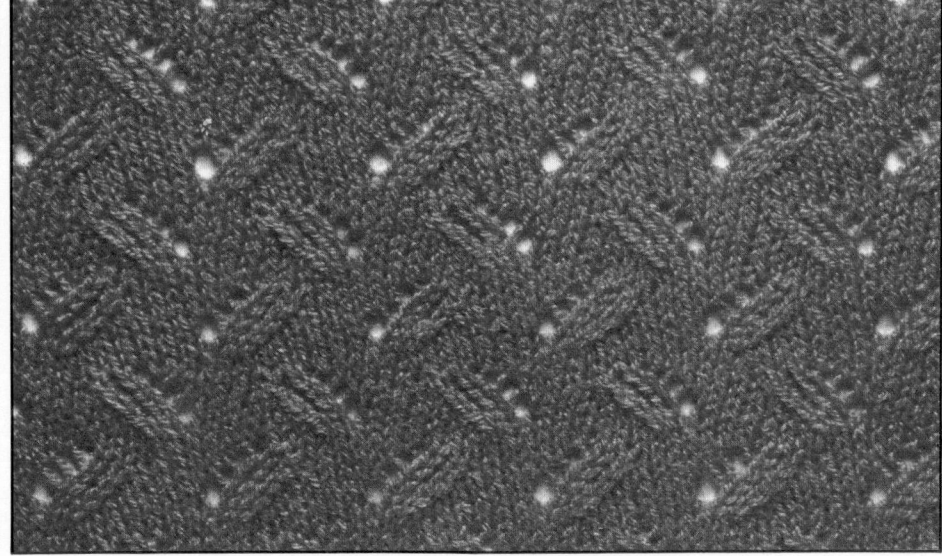

Cast on a multiple of 9 sts plus 3 extra.
1st row (RS) K to end.
2nd row P to end.
3rd row K3, *K2 tog, K1, yo, K6, rep from* to end.
4th row P1, *P6, yo, P1, P2 tog, rep from * ending with P2.
5th row K1, *K2 tog, K1, yo, K6, rep from * ending with K2.
6th row P3, *P6, yo, P1, P2 tog, rep from * to end.
7th and 8th rows As 1st and 2nd.
9th row *K6, yo, K1, sl 1, K1, psso, rep from * ending with K3.
10th row P2, *P2 tog tbl, P1, yo, P6, rep from * ending with P1.
11th row K2, *K6, yo, K1, sl 1, K1, psso, rep from * ending with K1.
12th row *P2 tog tbl, P1, yo, P6, rep from * ending with P3.
These 12 rows form the patt. Rep them throughout.

Raindrop eyelets

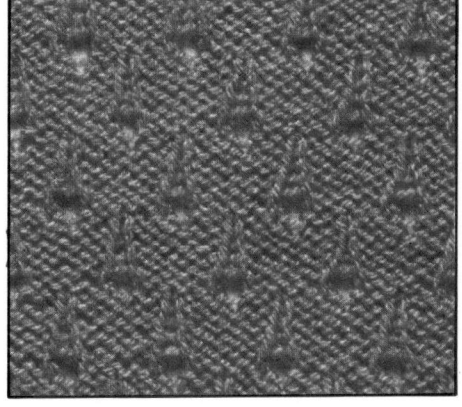

This is a pretty pattern for an easy-to-make purl fabric.
Cast on a multiple of 6 sts.
1st row (RS) *P4, yo, P2 tog, rep from * to end.
2nd, 4th and 6th rows K1, *P1, K5, rep from * ending with P1, K4.
3rd and 5th rows P4, *K1, P5, rep from * ending with K1, P1.
7th row P1, *yo, P2 tog, P4, rep from * ending with yo, P2 tog, P3.
8th, 10th and 12th rows K4, *P1, K5, rep from * ending with P1, K1.
9th and 11th rows P1, *K1, P5, rep from * ending with K1, P4.
These 12 rows form the patt. Rep them throughout.

Fred Mancini

Skirt and shawl

This soft gathered skirt has a pretty matching shawl.

Sizes
Skirt to fit 34-38in (87-97cm) hips.
Length, 27in (68cm).
Shawl 50in (126cm) x 21in (54cm).

Materials
Sport yarn
Skirt *9oz (250g) in main color (A)*
1oz (25g) in contrasting color (B)
Waist length of 1in (2.5cm)-wide elastic
Shawl *4oz (100g) in main color (A)*
1oz (25g) in contrasting color (B)
1 pair No. 5 (4mm) knitting needles
3½yd (3.2m) of ½in (1.2cm)-wide ribbon

Gauge
24 sts and 28 rows to 4in (10cm) in stockinette st on No. 5 (4mm) needles.

Skirt

Back
Using No. 5 (4mm) needles and B, cast on 150 sts. **Beg with a K row, work 6 rows stockinette st.
Next row (hem row) K1, *yo, K2 tog, rep from * to last st, K1.
P1 row and K1 row. Cut off B and join in A. **
Work 5 more rows stockinette st. Beg patt.
1st row (RS) K to end.
2nd and foll alternate rows P to end.

BACK
24½in
FRONT
27in

Brian Mayor

Victor Yuan

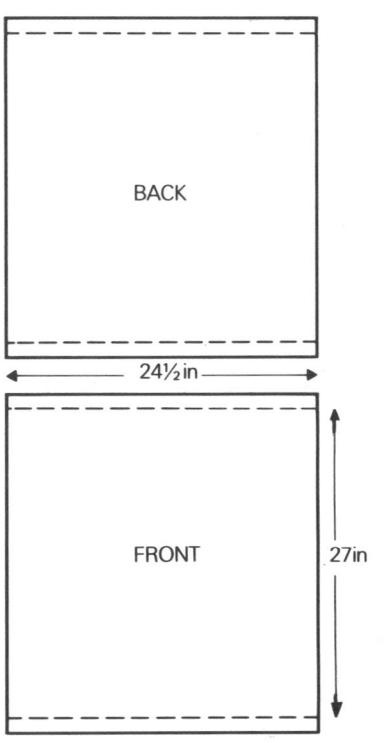

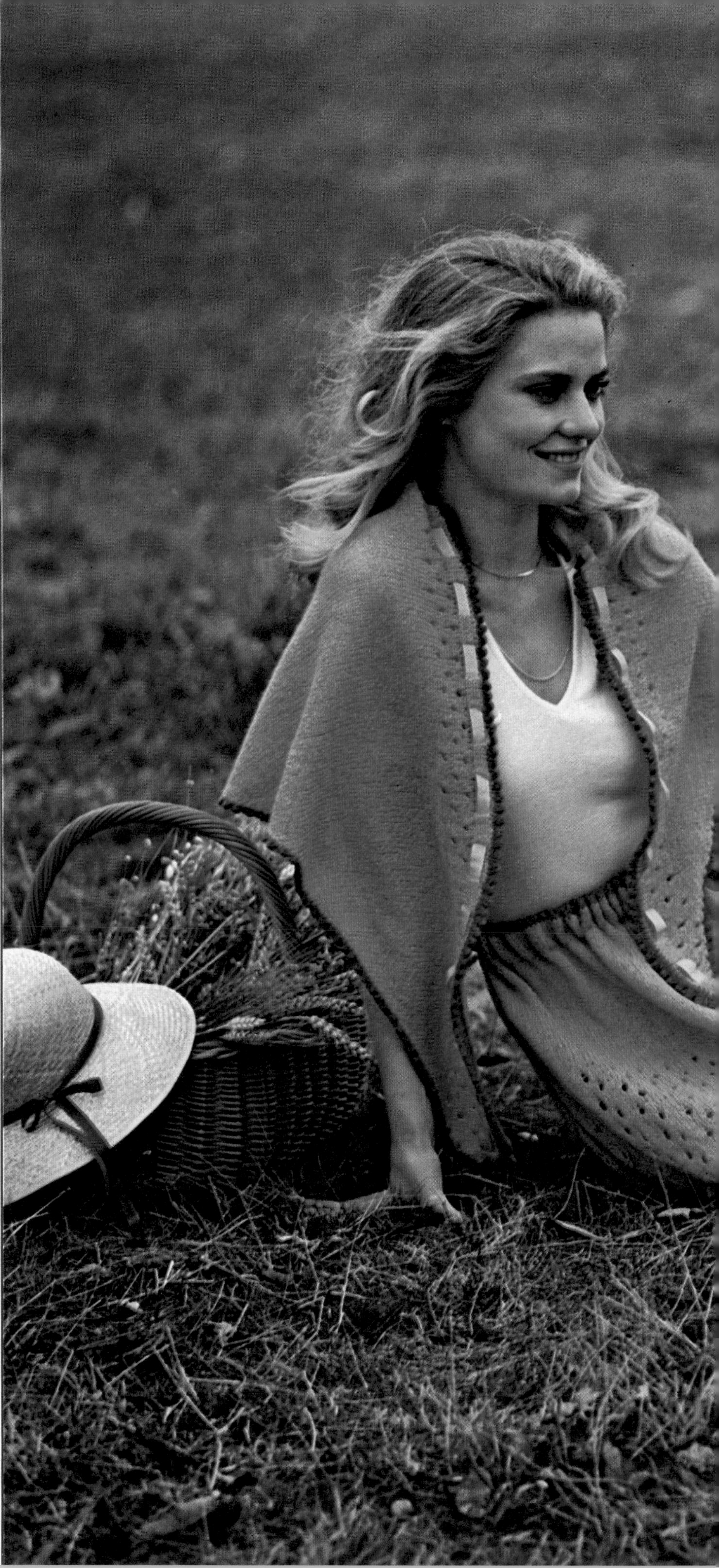

3rd row *K4, yo, K2 tog, rep from * to end.

5th row K to end.

7th row K2, *yo, K2 tog, K4, rep from * ending last rep with K2 instead of K4.

8th row P to end.

These 8 rows form patt. Rep throughout until work measures 8in (20cm) less than length required. Cont in stockinette st until work measures 28in (71cm) from hem row; end with P row. Cut off A and join in B. K1 row and P1 row.

Next row (waist row) K1, *yo, K2 tog, rep from * to last st, K1. Beg with P row, work 9 rows stockinette st. Bind off.

Front

Work as for back.

To finish

Press or block according to yarn used. Join side seams. Fold hem to WS and sew in place. Fold waistband to WS and sew in place leaving opening to insert elastic. Sew up opening after inserting elastic. Press seams. Thread ribbons through as desired.

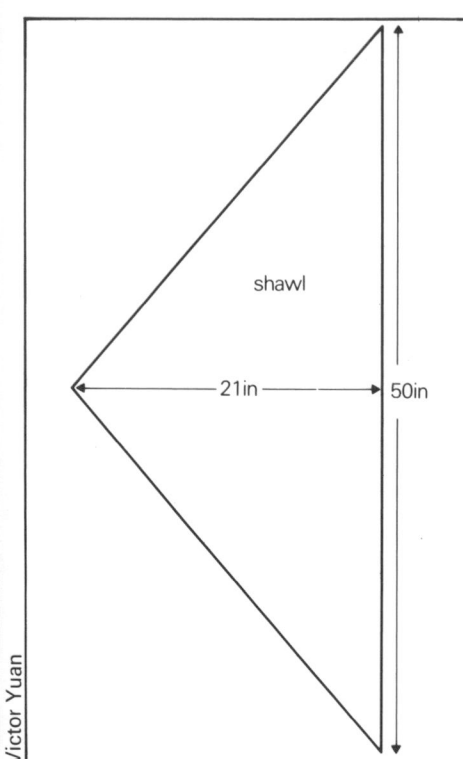

Shawl

Using No. 5 (4mm) needles and B, cast on 303 sts. Work as for skirt back from ** to **. Beg patt and shape as foll:

1st row (RS) K2 tog, K to last 2 sts, K2 tog.
2nd and foll alternate rows P2 tog, P to last 2 sts, P2 tog.
3rd row K2 tog, yo, K2 tog, *K4, yo, K2 tog, rep from * to last 7 sts, K3, K2 tog, yo, K2 tog.
5th row As 1st.
7th row K2 tog, K5, *yo, K2 tog, K4, rep from * to last 2 sts, K2 tog.
9th row As 1st.
11th row K2 tog, K4, *yo, K2 tog, K4, rep from * to last 7 sts, yo, K2 tog, K3, K2 tog.
13th row As 1st.
15th row K2 tog, K3, *yo, K2 tog, K4, rep from * to last 6 sts, yo, K2 tog, K2, K2 tog.
16th row As 2nd.
Beg with a K row, cont in stockinette st, dec one st at each end of every row until 3 sts rem. Bind off.

Edging

Using No. 5 (4mm) needles, B and with RS facing, pick up and K 154 sts along one diagonal edge. P 1 row.
Next row (picot row) K1, *yo, K2 tog, rep from * to last st, K1.
P 1 row and K 1 row.
Bind off.
Complete the other diagonal edge in the same way.

To finish

Press or block as for skirt. Fold all edges to WS along picots and sew in place. Thread ribbons through as desired.

shawl

21in

50in

Knitting / COURSE 44

*Facing hems with ribbon
*Finishing buttonholes with ribbon facing
*Patterns for a woman's jacket and cardigan

Facing hems with ribbon

A neatly finished hem on a jacket, cardigan or skirt adds a professional touch to the way a garment looks and hangs. Ribbon facings can be used on special garments if you want to avoid the bulk of a knitted hem or facing; this kind of facing is also a method of finishing and reinforcing buttonholes. There are several types of ribbon suitable for facing. They are all straight-grained, not cut on the bias, not too stiff, are available in various widths and do not ravel. Unless you want a neutral color like black, white, or beige, you may have difficulty finding a shade to match your yarn. If you feel that the colors available are not suitable, you might consider dyeing white ribbon the color you need to match.

How to miter a corner

1 Cut the ribbon to the length needed, allowing a little extra for overlap if it is to be joined. The dotted lines on the drawing (above) of the yellow cardigan on page 42 indicate the edges to be faced—the outer edges of the completed garment, including the pocket top edges.

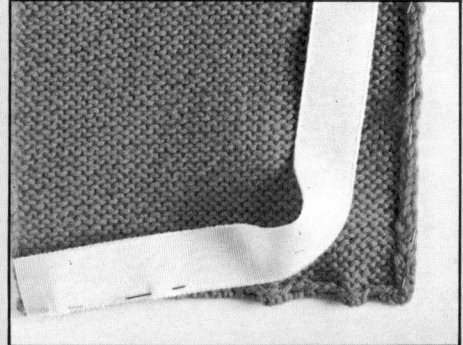

2 Turn under two rows of knitting at the lower edge, or one to two stitches at the side edge, to the wrong side of the fabric. Pin the ribbon in place along the outer edge; if you have to join the ribbon, place the seam as unobtrusively as possible, perhaps at the side seam.

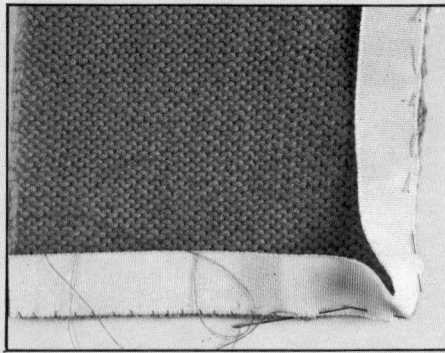

3 When you reach a corner where the two edges are at right angles to each other, continue to pin at the outer edge only, then slip stitch the ribbon in place at this edge using a matching sewing thread (here it is a contrasting color for clarity).

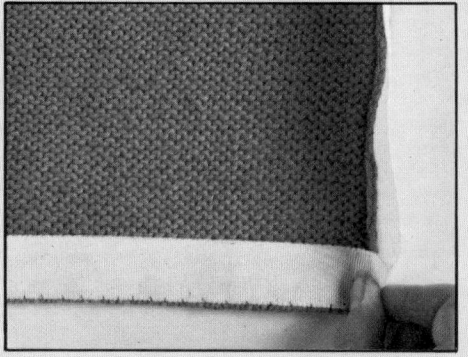

4 Now pin the inner edge of the ribbon in place, folding the corners as they are reached to form a miter: take the ribbon completely to the end of one edge, then fold the extra ribbon into a neat triangular shape with one of the sides running diagonally between the outer corner and inner edge of the ribbon.

5 Slip stitch the ribbon along the inner edges, joining any mitered corners in the same way. On the right side of the fabric, the edges are turned under. The ribbon finishes them neatly without adding bulk.

6 When facing the lower edge of the sleeves allow $\frac{5}{8}$in (1.5cm) at each end of the ribbon for a seam. Turn under the seam allowance, sew ribbon to fabric as explained above, then join the ends of the ribbon together neatly.

How to face around a curve

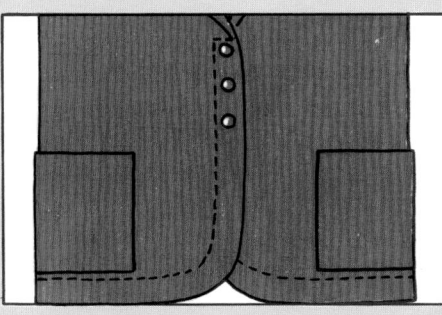 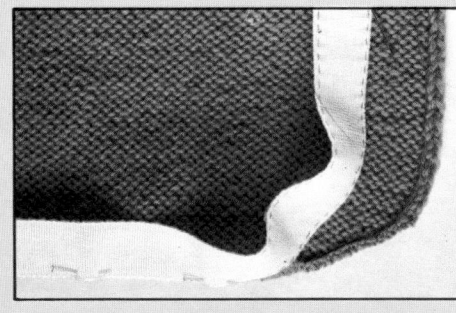 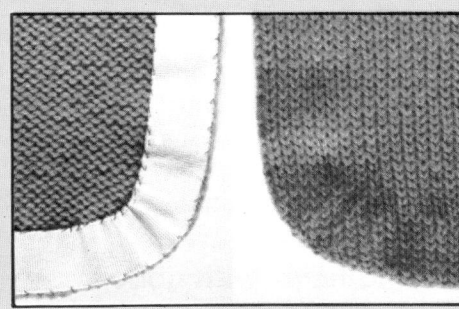

1 This drawing shows the green jacket on page 42. The dotted lines indicate the edges to be faced, including the curved edge of the lower fronts. Cut the ribbon to the required length, allowing extra for gathering around the corners.

2 Prepare the outer edge of the knitting and pin ribbon as shown in step 2 on page 39. About 1 in (3cm) before the curve, make small running stitches on each side of the ribbon; these should extend a short distance past the corner to allow the ribbon to be gathered.

3 Gather the stitches up so that the outer edge fits the curve, and continue to pin the ribbon in place around the outer edge. Complete the facing as shown for mitering a corner, distributing the gathers evenly around the inner curve.

Finishing buttonholes with ribbon facing

A ribbon facing is a way of adding extra strength to the buttonhole—and the button—edges of a knitted fabric. Choose a straight-grained ribbon to match the fabric.

Measure the length of the ribbon you need along the knitted edge; be careful not to stretch the knitting.

The button band facing must match the buttonhole band in length to ensure an even fit when the two edges are together. The buttonholes have already been worked in the main fabric and are cut in the ribbon after it is sewn in place. Buttonhole stitching adds a finishing touch.

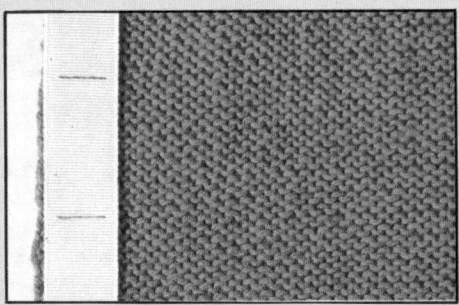 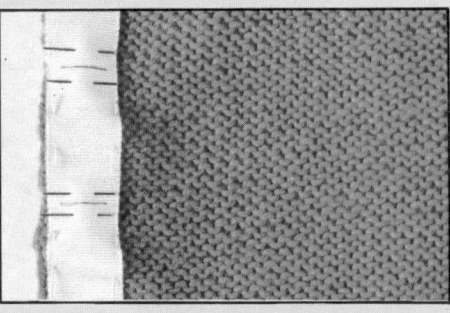

1 The ribbon must be wide enough to cover the buttonholes, allowing an extra $\frac{1}{2}$ in (1.2cm) on each side and at each end. Do not stretch the knitting when you measure a piece of ribbon or the buttonhole band will be stretched. Cut the ribbon for the button band at the same time to guarantee a perfect match.

2 Turn any edges of knitting that need finishing to the wrong side and baste to hold in place. Fold under raw ends on the ribbon and pin it in place on the wrong side of the fabric. Ease into place and check that the buttonholes are evenly spaced. Pin the ribbon on each side of every buttonhole to hold it in place.

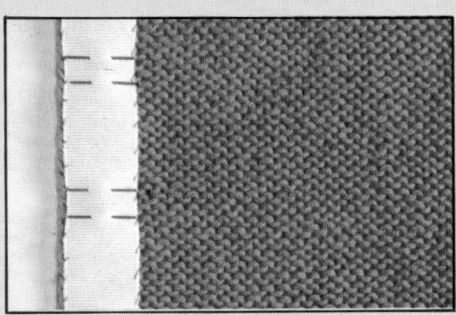 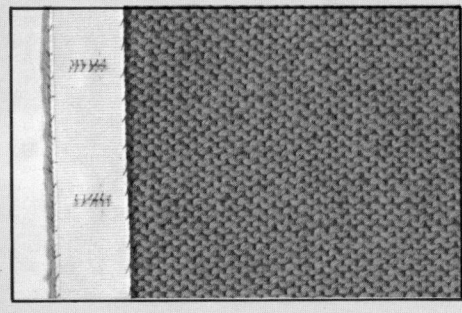 

3 Slip stitch the ribbon in place around the edges. Carefully cut the buttonholes in the ribbon, making sure they are exactly the same size as the knitted buttonholes; use a single-edged razor blade or a small pair of sharp scissors.

4 To keep the edges together, overcast around each buttonhole, sewing through the ribbon and knitted fabric with small but fairly widely spaced stitches. Remove the pins from around the buttonholes.

5 Add the finishing touch with buttonhole stitches: with the right side of the work facing and using a needle threaded with matching silk thread, join the thread at at the lower left-hand edge of the buttonhole. Insert the needle from front to back a short distance down from the lower edge of the buttonhole and wind the thread around the needle.

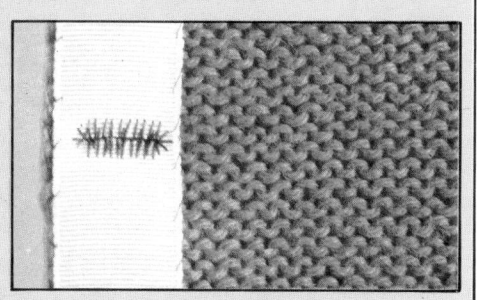

Fred Mancini

6 To complete one stitch draw the needle through; the thread looped around the needle forms a neat knot exactly on the lower edge of the buttonhole. Continue working along the lower edge in this way; turn the corner by working three stitches.

7 Turn the buttonhole upside down so that the top edge becomes the lower edge and complete to match the other side. On the right side of the work the knots securing the stitches make a neat border around the edges of the buttonhole.

8 On the wrong side of the work the overcast edges of the ribbon are neatly finished by the buttonhole stitches. Do not work too many stitches around the hole or it will become stretched, but too few stitches make the hole smaller than intended.

Woman's jacket and cardigan

The classic cover-ups on the following page will see you through spring or fall.

Green jacket

Sizes

To fit 32[34:36:38]in (83[87:92:97]cm) bust.
Length, 22[22:23:23]in (56[56:58:58]cm); Sleeve seam, 16½[17:17½:18]in (42[43:44:45]cm).

Note Directions for larger sizes are in brackets []; if there is only one set of figures it applies to all sizes.

Materials

19[20:21:22] × 1oz (25g) balls of medium-weight chenille yarn
No. 8 (5½mm) knitting needles
Three buttons; stitch holder
3¼yd (3m) of 1in (2.5cm)-wide ribbon for facing

Gauge

16 sts and 24 rows to 4in (10cm) in reverse stockinette st on No. 8 (5½mm) needles.

Back

Using No. 8 (5½mm) needles cast on 72[76:80:84] sts loosely. Beg with a P row, cont in rev stockinette st for 20[20:22:22] rows. Dec one st at each end of next and every foll 6th row until there are 64[68:72:76] sts. Cont straight for a further 21 rows. Now inc one st at each end of next and every foll 8th row until there are 70[74:78:82] sts. Cont straight for a further 9 rows.

Shape armholes

Bind off 2 sts at beg of next 2 rows, then dec one st at each end of next and foll alternate row. 62[66:70:74] sts. Cont straight until armhole measures 8[8:8½:8½]in (20[20:21:21]cm); end with K row.

Shape shoulders

Bind off 5 sts at beg of next 4 rows and 4[5:6:7] sts at beg of foll 4 rows. Cut off yarn and leave rem 26 sts on a holder.

Left front

Using No. 8 (5½mm) needles cast on 30[32:34:36] sts loosely. Beg with a P row, cont in rev stockinette st and shape front edge as foll:
Next row Work to end.
Next row Cast on 2, work to end.
Next row Work to last st, inc in last st. Rep last 2 rows twice more.
Next row Inc in first st, work to end. 40[42:44:46] sts.
Cont straight for a further 12[12:14:14] rows. Dec one st at beg of next and every foll 6th row until there are 36[38:40:42] sts. Cont straight for a further 21 rows. Inc one st at beg of next and every foll 8th row until there are 39[41:43:45] sts, ending with a P row.

Shape front edge

Bind off 4 sts at beg of next row. Work 1 row. Dec one st at front edge on next and every foll 3rd row until 32[34:36:38] sts rem.

Shape armhole

Cont to dec one st at front edge on every 3rd row, bind off 2 sts at beg of next row, work 1 row, then dec one st at armhole edge on next and foll alternate row. Keep armhole edge straight, cont to shape front edge on every 3rd row until 18[20:22:24] sts rem. Place marker at front edge. Cont straight until armhole measures 8[8:8½:8½]in (20[20:21:21]cm); end at armhole edge.

Shape shoulder

Bind off 5 sts at beg of next and foll alternate row and 4[5:6:7] sts at beg of foll alternate row. Work 1 row. Bind off. Mark 3 button positions, the first 5½in (14cm) from lower edge, the last 2½in (6cm) from beg of front shaping and the other one evenly spaced between.

Right front

Working 1 extra row before neck and armhole shaping, work as for left front reversing shaping and making buttonholes to correspond with markers thus: **1st buttonhole row** P4, bind off 3, P to end. **2nd buttonhole row** K to end casting on 3 sts over those bound off on previous row.

Sleeves

Cast on 38[40:42:44] sts loosely. Beg with a P row, cont in rev stockinette st but inc one st at each end of every foll 20th row until there are 46[48:50:52] sts. Cont straight until work measures 16½[17:17½:18]in (42[43:44:45]cm); end with K row.

Shape top

Bind off 2 sts at beg of next 2 rows. Dec one st at each end of next and every foll 4th row until 34[36:38:40] sts rem, then at each end of every other row until 24 sts rem. Bind off 3 sts at beg of next 4 rows.
Bind off.

Left front lapel

With WS facing join on yarn and pick up and K 28 sts between beg of front shaping and marker.
K 3 rows, so ending at "top" of lapel.
*Next row** K24, turn and K to end.
Next row K16, turn and K to end.
Next row K8, turn and K to end.
K 2 rows across all sts.* Rep from * to * once more. K 1 row.
Bind off.

Right front lapel

Work as given for left front lapel, but K 2 rows, so ending at "top," then K 2 rows before binding off.

Collar

Join shoulder seams. With WS facing join on yarn and pick up and K 66 sts between markers including sts on holder. Work in garter st for 3in (8cm). Bind off.

Patch pockets (make 2)

Using No. 8 (5½mm) needles cast on 20 sts. Beg with a P row, cont in rev stockinette st for 5½in (14cm). Bind off.

To finish

Set in sleeves, then join right side and sleeve seams. Sew ribbon facing around outer edge of jacket, beg and ending at base of lapel, and lower edge of sleeves. Cut buttonholes in ribbon and buttonhole stitch through both knitting and ribbon. Sew top of lapel to collar for ¾in (2cm). Sew on the buttons. Sew on pockets.

Yellow cardigan

Sizes

To fit 32[34:36:38]in (83[87:92:97]cm) bust. Length, 23½[24:25:25½]in (60[61: 63:64]cm).
Sleeve seam, as green jacket.
Note Directions for larger sizes are in brackets []; if there is only one set of figures it applies to all sizes.

Materials

*17[18:19:20] × 1oz (25g) balls of medium-weight chenille yarn
No. 8 (5½mm) knitting needles
Six buttons
3¼yd (3m) of 1in (2.5cm)-wide ribbon for facing*

Gauge

16 sts and 24 rows to 4in (10cm) in reverse stockinette st on No. 8 (5½mm) needles.

Back

Using No. 8 (5½mm) needles cast on 70[74:78:82] sts loosely. Beg with a P row, cont in rev stockinette st until work measures 16[16:16½:17]in (41[41:42: 43]cm).

Shape armholes

Bind off 3 sts at beg of next 2 rows, then dec one st at each end of next and every other row until 56[60:64:68] sts rem. Cont straight until armhole measures 7½[8:8½:8½]in (19[20:21:21]cm); end with K row.

Shape shoulders

Bind off 4 sts at beg of next 4 rows and 5[6:6:7] sts at beg of foll 4 rows. Bind off rem 20[20:24:24] sts.

Left front

Using No. 8 (5½mm) needles cast on

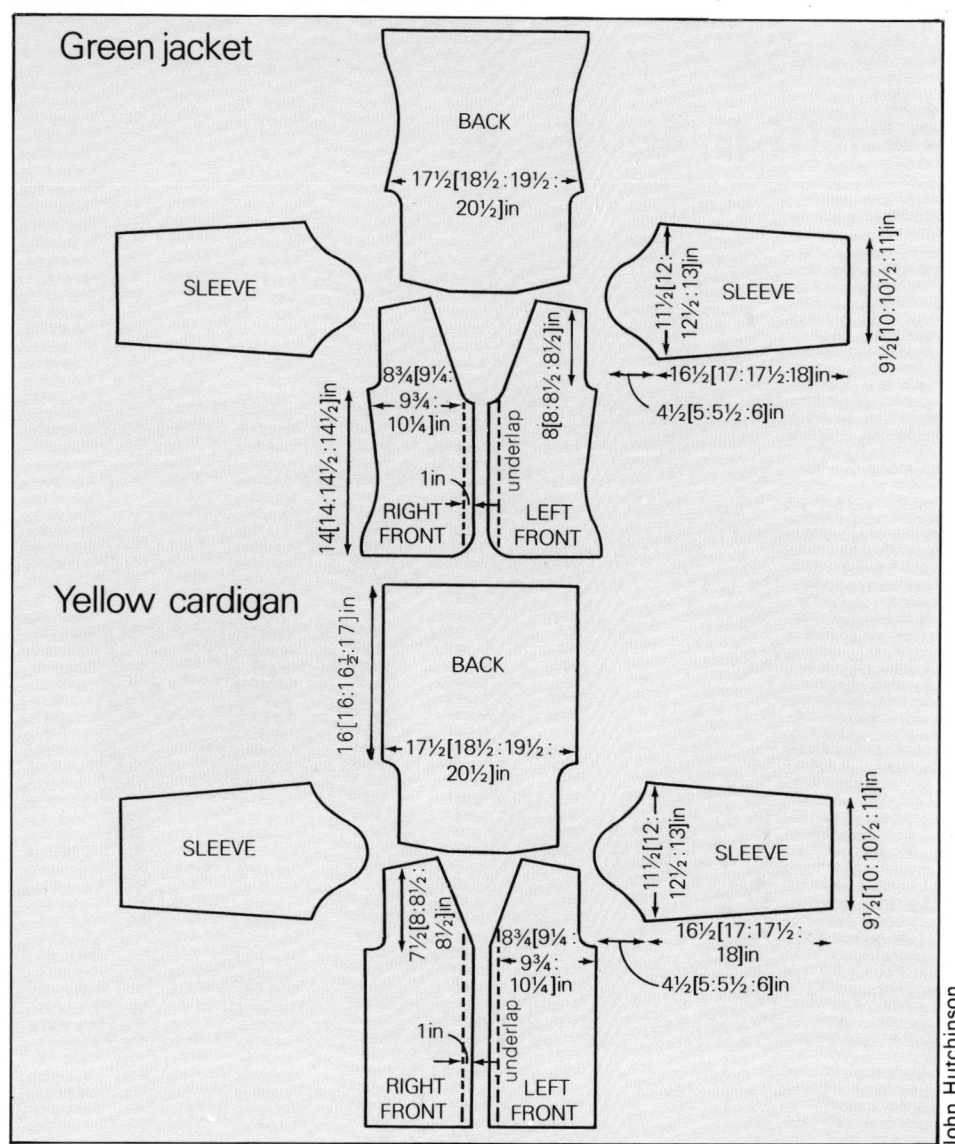

38[40:42:44] sts loosely. Beg with a P row, cont in rev stockinette st until work measures 16[16:16½:17]in (41[41:42: 43]cm); end with K row.

Shape armhole and front edge

Bind off 3 sts at beg of next row. Work 1 row. Dec one st at armhole edge on next and 3 foll alternate rows *and at same time* dec one st at front edge on next and every foll 3rd row until 18[20:20:22] sts rem. Cont straight until front measures same as back to shoulder ending at armhole edge.

Shape shoulder

Bind off 4 sts at beg of next and foll alternate row, then 5[6:6:7] sts on foll alternate row. Work 1 row. Bind off. Mark 6 button positions, the first 1in (3cm) from lower edge, the last level with beg of front shaping and the others evenly spaced between.

Right front

Work as for left front reversing all shaping and making buttonholes to correspond with markers thus: **1st buttonhole row** (RS) P4, bind off 3, P to end. **2nd buttonhole row** K to end, casting on 3 sts over those bound off on previous row.

Sleeves

Using No. 8 (5½mm) needles cast on 38[40:42:44] sts. Beg with P row, cont in rev stockinette st but inc one st at each end of every foll 20th row until there are 46[48:50:52] sts. Cont straight until work measures 16½[17:17½:18]in (42[43:44: 45]cm); end with K row.

Shape top

Bind off 2 sts at beg of next 2 rows. Dec one st at each end of next and every foll 4th row until 34[36:38:40] sts rem, then at each end of every foll alternate row until 24 sts rem. Bind off 3 sts at beg of next 4 rows. Bind off.

Patch pockets (make 2)

Using No. 8 (5½mm) needles cast on 20 sts. Beg with P row, cont in rev stockinette st for 5½in (14cm). Bind off.

To finish

Join shoulder seams. Set in sleeves. Join side and sleeve seams. Sew ribbon facing around outer edge and lower edge of sleeves. Cut buttonholes in ribbon and sew buttonholes. Sew on buttons and pockets.

Working right and left crossed stitches

In ''Triple bud pattern'' (see Stitch Wise, page 46) the stems of the flowers are single knit stitches against a purl background. The stitches are emphasized by slipping them on WS rows.

After a number of rows the stem splits into three to support the buds: this is done by increasing the single stem stitch to three, then the right and left cross techniques are applied to move the outer stems one stitch over on every RS row while the center stem stitch remains in the same place. These step-by-step photographs illustrate the directions for crossing stitches given in the 9th pattern row.

1 Two rows before the crossed stitches prepare for the technique by making three stitches out of the single stem stitch—slip, purl and slip these stitches on the following row (see 7th and 8th pattern rows).

2 To work a right cross, purl to within one stitch of the stem group. Move the yarn to the back and slip the next purl stitch. Drop the first stitch of the stem group and leave it at the front of the work, then slip the last purl stitch back onto the left-hand needle.

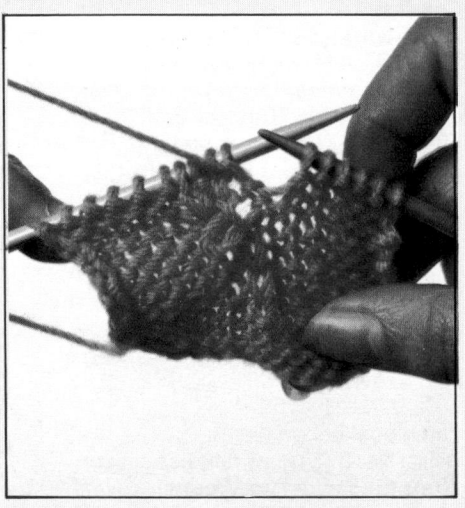

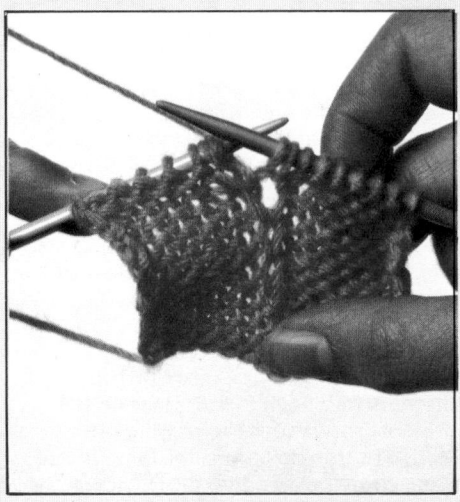

3 Use the right-hand needle point to pick up the right-hand dropped stitch and replace it on the left-hand needle. Knit the dropped stitch and purl the following one. The right cross is now complete: note that the two stitches have changed position.

4 Knit the next stitch to form the center stem of the three. Drop the next stitch off the left-hand needle and leave it at the front of the work. Purl the following stitch.

5 Replace the last stitch on the left-hand needle and knit it. The left cross is now complete and there are now three stems. On following RS rows the central stem remains the same while the outer ones move farther to the right and left by crossed stitch techniques.

Working long stitch "petals"

Long, loose stitches on the surface of the fabric are often used in knitting to give it an interesting texture; in slip stitch patterns they can look extremely colorful. In "Flower arrangement" (see Stitch Wise, page 47) long stitches have a pictorial effect; here they form petals on each side of a flower stem.

The stitches are picked up from the base of the stem after a number of rows have been worked to complete the stem. Take time and be careful when pulling the long stitch to the height of the rest of the knitting; simply tugging it up will pucker and distort the fabric.

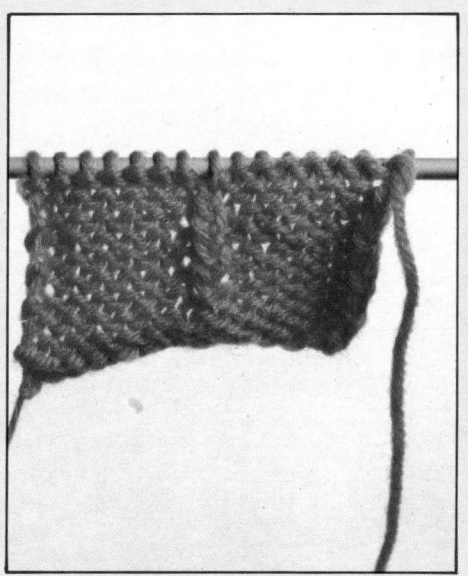

1 The stem of the flower is worked before the petals: it is a single knit stitch against six rows of purl background. On each row the stem is emphasized by working into the back of the stitch.

2 On the 7th pattern row, purl to within four stitches of the stem. With the yarn at the back of the work, insert the right-hand needle point from front to back through the fabric at the right of the stem stitch in the first pattern row. Hook the needle point through the loop of a stitch and draw it through. The right-hand needle point and new loop are now lying entirely on the front of the fabric.

3 Draw a long, loose loop up to the height of the work on the left-hand needle. It may be fairly difficult to draw the loop up, so place your left thumb on the base of the stem to steady the work. Knit the next stitch, then pass the long loop over it.

4 Purl three stitches, knit the stem stitch through the back of the loop, then purl three more stitches. Now take the yarn to the back of the work and pick up another long loop from the first row at the left of the stem.

5 Knit the next stitch and pass the second long loop over it.
The long stitches now form "petals" on each side of the stem. These extra stitches are rapidly decreased by passing them over the knitted stitches, which also anchors the petals in the correct position. The long stitches must lie flat and not cause the fabric to pucker; if necessary, ease the stitches to make them longer.

Fred Mancini

Flower pattern and fabrics

Tyrolean flower border

This is an overall pattern based on the panel used for the fronts of the sweater on page 48. The design is a combination of techniques already covered, including slip stitch patterning, making bobble stitches (for the flowers) and long dropped stitches (for the stems). Here the pattern is shown in alternating bands of contrasting colors. A single row of this knitted-in "embroidery" makes an interesting border design.

For one band of pattern you need three colors, A, B and C. Using A, cast on a multiple of 10sts plus 3 extra.

1st row Using A, K to end.
2nd row Using A, P to end.
3rd row Using B, K to end.
4th row Using B, K5, *K3 winding yarn 3 times around needle for each st, K7, rep from * ending with K5 instead of K7.
5th row Using A, K1, *sl1 with yarn at back, K3, sl3 dropping extra loops, K3, rep from * to last 2sts, sl1, K1.
6th row Using A, P1, *sl1 with yarn in front, P3, sl3, P3, rep from * to last 2sts, sl1, P1.
7th row Using A, K5, *sl3 with yarn at back, K7, rep from * ending with K5

instead of K7.
8th row As 7th, but P instead of K and keep yarn in front when slipping sts.
9th row Using A, K3*, sl2 with yarn at back, drop next st (first in B) off needle at front of work, replace 2 slipped sts on left-hand needle, pick up dropped st in B and K it, K3, drop next st (third in B) off needle at front of work, K2, pick up dropped st in B and K it, K3, rep from * to end.
10th row Using C, P1, sl2 with yarn in front, *(P1, K1, P1 all into next st, sl2) twice, P1, K1, P1 all into next st, sl3, rep from * ending with (P1, K1, P1 all into next st, sl2) 3 times, P1.
11th row Using C, K1, sl2 with yarn at back, *make bobble (MB) as foll: P3, turn and K3, turn and sl1, K2 tog, psso, (sl2, MB) twice, sl3, rep from * ending with (MB, sl2) 3 times, K1.
12th row Using A, P to end, working into back of bobble sts.
13th and 14th rows As 1st and 2nd. These 14 rows form the patt. Rep them throughout. Choose 3 different colors for next repeat of pattern and work in alternating rows of color.

Triple bud pattern

Alternating sprigs of three buds branching off a middle stem form an overall textured stitch on a purl background. The stems are slipped knit stitches carried up through the fabric to give a raised chain effect. The buds are bobble stitches and the stems split into three, using crossed stitch techniques. Cast on a multiple of 16sts plus 5 extra.
1st row (RS) P2, *(K1, yo, K1, yo, K1) all into next st—called inc 5—, P3, K1, P3, rep from * to last 3 sts, P3.
2nd row K3, *K3, sl1 with yarn at front, K3, P5, rep from * to last 2 sts, K2.
3rd row P2, *K5, P3, inc 5, P3, K5, P3, K1, P3, rep from * to last 3 sts, P3.
4th row K3, *K3, sl1 with yarn at front, K3, P1, P3 tog, P1, K3, P5, K3, P1, P3 tog, P1, rep from * to last 2sts, K2.
5th row P2, *sl1 with yarn at back, K2 tog, psso, P3, K5, P3, sl1, K2 tog, psso, P3, K1, P3, rep from * to last 3sts, P3.
6th row K6, *sl1 with yarn at front, K7, P1, P3 tog, P1, K7, rep from * ending with K6 instead of K7.
7th row P6, *sl1 with yarn at back, K2 tog, psso, P5, P2 tog, (K1, yo, K1) into next st, P2 tog, P5, rep from * ending with P4 instead of P5.
8th row K5, *sl1 with yarn in front, P1, sl1, K13, rep from * to end.
9th row P12, *sl1 with yarn at back, drop next st off needle to front of work, sl last slipped st back onto left-hand needle, pick up dropped st and K it, P1—called right cross (RC)—, K1, drop next st off needle to front of work, P1, pick up dropped st and K it—called left cross (LC)—, P11, rep from * ending with P4 instead of P11.
10th row K4, *(sl1 with yarn in front, K1) twice, sl1, K11, rep from * to last st, K1.
11th row P11, *RC, P1, K1, P1, LC, P9,

rep from * ending with P3.
12th row K3, *(sl1 with yarn in front, K2) twice, sl1, K9, rep from * to last 2sts, K2.
13th row P10, *RC, P2, K1, P2, LC, P7, rep from * ending with P2.
14th row K2, *(sl1 with yarn in front, K3) twice, sl1, K7, rep from * to last 3sts, K3.
15th row P3, *P3, K1, P3, inc 5, rep from * to last 2sts, P2.
16th row K2, *P5, K3, sl1 with yarn in front, K3, rep from * to last 3sts, K3.
17th row P3, *P3, K1, P3, K5, P3, inc 5, P3, K5, rep from * to last 2sts, P2.
18th row K2, *P1, K3 tog, P1, K3, P5, K3, P1, P3 tog, P1, K3, sl1 with yarn in front, K3, rep from * to last 3sts, K3.
19th row P3, *P3, K1, P3, sl1 with yarn at back, K2 tog, psso, P3, K5, P3, sl1, K2 tog, psso, rep from * to last 2sts, P2.
20th row K6, *P1, P3 tog, P1, K7, sl1 with yarn in front, K7, rep from * ending with K6.
21st row P4, *P2 tog, (K1, yo, K1) into next st, P2 tog, P5, sl1 with yarn at back, K2 tog, psso, P5, rep from * to last st, P1.
22nd row *K13, sl1 with yarn in front, P1, sl1, rep from * to last 5sts, K5.
23rd row P4, *RC, K1, LC, P11, rep from * to last st, P1.
24th row K12, *(sl1 with yarn at back, K1) twice, sl1, K11, rep from * ending with K4.
25th row P3, *RC, P1, K1, P1, LC, P9, rep from * to last 2sts, P2.
26th row K11, *(sl1 with yarn in front, K2) twice, sl1, K9, rep from * ending with K3.
27th row P2, *RC, P2, K1, P2, LC, P7, rep from * to last 3sts, P3.
28th row K10, *(sl1 with yarn at front, K3) twice, sl1, K7, rep from *, end with K2.
These 28 rows form patt. Rep throughout.

Flower arrangement

Each flower in this pretty fabric is made from only one stitch the same as a bobble. The stems are emphasized by twisting the stitch (working into the back of it) and the petals are a new type of long stitch.
For an overall pattern cast on a multiple of 12sts plus 1 extra.
1st row (RS) P12, *K1 tbl, P11, rep from * to last st, P1.
2nd row K12, *P1 tbl, K11, rep from * to last st, K1.
3rd-6th rows Rep 1st and 2nd rows twice.
7th row P8, *with yarn at back, insert right-hand needle from front to back through fabric at right of twisted K st in 1st row and draw a long, loose loop up to height of work on needle, with loop on right-hand needle, K next st and pass loop over st, P3, K1 tbl, P3, with yarn at back, draw up another loop from left of st in 1st row, with loop on right-hand needle, K next st and pass loop over, P3, rep from * to last 5sts, P5.
8th row As 2nd.
9th row P12, *(K1, yo) 3 times and K1 all into same st—called inc 7—, P11, rep from * to last st, P1.

10th row K12, *P7, K11, rep from * to last st, K1.
11th row P12, *K2 tog tbl, K3 tog tbl, K2 tog, P11, rep from * to last st, P1.
12th row K12, *P3 tog, K11, rep from * to last st, K1.
13th row P6, *K1 tbl, P11, rep from * ending with P6.
14th row K6, *P1 tbl, K11, rep from * ending with K6.
15th-18th rows Rep 13th and 14th rows twice.
19th row P2, *with yarn at back, draw a long loop from right of twisted K st in 13th row and pass loop over next st as before, P3, K1 tbl, P3, draw another loop from left of same st and pass over next st as before, P3, rep from * ending with P2.
20th row As 14th.
21st row P6, *inc 7, P11, rep from *ending with P6.
22nd row K6, *P7, K11, rep from * ending with K6.
23rd row P6, *K2 tog tbl, K3 tog tbl, K2 tog, P11, rep from * ending with P6.
24th row K6, *P3 tog, K11, rep from * ending with K6.
These 24 rows form patt. Rep throughout.

Fred Mancini

Tyrolean sweater

This Alpine-fresh sweater, with its delicate flower decoration, leg-of-mutton sleeves and flared cuffs, is the perfect cover-up for a cool spring day.

Sizes

To fit 32[34:36:38]in (83[87:92:97]cm) bust.

Length from shoulder, 19½[19½:20½: 20½]in (49.5[49.5:52:52]cm).

Sleeve seam, 17[18:18:18½]in (43[45.5: 45.5:47]cm).

Note Directions for larger sizes are in brackets []; where there is only one set of figures it applies to all sizes.

Materials

15[15:16:16]oz (400[400:450:450]g) of a sport yarn in main color (A)

2oz (50g) each in contrasting colors (B and C)

1 pair No. 3 (3¼mm) knitting needles

Cable needle

5 buttons

Gauge

28sts and 36 rows to 4in (10cm) in stockinette st on No. 3 (3¼mm) needles.

Back

Using No. 3 (3¼mm) needles and B, cast on 132[142:152:162]sts. **K2 rows. Cut off B and join in A. Beg bud patt.

1st row (WS) P to end.

2nd row K8, *(K1, yo, K1, yo, K1) all into next st, K9, rep from * ending with K3 instead of K9.

3rd row P3, *P5 winding yarn twice around needle for each st, P9, rep from * ending with P8.

4th row K8, *keeping yarn at back, sl5 dropping extra loops, K9, rep from * ending with K3.

5th row P3, *keeping yarn at front, sl5, P9, rep from * ending with P8.

6th row K8, *sl next 3sts **tog** knitwise, K2 tog, pass slipped sts all over K2 tog, K9, rep from * ending with K3.

7th row P to end.

8th row K3, *(K1, yo, K1, yo, K1) all into next st, K9, rep from * ending with K8.

9th row P8, *P5 winding yarn twice around needle for each st, P9, rep from * ending with P3.

10th row K3, *keeping yarn at back, sl5 dropping extra loops, K9, rep from * ending with K8.

11th row P8, *keeping yarn at front, sl5, P9, rep from * ending with P3.

12th row K3, *sl next 3sts **tog** knitwise, K2 tog, pass slipped sts all over K2 tog, K9, rep from * ending with K8.

These 12 rows form patt. Rep them twice more **.

Next row P2[6:3:0], *P2 tog, P7[6:6:6], rep from * 13[15:17:19] times more, P2 tog, P2[6:3:0]. 117[125:133:141] sts.

Next row K1, *P1, K1, rep from * to end.

Next row P1, *K1, P1, rep from * to end.

BACK

16[17:18:19]in

6¼[6¼:8:8]in

17[18:18: 18½]in

SLEEVE

16½[16½:18:18]in

13½[13½: 14½:14½]in

SLEEVE

7[7: 7½:7½]in

8½[9:9½:10]in

8½[8½:9:9]in

4in

RIGHT FRONT

LEFT FRONT

½ in overlap

John Hutchinson

Cont in ribbing until work measures 8½[8½:9:9]in (21.5[21.5:23:23]cm) from beg of ribbing.

Shape armholes
Bind off 7sts at beg of next 2 rows. Dec one st at each end of every row until 89[97:105:113]sts rem. Cont straight until armholes measure 7[7:7½:7½]in (18[18:19:19]cm).

Shape shoulders
Bind off 8sts at beg of next 6 rows and 5[7:9:11]sts at beg of foll 2 rows. Bind off rem 31[35:39:43]sts.

Left front
Using No. 3 (3¼mm) needles and B, cast on 82[82:92:92]sts. Work from ** to ** as for back.
Next row P4[4:3:0], *P2 tog, P4[7:4:7], rep from * 11[7:13:9] times more, P2 tog, P4[4:3:0]. 69[73:77:81]sts.
Beg ribbing and flower border panel.
1st row (RS) (K1, P1) 12[13:14:15] times, K13 A, (P1, K1) 16[17:18:19] times.
2nd row Rib 32[34:36:38], P13 A, rib 24[26:28:30].
3rd row Rib 24[26:28:30], K13 B, rib 32[34:36:38].
4th row Rib 32[34:36:38], K5 B, K3 winding yarn 3 times around needle for each st, K5 B, cut off B, rib 24[26:28:30].
5th row Rib 24[26:28:30], K1, sl1 with yarn at back, K3, sl3 dropping extra loops, K3, sl1, K1, rib to end.
6th row Rib 32[34:36:38], P1, sl1 with yarn in front, P3, sl3, P3, sl1, P1, rib to end.
7th row Rib 24[26:28:30], K5, sl3 with yarn at back, K5, rib to end.
8th row Rib 32[34:36:38], P5, sl3 with yarn in front, P5, rib to end.
9th row Rib 24[26:28:30], K3, sl2 with yarn at back, drop next st off needle at front of work, replace 2 slipped sts on left-hand needle, pick up dropped st and K it, K3, drop next st off needle at front of work, K2, pick up dropped st and K it, K3, rib to end.
10th row Rib 32[34:36:38], P3 in A, (P1, K1, P1 all into next st in C, sl2) twice, P1, K1, P1 all into next st in C, P3A, rib to end.
11th row Rib 24[26:28:30] in A, K3, (make bobble in C as foll: P3, turn and K3, turn and sl1, K2 tog, psso, K2 A) twice, make bobble in C, K3 A, cut off C, rib to end.
12th row Rib 32[34:36:38], P13 working into back of bobble sts, rib to end.
13th row As 1st.
14th row As 2nd.
These 14 rows form patt. Cont in patt until work measures 7½[7½:8:8]in (19[19:20.5:20.5]cm) from beg of ribbing; end with a RS row. Dec one st at beg of next and every foll alternate row until work measures 8½[8½:9:9]in (21.5[21.5:23:23]cm) from beg of ribbing; end with a WS row.

Shape armhole
Bind off 7sts at beg of next row. Cont to dec one st at front edge as before, dec one st at armhole edge on next 7 rows. Dec at front edge only until 29[31:33:35]sts rem. Cont straight until armhole measures 7[7:7½:7½]in (18[18:19:19]cm); end with a WS row.

Shape shoulder
Bind off at beg of next and foll alternate rows 8sts 3 times. Work 1 row. Bind off rem 5[7:9:11]sts.

Right front
Work as for left front, reversing shaping and position of ribbing and flower border panel as foll:
1st row (K1, P1) 16[17:18:19] times, K13 A, (P1, K1) 12[13:14:15] times. Patt 3 more rows.
Next row (buttonhole row) Rib 3, bind off 2sts, patt to end.
Next row Patt to end, casting on 2sts over those bound off in previous row. Make 4 more buttonholes 1¾in (4.5cm) apart.

Sleeves
Using No. 3 (3¼mm) needles and B, cast on 82[82:92:92]sts. K2 rows. Cut off B and join in A. Work 19 rows bud patt as for back.
Next row K1 [1:5:5], *K2 tog, K11 [11:6:6], rep from * 5[5:9:9] times more, K2 tog, K1 [1:5:5]. 75[75:81:81]sts.
Beg first row with P1, cont in K1, P1 ribbing, inc one st at each end of every 10th[10th:8th:8th] row until there are 91[91:101:101]sts.
Cont straight until sleeve measures 11½[12:12:12]in (29[30.5:30.5:30.5]cm) from beg of ribbing, end with a WS row and inc one st at end of last row. 92[92:102:102]sts.
Work 3½[4:4:4½]in (9[10:10:11.5]cm) in bud patt, end with a WS row.

Shape top
Bind off 7sts at beg of next 2 rows. Dec one st at each end of every foll 4th row 5 times in all, then at each end of every foll alternate row until 27 sts rem. Bind off.

To finish
Press under damp cloth with warm iron, omitting ribbing.
Join shoulder seams.
Set in sleeves, gathering around top 8in (20cm) to fit along shoulder edge. Join side and sleeves seams.
Border Using No. 3 (3¼mm) needles, B and with RS facing, pick up and K 80[80:84:84]sts along right front edge to shaping, 70[70:74:74]sts along shaped front edge and 15[17:19:21]sts to center back neck. Bind off knitwise on WS. Work similar border on left side. Press seams and border. Sew on buttons.

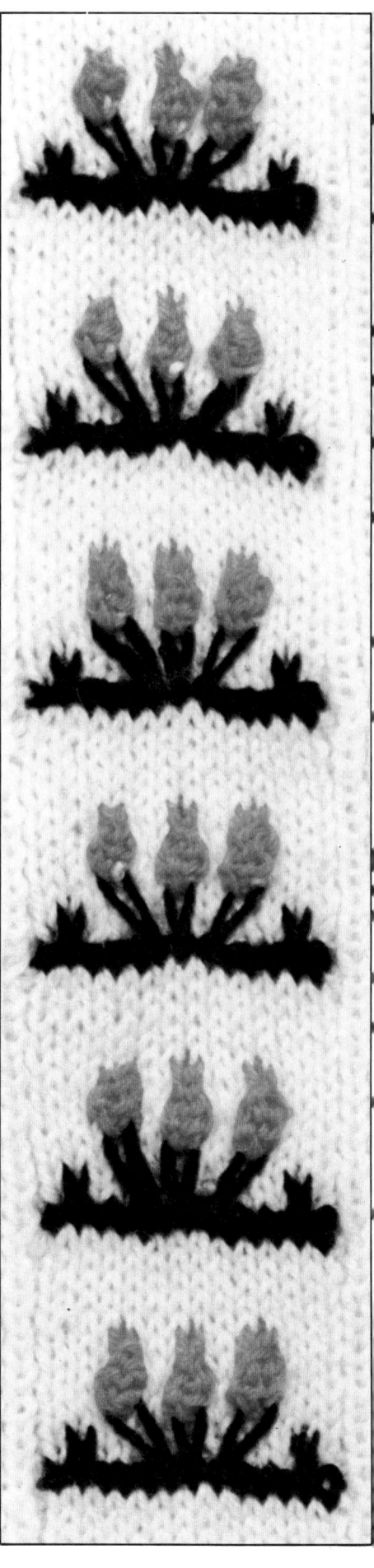

Knitting/COURSE 46

Knitting with beads

The bead knitting of the 18th and 19th centuries illustrates the beautiful results that can be achieved by adding beads to knitted garments and accessories. Today, with the wide range of wooden, plastic, and glass beads available, the possibilities for bead knitting seem endless.

With a little practice the technique of knitting with beads should present few problems even to the less advanced knitter. There are two traditional methods for adding beads to knitting: one is called bead knitting and the other beaded knitting. In bead knitting the beads are worked into the knitted fabric so that each bead covers a stitch. In beaded knitting, however, the beads lie between the stitches. Instructions for bead knitting are given here and those for beaded knitting are in the next course, which also explains the application of sequins.

Threading beads

When knitting with beads it is important to choose ones that will be suitable for the type of yarn you are using. The yarn should pass easily through the eye of the bead; if the eye is too small (or the yarn too thick) the yarn could easily become frayed. Equally important is the weight of the beads. Knitting will sag if the beads are too heavy; if large beads are needed it would be wise to use plastic or wooden ones instead of glass. Before beginning bead knitting, you must thread the beads onto the knitting yarn. This process is simple if only one type of bead is being used throughout. But when working a pattern that calls for more than one type of bead, the knitter must follow a charted design while threading, as shown on the next page.

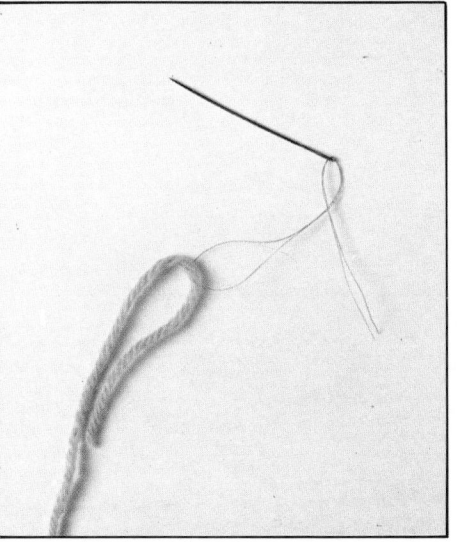

1 It is not always possible to thread the knitting yarn through a needle thin enough to pass through the eye of the beads. In this case, thread both ends of a short piece of strong cotton thread through the needle. Then pass the end of the knitting yarn through the thread loop and double it back.

2 When using a single type of bead which has come already strung, pass the needle through several beads at a time and then pull them off the string and slide them down the needle and thread onto the knitting yarn.

Charts for bead patterns

A variety of designs can be made by arranging different types or colors of beads together. This, however, necessitates threading the beads in correct sequence by using a knitting chart. Follow the threading instructions carefully so that you will not have to break your yarn and rethread the pattern. Bead knitting is not as easily undone as ordinary knitting, so take a little extra time threading in the right order before beginning your knitting.

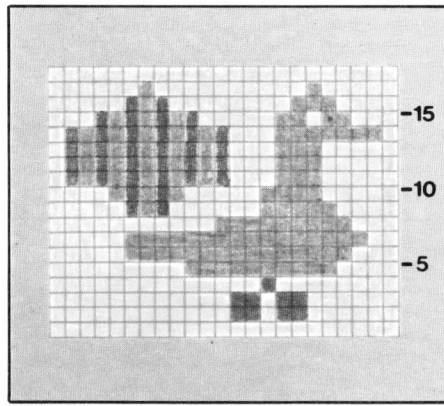

1 If you are knitting a design which is entirely covered with beads, each square on the knitting chart corresponds to a bead. Remember when working with a chart that the first row is the bottom row of the chart and is read from right to left.

2 Thread the beads onto the yarn in the correct order. The last bead to be threaded will be the first bead to be knitted, so that if there are an even number of rows in the pattern, begin threading from the right side of the top row of the chart.

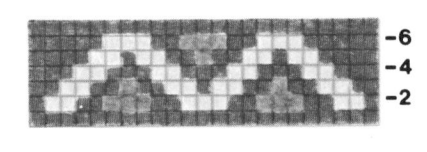

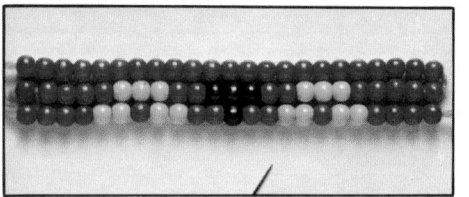

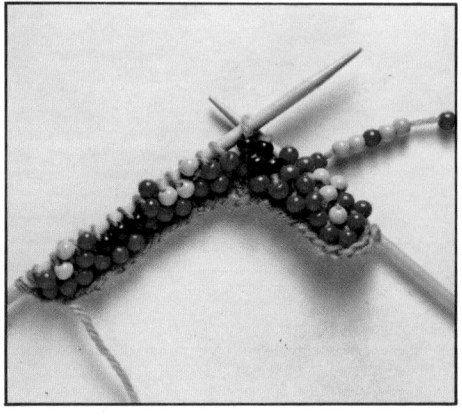

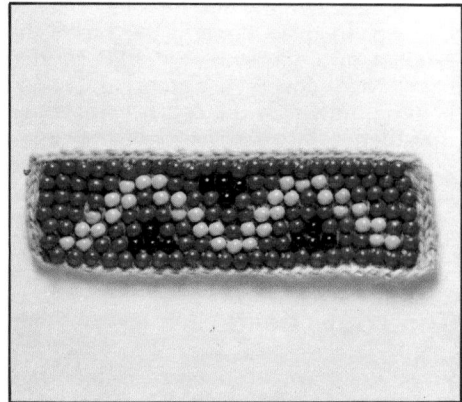

3 If there are an odd number of rows in the chart, begin threading from the left side of the top row.

4 After the beads are threaded, knit them off in the method shown right, adding one bead with each stitch.

5 Each bead should be big enough to cover each stitch but not big enough to cause the fabric to curl up.

Charts for bead motifs

A solid bead-covered fabric is most suitable for small articles such as clutch purses, belts or bracelets, but individual motifs can be sprinkled over large items very effectively. Following a chart for threading is necessary for bead motifs only if more than one type or color of bead is being used.

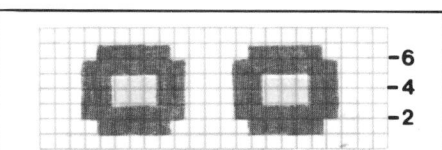

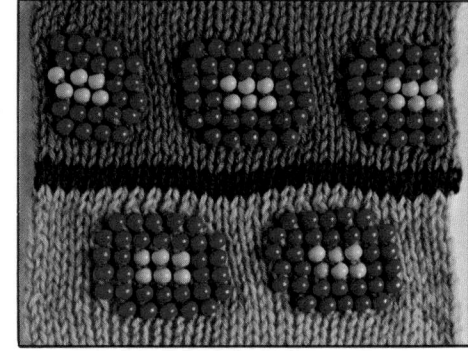

1 The colored squares on the chart represent the beads and the white ones the knitted fabric. Thread the beads so that the last bead is threaded first.

2 An interesting result is achieved by repeating a motif in stripes of different colors.

Bead knitting

In bead knitting the crossed knit and purl stitch is most commonly used for applying the beads. Although it is possible to use the ordinary knit stitch, the crossed stitch has three advantages. First, because the stitch is crossed, the bead will lie over both sides of each loop and can therefore cover it completely, which is important if you want to create an entirely beaded surface. Second, the bead will protrude instead of sinking into the fabric. And, third, when a knit stitch is crossed it tightens and thus holds the bead securely in place, preventing it from slipping through to the back of the work. Choose knitting needles that will produce a loop which the beads can pass through easily. The following instructions show how to work both the knit and the purl row. The knit row is easier to master and it is probably no coincidence that most historical examples of bead knitting appear on articles which have been knitted in the round in which only the knit stitch was used. Because the stitches are crossed by the succeeding row, remember when working scattered motifs to cross the stitches which hold beads in the following row even if you are not adding a bead in that particular stitch.

Knit row

1 Knit to the position of the first bead stitch. When working a bead-covered surface, allow at least two plain stitches at each edge.

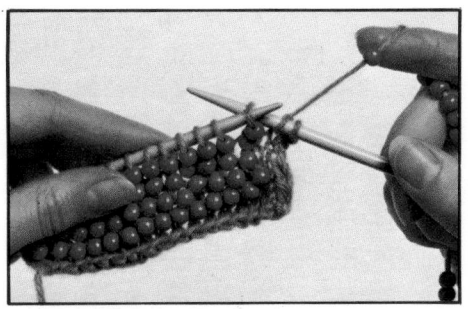

2 At the bead stitch insert the right-hand needle into the back of the next stitch, which creates a crossed knit stitch instead of a plain one.

3 Next slide the bead up to the work.

4 Wrap the yarn around the top of the right-hand needle in the usual way. The bead should now be positioned at the back of the work.

5 Keeping both needles in the well-opened loop, push the bead through to the front with the left forefinger.

6 After the right-hand needle has drawn the new loop through, the stitch is dropped from the left-hand needle and the next bead stitch is worked the same way.

Purl row

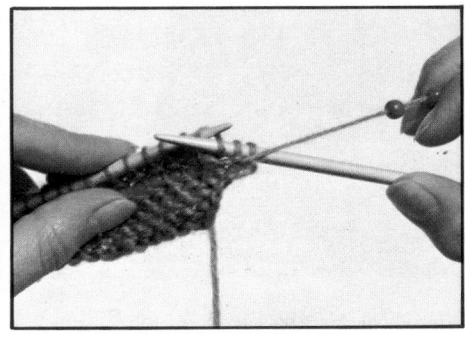

1 On the purl row, again work at least the first two stitches without beads. At the bead stitch insert right-hand needle into the back of the next stitch.

2 Wrap the yarn around the top of the right-hand needle before pushing the bead too close.

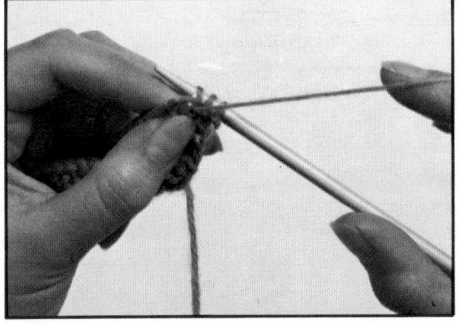

3 Slide the bead up to the work and pass the right-hand needle through the loop using the left thumb to push the bead through at the same time.

Fred Mancini

Woman's bead-knitted cardigan

Beads — in shades of blue, white, cream and orange — sprinkled on one shoulder add an individual touch to the lines of this elegant cross-over sweater. The picot edging gives a professional finish to the garment. You can practice bead knitting while you treat yourself to something special.

Sizes
To fit 32[34:36]in (83[87:91]cm) bust.
Length, 19½[20½:21½]in (50[52:54]cm).
Sleeve seam, 17[17¼:17¾]in (43[44:45]cm.
Note Directions for larger sizes are in brackets []; if there is only one set of figures it applies to all sizes.

Materials
11[12:13]oz (300[325:350]g) of a fingering yarn
1 pair each Nos. 2 and 3 (2¾ and 3¼mm) knitting needles
No. 2 (2¾mm) circular needle
Beads as needed
Two buttons, stitch holder

Gauge
28 sts and 36 rows to 4in (10cm) in stockinette st on No. 3 (3¼mm) needles.

Left front
Using No. 2 (2¾mm) needles cast on 95[103:111] sts. Beg with a K row, work 15 rows stockinette st.
Picot row K1, *yo, K2 tog, rep from * to end.
Change to No. 3 (3¼mm) needles and beg with a K row, work 16 rows stockinette st. * *
Shape sides and front edge
Next row Inc in first st, K to end.
Next row Bind off 2, P to end.
Next row K to last 2 sts, K2 tog.
Cont to inc at side edge on every 12th row 8 times more and *at the same time* cont to dec at front edge on next 3[7:11] rows, then on every alternate row until 51[55:59] sts rem; end with a P row.
Shape armhole
Cont to dec at front edge on every 4th row 16[17:18] times, and *at the same time* at armhole edge bind off 3 sts at beg of next row, 2 sts at beg of foll 2 alternate rows, then dec one st at beg of foll 3[4:5] alternate rows. Cont straight until armhole measures 7[7½:8]in (18[19:20]cm; end with a P row.
Shape shoulder
Bind off 5[5:6] sts at beg of next and

foll 3 alternate rows. P 1 row. Bind off.

Right front
First, pin out left front with wrong side of work facing and plan position of bead pattern on top part of front. Work right front to match left front, reversing all shaping. After armhole shaping has been completed, thread the required beads onto the ball of yarn, following the chart, right, and starting with the last bead to be worked. Cont to work right front, knitting beads in patt as shown on chart. There is a note on the chart about

threading flowers.

Back
Work as for left front to **.
Cont in stockinette st, inc one st at each
end of next and every foll 12th row until
there are 113[121:129] sts. Cont straight
until work measures the same as fronts
to armholes; end with a P row.

Shape armholes
Bind off 3 sts at beg of next 2 rows,
2 sts at beg of next 4 rows, then dec one
st at each end of next and foll 2[3:4]
alternate rows. Cont straight until
armholes measure the same as front
armholes to shoulder seams; end with
a P row.

Shape shoulders
Bind off 5[5:6] sts at beg of next 8 rows
and 5[7:5] sts at beg of foll 2 rows.
Cut off yarn and leave rem 43[45:47]
sts on a holder.

Sleeves
Using No. 2 (2¾mm) needles cast on
51[55:59] sts and work as for left front
to **. Cont in stockinette st, but inc
one st at each end of next and every foll
8th row until there are 85[89:93] sts.
Cont straight until sleeve measures
17[17¼:17¾]in (43[44:45]cm) from
picot row; end with a P row.

Shape top
Bind off 3 sts at beg of next 2 rows, then
2 sts at beg of next 4 rows. Dec one st
at each end of next and every foll alternate
row until 45[47:49] sts rem; end with a
P row. Bind off 2 sts at beg of next 8
rows, 3 sts at beg of next 4 rows then 4
sts at beg of next 2 rows. Bind off.
Note When the first sleeve has been
completed, pin it out and plan the patt.
Work second sleeve knitting in beads as
indicated on chart.

Front border
Join shoulder seams. Using No. 2
(2¾mm) circular needle and with RS
facing, join yarn to picot row on right
front and pick up and K 177[183:189] sts
along front edge to shoulder, K back
neck sts from holder, then pick up and K
177[183:189] sts along left front edge
ending at picot row. Beg with a P row,
work 6 rows stockinette st.
Picot row K1, *yo, K2 tog, rep from *
to end.
Beg with a K row, work 5 rows stockinette
st. Bind off.

To finish
Press or block work, according to yarn
used. If pressing, be careful when
pressing over the beads. Set in sleeves,
then join side and sleeve seams. Turn
all edges on picot rows to wrong side
and slip stitch in place. Sew a button
on left side seam and inside of right
side seam and make loops on each side
of front to fasten.

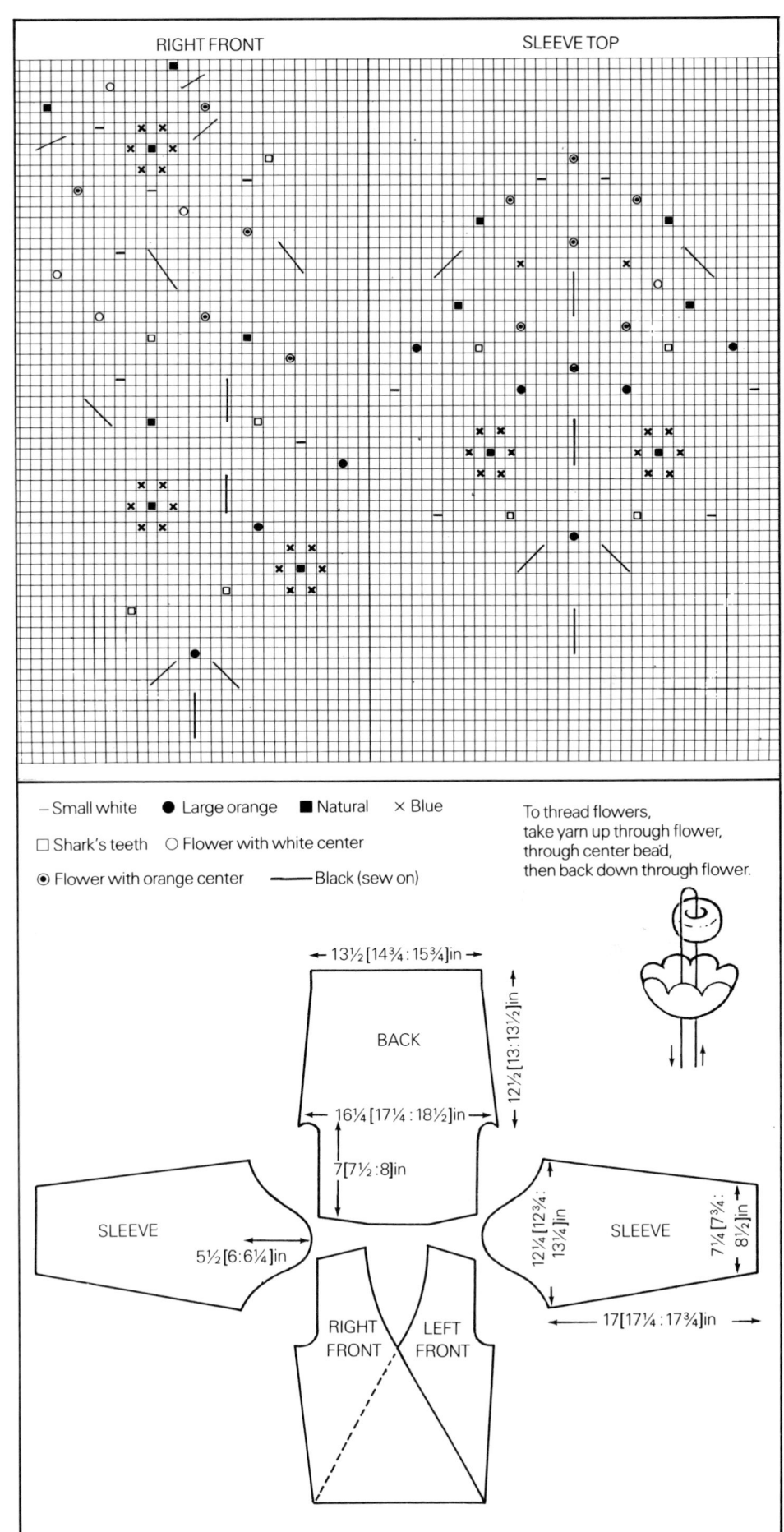

RIGHT FRONT   SLEEVE TOP

− Small white   ● Large orange   ■ Natural   × Blue

□ Shark's teeth   ○ Flower with white center

⊙ Flower with orange center   —— Black (sew on)

To thread flowers,
take yarn up through flower,
through center bead,
then back down through flower.

← 13½[14¾:15¾]in →

BACK

12½[13:13½]in

← 16¼[17¼:18½]in →

7[7½:8]in

SLEEVE

5½[6:6¼]in

12¼[12¾:13¼]in

SLEEVE

7¼[7¾:8½]in

RIGHT FRONT   LEFT FRONT

← 17[17¼:17¾]in →

John Hutchinson

Sewing / COURSE 43

Applying a yoke to a dress

These directions are for applying a rectangular yoke to the front of a dress. By turning under the seam allowances of the yoke before you sew it in place, you can avoid tricky mitering at the lower corners.

In the step-by-step photographs here, the main part of the dress below the yoke is gathered for fullness, since in this case the yoke is applied to a maternity dress. The same principles apply even if the garment is a slimline one.

1 Turn under the seam allowances along the side and lower edges of the front yoke section. Baste and press flat.

2 On the main dress section, staystitch down both side yoke seamlines. Mark the corners of the seamline with tailor's tacks. Run two rows of gathering across the lower edge of the yoke on the main dress section, on each side of the seamline, between the tailor's tacks.

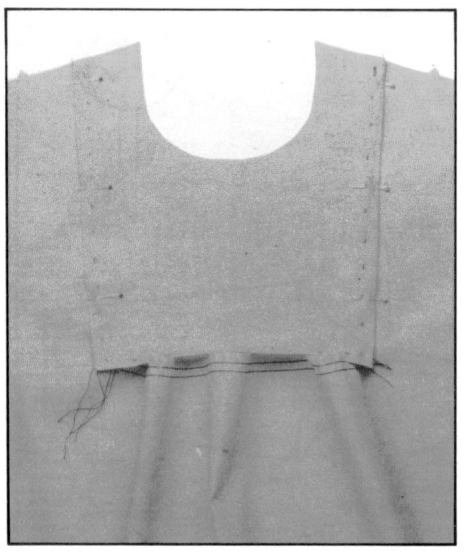

3 With dress front and yoke right side up, align the folded edge of the yoke with the seamline of the dress. Pin the yoke to the dress along the side edges.

4 Across the lower seamline of the dress front, pull up the gathering to fit the yoke and anchor the threads on a pin. Baste the yoke in place, spreading the gathers evenly.

5 On the right side, topstitch the yoke to the dress, stitching close to the folded edge of the yoke as shown. Remove all basting. On the inside, trim seam allowances and finish by overcasting together. Press seam toward the yoke.

Mitered corner on a ribbon trim

On the maternity dress on page 59, the seamline between the yoke and the dress (and also between the fabric trim on the cuffs and the dress) is finished by covering with a strip of ribbon sewn in place on each side of the seamline. At the lower edge of the yoke, the ribbon is mitered, or folded so that it turns the corner neatly.

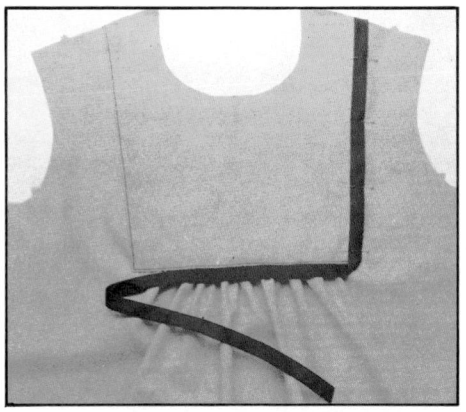

1 With the right side of the fabric and the ribbon face up, pin and baste the ribbon over the seamline as far as the corner. With the outer edge of the ribbon basted in place as far as the outer point of the corner, fold the ribbon under, so that the wrong side of the ribbon is up and lying parallel to the seamline to be covered.

2 Fold the ribbon up, so that the right side is showing. This will form the miter. Reverse the procedure for the other corner of the yoke. Baste and topstitch the ribbon in place, sewing close to both edges. Press.

Mitered corner on a fabric hem

Many dresses, particularly slim-fitting ones or those designed to be worn over slacks, have a slit up the side for about 6in (15cm) to allow for ease of movement. The facing down the sides of the slit is the same as the hem allowance across the bottom of the dress, and for a neat finish, the fabric should be mitered on the inside to avoid unattractive seams at the corners of the dress, which often show when you walk.

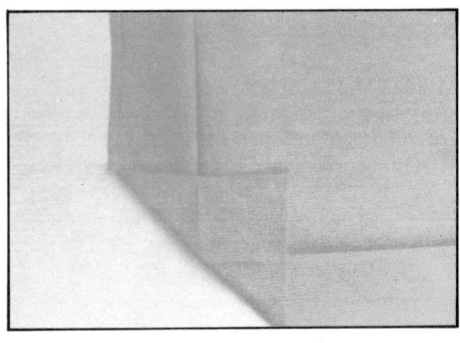

1 Stitch the side seam to the point marked at the upper end of the slit. Turn in the raw edge of the hem and side seam allowance $\frac{1}{4}$in (6mm) and press.

2 Turn hem allowance up and side facing to inside. Measure width of allowances evenly. Press folded edges only. Turn fabric back again and turn in the corner so that the diagonal foldline coincides with the corner of the side and hem foldlines. Press to mark foldline. This diagonal fold indicates the position of the stitching line for the miter.

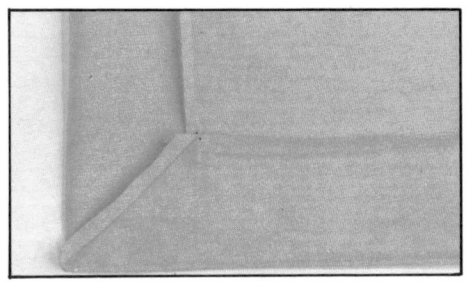

3 Turning the section to the right side, fold the hem to match the side facing, right sides together, so that the foldlines match. Baste and stitch along crease to corner at outer edge of hem. Cut off corner, leaving a $\frac{1}{4}$in (6mm) border.

4 Press the mitered seam open.

5 Turn the hem and facing allowances to the inside. Finish the edges of the hem and facing by stitching close to the folded inner edges. Baste around hem. Sew hem and facing to dress, using invisible hemming stitch.

Mike Berend

Stretch front panel for maternity slacks

During the early months of pregnancy, slacks may be worn with a simple elasticized waist, formed by threading elastic through a casing at the waist. However, in the later months, it is more comfortable to wear slacks with a stretch panel at the front and no elastic over the stomach.

A stretch knit fabric is probably the most suitable material for the panel. Use a synthetic knit if the slacks are made in a synthetic fabric, and cotton knit for cotton slacks. (See Sewing course 16, Volume 4, page 60, for notes on sewing stretch fabrics.)

The maternity slacks shown on page 62 can be made either with a stretch front panel or with a plain casing (see the directions for adapting the pattern.)

When buying elastic for the waist, choose a fairly pliable elastic, like the kind used for elasticized waists such as the ones used on the shorts shown in Volume 8, page 80. It is impossible to make adjustable button-holes, which are needed to make the waistband, if you use a deeply ribbed elastic.

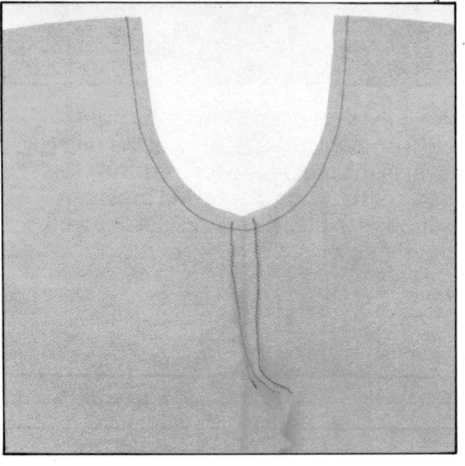

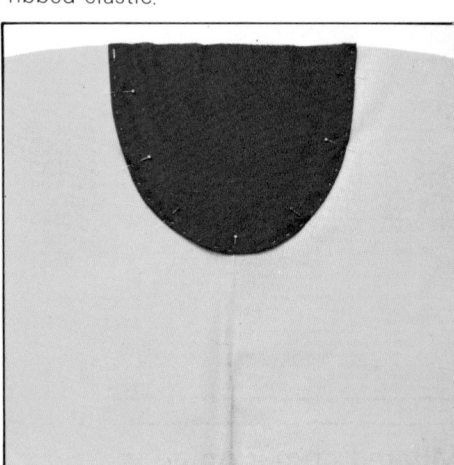

1 With right sides together stitch the front crotch seam to within 1½in (3.5cm) of inside leg seam.
Finish and press seam open. If necessary clip the curves to make the seams lie flat. To prevent stretching, staystitch around the curved edges at the front of the slacks and around the panel.

2 Turn in ⅝in (1.5cm) seam allowance around the curved edge of the front panel and baste. Press flat.

3 With right side up, pin and baste the panel to the slacks front. Stitch close to the outer edge of panel, stitching only to the casing foldline.

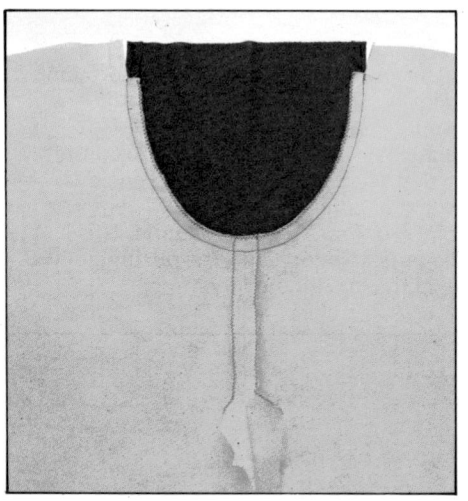

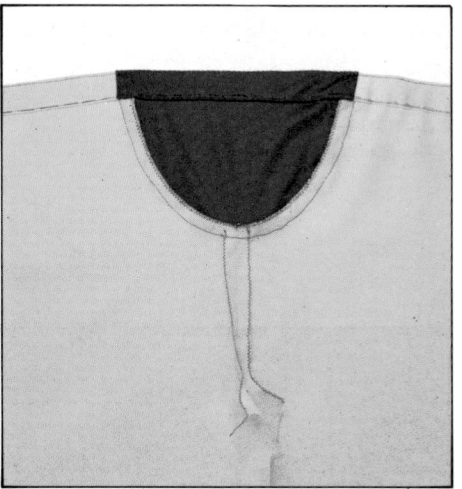

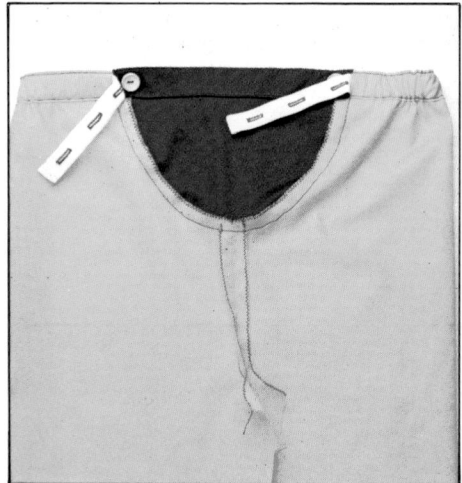

4 Clip the slacks seam allowance at the foldline to stitching. Press back. Finish the seam edges by overcasting them together. Sew slacks front to back down side seams. Press open.

5 To form the casing, turn in ¼in (6mm) around top edge. Then fold top edge to inside along foldline. Baste and stitch close to both edges. Press. When stitching across the front panel, stretch the fabric slightly to prevent the stitches from breaking when the panel is stretched; or use a zig-zag stitch if your machine has one.

6 Cut a piece of elastic, allowing approximately 6in (15cm) extra at each end to extend beyond the front panel seams. Cut off the extra and finish the ends. Make 3 evenly spaced ⅝in (1.5cm) buttonholes in each end of the elastic. Thread the elastic through the casing so that the ends extend from openings. Sew a button on each side of the front panel and fasten elastic in place.

Maternity dress and slacks

Pregnancy need not mean that you cannot look fashionable. This smock dress, with contrasting yoke and cuffs, can be worn through every stage of pregnancy. The matching slacks give additional warmth.

Dress

Adapting the pattern

Measurements
The pattern for the dress is adapted from the basic dress in the Stitch by Stitch Pattern Pack, which is available in sizes 10 to 20, corresponding to sizes 8 to 18 in ready-made clothes.

Materials
  2 sheets of tracing paper, at least
    36 x 50in (90cm x 130cm)
  Pencil
  Yardstick

1 Trace the dress front pattern, leaving 4in (10cm) of extra paper down the center front and at side edges. Omit waist dart. Cut the seam allowance away from the front neck edge; this edge is bound.
2 To move the dart allowance to the yoke seam, extend the bust dart line by 2in (5cm). From the center of the shoulder line draw a line to this point of the dart. Slash along this line from the shoulder to point. Close the side bust dart and tape in place. This will open the pattern at the shoulder.

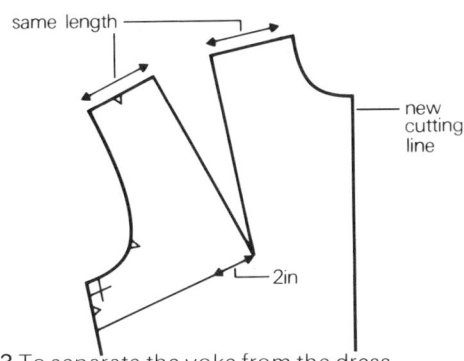

3 To separate the yoke from the dress, lay another piece of tracing paper over the bodice section of the dress. Trace the center front, neck, shoulder and side edges of the yoke. Join the dart point

Victor Yuan

and the center front edge with a straight horizontal line. Add $\frac{5}{8}$in (1.5cm) seam allowance to outer edges of yoke.

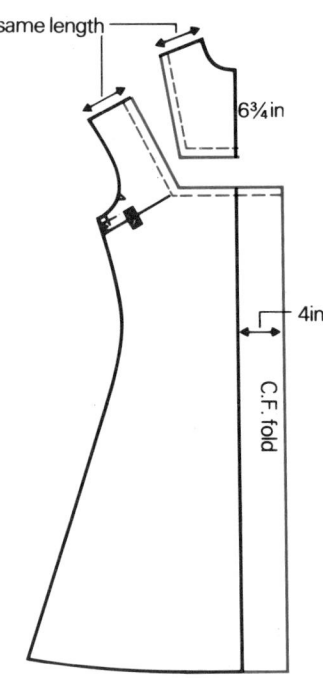

same length

6¾ in

4in

C.F. fold

4 To allow for gathering across the dress front, extend the front foldline out 4in (10cm) from the yoke line to the lower edge. For sizes 18 and 20 extend front foldline out 3in (7.5cm) from the yoke line to the lower edge. Add $\frac{5}{8}$in (1.5cm) seam allowance to the yoke seamlines.

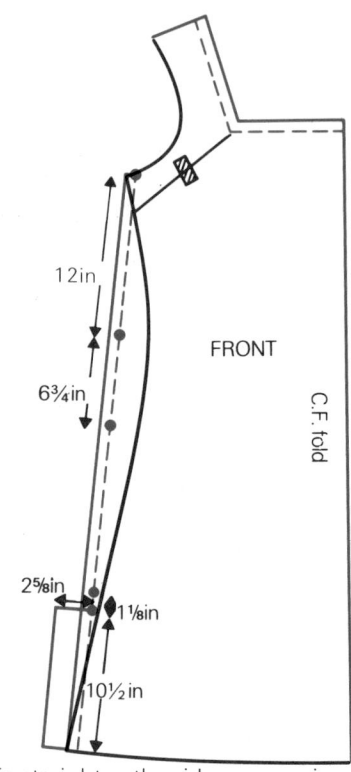

12in

6¾ in

FRONT

C.F. fold

2⅝in

1⅛in

10½ in

5 To straighten the side seam, using a yardstick draw a line from the side

cutting line at the armhole to the cutting line at the hem. Mark in the $\frac{5}{8}$in (1.5cm) seam allowance. To mark the length of the side slit and to allow for the facing, measure up the side seamline from the lower edge of dress 10½in (26.5cm) and mark. The side seam is sewn to this point. For the facing, measure up a further 1⅛in (3cm) and out 2⅝in (6.5cm) from the seamline. Draw a line to the lower edge.
6 To mark the pocket position, measure down the side seam from the armhole seamline 12in (30cm) and a further 6¾in (17cm). The pocket is stitched between these two points.

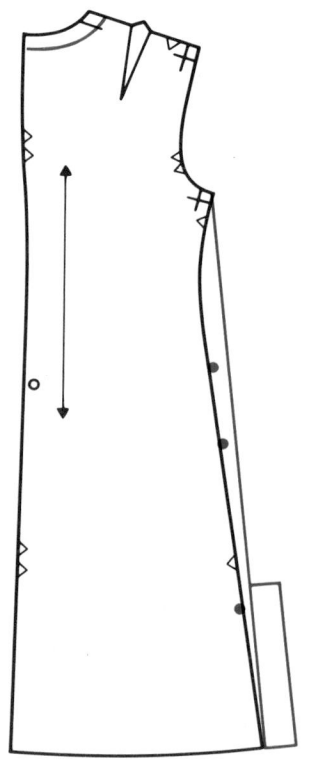

7 Trace the dress back pattern, leaving extra at the side edge. Omit the waist dart. Cut the seam allowance away from the neck edge, as this edge is bound. To straighten the side seam, use a yardstick to draw a line from the side cutting line at the armhole to the cutting line at the hem. Mark the $\frac{5}{8}$in (1.5cm) seam allowance.
Mark the length of the side slit, draw the slit facing and mark pocket position as directed for the dress front, using the same measurements.

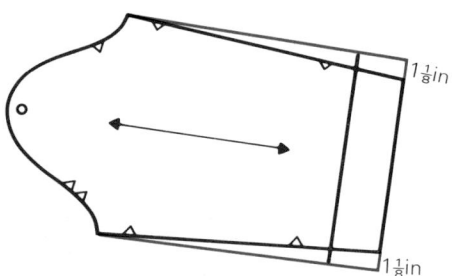

1⅛in

1⅛in

8 Trace the sleeve pattern, allowing extra paper at the sides. To make the

sleeve wider at the wrist, measure out 1⅛in (3cm) from each side at the lower edge. Draw the new side cutting lines from the armhole to these points. Mark new seam allowances.

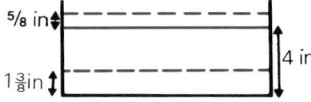

$\frac{5}{8}$ in

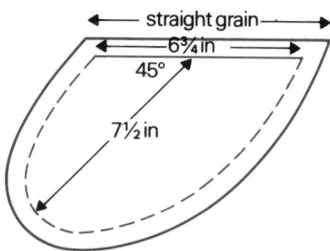

1⅜in

4 in

9 Draw a new cutting line 4in (10cm) from the edge. Mark $\frac{5}{8}$in (1.5cm) seam allowance above it. Cut away bottom piece and trace it, adding seam allowance to top edge. Draw 1⅜in (3.5cm) hem allowance. This piece is for contrasting trim.

straight grain

6¾in

45°

7½in

10 For the pocket, draw a straight line 6¾in (17cm) long. Mark a point halfway down this line and from this point, slanting down at an angle of 45°, measure and mark a point 7½in (19cm) away. Using a flexible curve, join the ends of the 6¾in (17cm) line to the marked point, making a deep, slanted bag-shaped pocket. Add $\frac{5}{8}$in (1.5cm) seam allowances all around. The pocket straight edge is placed on the straight grain (lengthwise or crosswise) when cutting.

Slacks

Adapting the pattern

Measurements
The pattern is adapted from the basic pants pattern in the Stitch by Stitch Pattern Pack, which is available in sizes 10 to 20, corresponding to sizes 8 to 18 in ready-made clothes.

Materials
*1 sheet of tracing paper at least 36 x 50in (90 x 130cm)
Pencil, flexible curve, yardstick
Right triangle*

Note Maternity slacks are cut with a higher waist to fit over the "bump."
1 Trace the front pattern, omitting dart. Extend center front cutting line up 3½in (9cm). Extend the grain line up ¾in (2cm) beyond the waist cutting line. Using the triangles, square out from the top of the grain line beyond the side edge. Measure out 2in (5cm) along this line from the original side cutting line at the waist and mark.
2 Before completing the side edge and the top edge, you must alter the width of the leg. The slacks are cut to fit closely.

around the ankle. Therefore, determine the length necessary and shorten the pattern to the finished length. Leave extra paper for the hem. At the lower edge measure in 2in (5cm) from the inside and side edges and mark. Using a yardstick draw a line to connect the mark from the waist to the hem. This is the side cutting line. For the inside cutting line, draw a line from the mark at the hem, tapering into the original cutting line at the notch.
3 To complete the side and top edge, using a flexible curve, connect mark at side edge to new center front, making a slight curve over the middle. This will be the foldline for casing. For casing, add 1⅜in (3.5cm) to this edge. Extend center front and side edges to new cutting line.

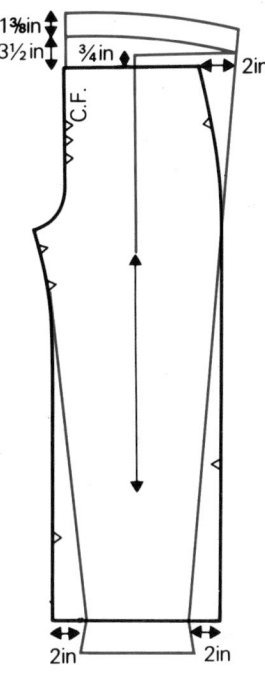

4 Before cutting around the new slacks shape, shape the outer edges of the hem allowance. Add 2in (5cm) to the lower

edge of pattern. Fold the hem allowance up along hemline fold. Trace the side edges.
5 Turn hem down and cut around the new slacks shape.
6 Trace the slacks back pattern, omitting the dart. Extend the back cutting line up ¾in (2cm). Extend the grain line up ⅜in (1cm) beyond the waist cutting line. Square out from the top of the grain line beyond the side edge. Measure out 2in (5cm) along this line from the original side cutting line at waist and mark. Draw a line to connect center back to side. This will be foldline for casing.

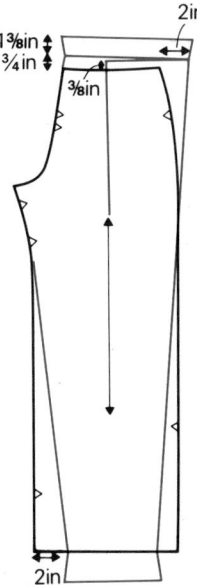

7 Following the directions given for the front, alter the length and width of the slacks leg using the same measurements. Add the hem allowance and the casing allowance to bottom and top edges, shaping center back and side edges as before.

Stretch front panel (optional)

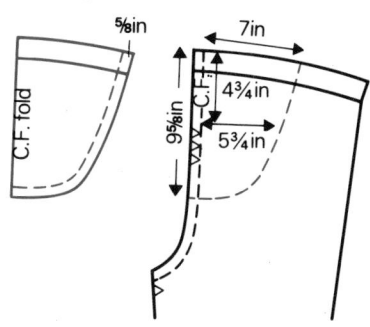

1 To cut a pattern for an optional front panel, alter the slacks front as shown on the left. Measure down the front seamline 9⅝in (24.5cm) and across 7in (17.5cm) along the top edge from the seamline. To mark the position for the curve, measure and mark a point 4¾in (12cm) down center front seamline and mark a point 5¾in (14.5cm) across from this point. Using a flexible curve, connect the mark at front to this center mark, then up to the mark at the top edge. Make the inner edge of the curve fairly deep.
2 Trace this panel and add ⅝in (1.5cm) seam allowance to curved edges of new pattern pieces. Trim seam allowance on front of panel section and cut panel once from stretch fabric, placing center on fold.

Directions for making

Key to adjusted pattern pieces

1 Dress front	Cut 1 on fold	
2 Dress back	Cut 2	
3 Dress sleeve	Cut 2	
1 Slacks front	Cut 2	
2 Slacks back	Cut 2	
A Front yoke	Cut 1 on fold	
B Pocket	Cut 4	
C Lower sleeve section	Cut 2 (contrast)	
D Front stretch panel	Cut 1 on fold	

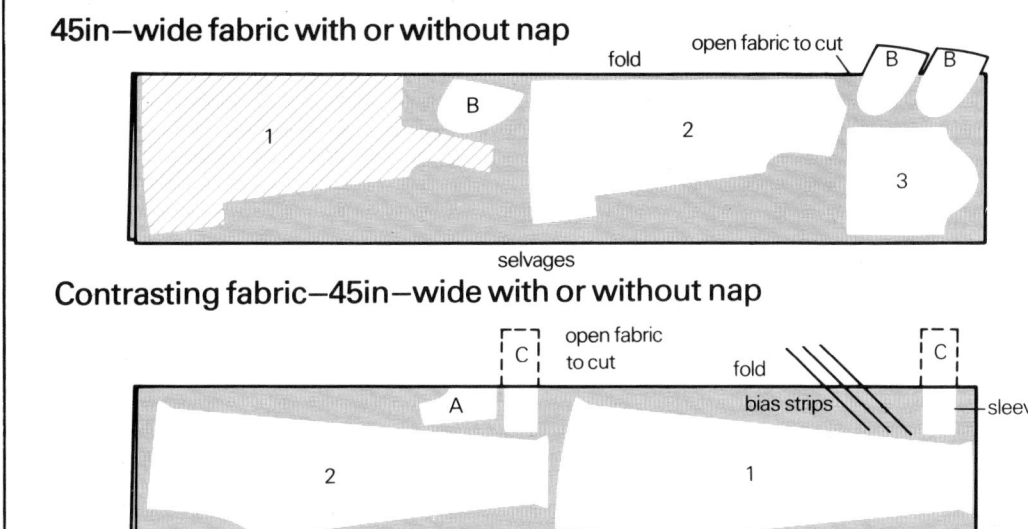

45in—wide fabric with or without nap

fold
open fabric to cut
B B
1
B
2
3
selvages

Contrasting fabric—45in—wide with or without nap

open fabric to cut
C
fold
C
bias strips
sleeve
A
2
1
selvages

54in- and 60in- wide stretch fabric

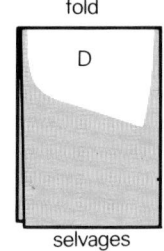

fold
D
selvages

Note For sizes 18 and 20. in order to cut the dress from 45in-wide fabric, the side slits should have rolled hems rather than wide facings.

Brian Mayor

Materials

*45in (115cm)-wide fabric with or
  without nap for main dress and
  sleeve sections:*
  Sizes 10, 12: 3⅜yd (3m)
  Sizes 14 to 20: 3½yd (3.2m)
*45in (115cm)-wide fabric with or
  without nap in contrasting fabric
  for yoke, sleeve trim and slacks*
  Sizes 10, 12: 2¾yd (2.5m)
  Sizes 14 to 20: 2⅞yd (2.6m)
*36in (90cm)-or 45in (115cm)-wide
  contrasting fabric for yoke and
  sleeve sections only:*
  Sizes 10, 12: ⅜yd (.4m)
  Sizes 14 to 20: ½yd (.5m)
54in (140cm) or 60in (150cm)-wide

*stretch fabric for panel (optional):
  For all sizes: ⅜yd (.3m)*
Thread
22in (56cm) zipper
Hook and eye
*2¾yd (2.5m) ½in-(1.2cm)-wide
  ribbon*
1⅛yd (1m) ¾in (2cm)-wide elastic
Two ½in (1.3cm) buttons (optional)

Suggested fabrics

Cotton, synthetics, cotton and wool
blends, synthetic blends.

Dress

1 Baste and stitch the front yoke section

to the dress front as shown on page 56.
To trim the yoke seamline with ribbon,
cut a piece of ribbon to the necessary
length, plus extra for folding under. With
the wrong side of the ribbon to the right
side of dress, baste the ribbon to the dress
over the yoke seamlines at the side edges
and above the seamline across the
bottom of yoke. Miter the corners of the
ribbon as explained on page 57.
Stitch ribbon in place. Remove all
basting and press.
2 Baste and stitch the back shoulder darts.
Press in. With right sides together, baste
and stitch center back seam to circle.
Press seam open. Insert zipper in back
opening as shown in Volume 4, page 68.

3 With right sides facing, baste and stitch the shoulder seams. Press seams open. To bind the neck edge, cut a strip of contrasting fabric to length required plus seam allowances (piece if necessary). Following directions in Volume 1, page 56, bind the neck edge of the dress. Sew a hook and eye to the top of opening.

4 With right sides together baste and stitch the side seams; make pockets in side seams as shown in Volume 5, page 72

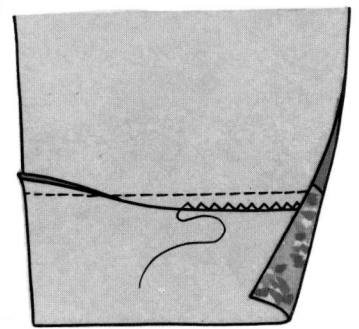

5 To make the sleeves, with right sides together, baste and stitch the contrasting section to the main sleeve. Trim seam allowance. Finish with zig-zag stitch and press down.

6 To trim the sleeve with ribbon, first cut four pieces of ribbon the width of the sleeves (two for each sleeve).

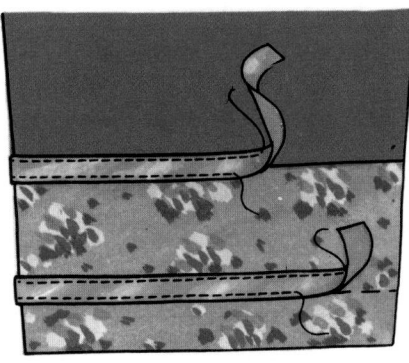

7 Baste and stitch one piece of ribbon to the lower edge of each sleeve with the outer edge of ribbon on the hemline, and the second piece of ribbon positioned so that it covers the seamline between the contrasting fabrics. With right sides together, sew the underarm seam. Press seam open. Turn sleeve hem up and blind hem as shown in Volume 4, page 72.

8 Prepare the sleeve cap for easing; with right sides together, matching shoulder points, notches and underarm seams, pin, baste and stitch the sleeve into armhole. Press seam allowances toward sleeve, clip underarm curves, and overcast raw edges together. Repeat for second sleeve.

9 Turn up the hem of the dress, mitering corners as shown on page 57. Topstitch around the front and back hemline and side slits, stitching $\frac{1}{4}$in (6mm) in from edges. Press.

Slacks

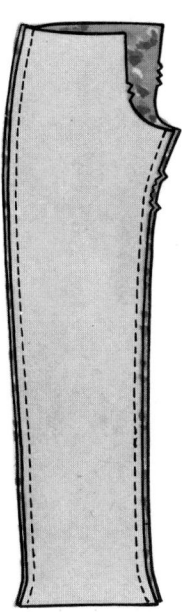

1 With right sides together, baste and stitch side and inside leg seams, easing fullness between the back notches to fit the front. Press seams open.

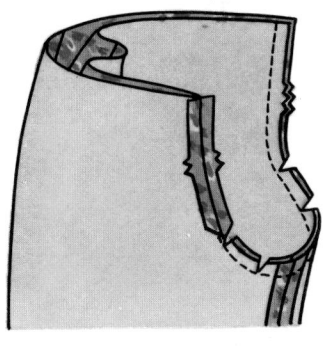

2 Turn one leg inside out and slip it inside the other leg. With right sides together, matching notches, baste and stitch the crotch seam. Clip curves. Press seam open.

3 Make the casing for the elasticized waist by turning in a $\frac{1}{4}$in (6mm) seam allowance and then the full width allowed for casing. Baste and stitch close to both folded edges, leaving about 1in (2-3cm) open at back seam for threading elastic. Cut elastic to fit, thread through casing, overlapping and stitching the ends together. Sew the opening closed.

4 Turn hems up as directed in Volume 1, page 65, for basic pants.

Stretch front panel (optional)
If inserting a stretch front panel, stitch the front crotch seam first, the panel is inserted as explained on page 58; side seam and inside leg seams are stitched; then the crotch seam is completed, stitching from back waist to the previous stitching at the front. Make the casing and elastic with button fastening as shown on page 58. Complete hems.

Terry Evans

Sewing / COURSE 44

* Lace Peter Pan collar bound with satin
* Attaching collar to neck edge with bias-cut binding
* Setting a gathered sleeve into armhole
* Pattern for a blouse with lace collar

Lace Peter Pan collar bound with satin

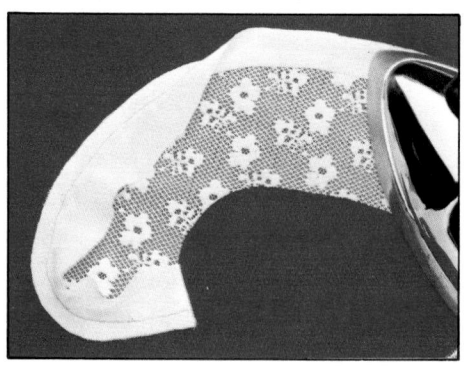
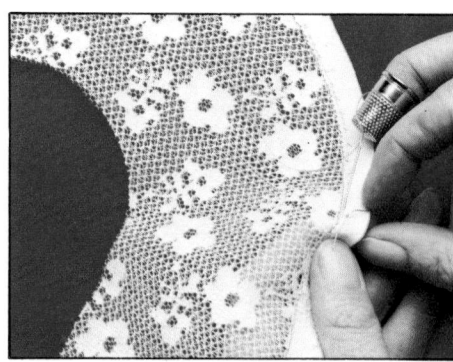

1 With wrong sides together, baste the net backing to the lace collar around all edges.

2 To bind outer edge of collar, measure the outer edge of the collar. Cut a 1⅝in (4cm)-wide bias strip of fabric this length. Starting at the front edge, with right sides together, baste and stitch the binding to the outer edge of collar, taking ⅜in (1cm) seam. Remove basting. Press binding away from collar. Turn in ⅜in (1cm) on outer edge of binding. Press.

3 Turn the binding under, enclosing the raw edges of the seam allowances. Baste and hem to the stitching line using invisible stitches.

Attaching collar to neck edge with bias-cut binding

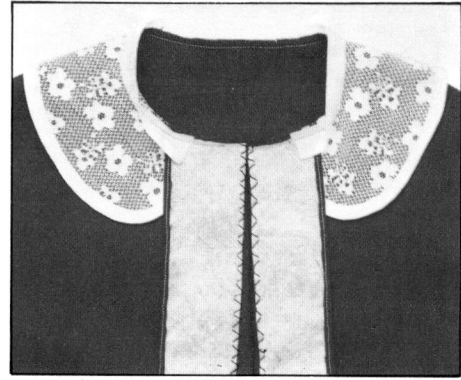
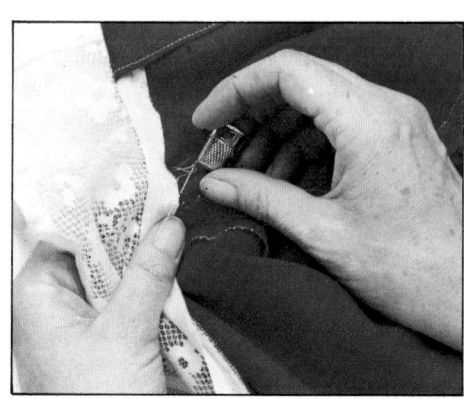

1 This method of applying the collar is used with a front facing. Before the collar is applied to the neck edge, the interfacing is attached to the front facing and the outer edge of the facing is finished. Baste the collar to the neck edge matching center fronts, center backs and shoulder markings. Fold the front facing on the foldline to the right side of the garment, taking it over the collar. Baste at neck edge.

2 Cut a bias strip of self fabric 1in (2.5cm) wide to fit the neck edge and overlap the facing on each side by ⅝in (1.5cm). With right sides together, baste the binding to the neck edge over collar and facing, matching all raw edges. Stitch around the neck to folded edge of front facings. Grade seam allowance, clip curves and cut across corners of facings.

3 Turn the front facings right side out. Press the neck seam allowance toward the bodice. The neck curve must be clipped enough to allow the seam allowance to lie flat. Fold under the raw edge of the binding and slip stitch to neck edge with small stitches.

Setting gathered sleeve into armhole

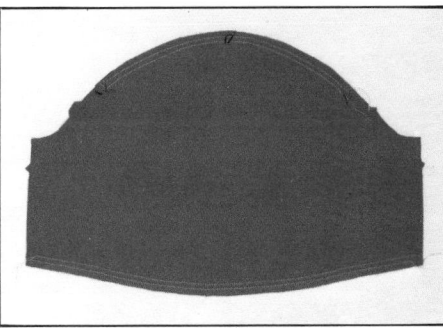

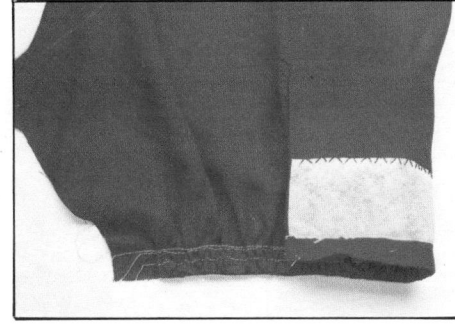

1 Prepare the sleeve for gathering by running two rows of gathering stitches around the sleeve to within 1⅝in (4cm) of the front and back notches. This will produce a puffy effect over the sleeve cap, instead of the usual slight fullness. Run two rows of gathering across the lower edge of the sleeve, starting and ending at the side seams.

2 With wrong sides together, fold cuff in half and press the folded edge. Open cuff out and baste interfacing to wrong side of cuff. Catch-stitch to the foldline. With right sides together, pin the interfaced edge of cuff to the lower edge of sleeve at the sides. Pull up the gathering threads until the sleeve fits the cuff. Spread the gathers evenly, pin, baste and stitch cuff in place. Trim seams. Press the seam allowance only, with point of the iron toward cuff.

3 With right sides together, baste and stitch the underarm seam of sleeve and cuff. Trim interfacing at seam and press seam open. Turn in ⅝in (1.5cm) along lower edge of cuff and press.

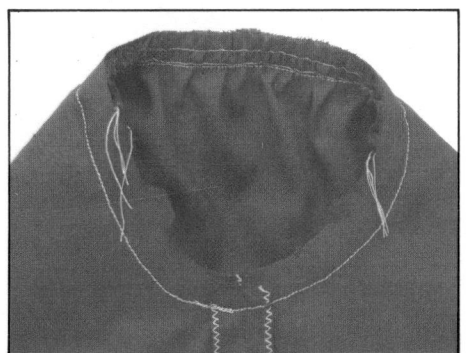

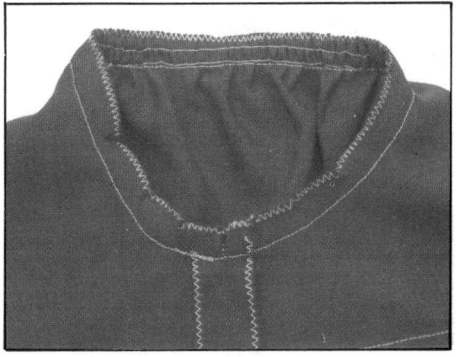

4 Fold cuff to inside along foldline and hem to stitching line. Press.

5 With right sides together, matching shoulder points, notches and underarm seams, pin sleeve into armhole. Pull up gathering threads until the sleeve fits the armhole. Baste, spreading the gathers evenly over the sleeve cap. Stitch with the sleeve facing up.

6 Using the point of the iron, press the armhole seam allowance to the seamline only, avoiding gathers on the sleeve section. Clip the curves. Turn the seam allowance into the sleeve and overcast raw edges together.

Mike Berend

Blouse with lace collar

This pretty blouse, with its lace collar, is part of a two-in-one outfit. In the next Sewing Course we give directions for the skirt, and for making a dress from the same pattern pieces.

Adapting the pattern

Measurements
The pattern for this blouse is made by altering the pattern for the basic shirt from the Stitch by Stitch Pattern Pack, available in sizes 10-20, which correspond to sizes 8-18 in ready-made clothes. The pattern for the Peter Pan collar can be found on a separate sheet in the pack.

Materials
3 sheets of tracing paper, 33½ × 18in (85 × 45cm)
Yardstick or ruler
Flexible curve; right triangle

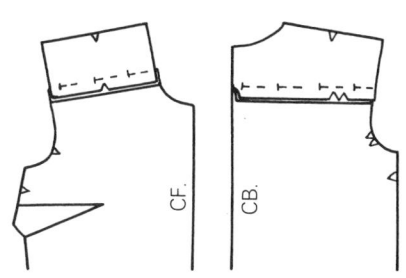

1 Pin the front yoke to the shirt front and the back yoke to the shirt back, making sure the seamlines are aligned. Trace both complete pieces, leaving extra paper at the center front edge for the facing. Cut out the pattern for the back.

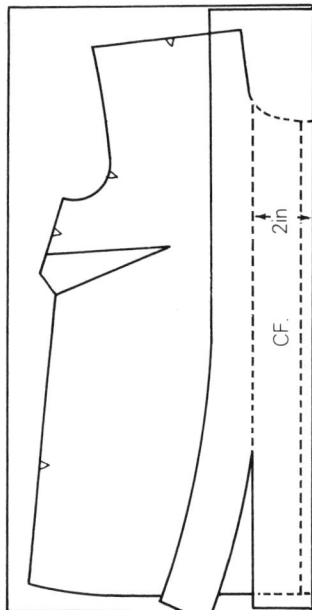

2 On the tracing of the front, draw a line $\frac{5}{8}$in (1.5cm) out from and parallel to center front line. Mark this as the foldline for facing. Fold the paper along this line and trace the front neck curve. For the width of the facing, measure out from the foldline 2in (5cm) and draw a line from neck edge to hem. Cut along this line. Cut out the rest of the front pattern. For front neck interfacings, use facing pattern as far as foldline.

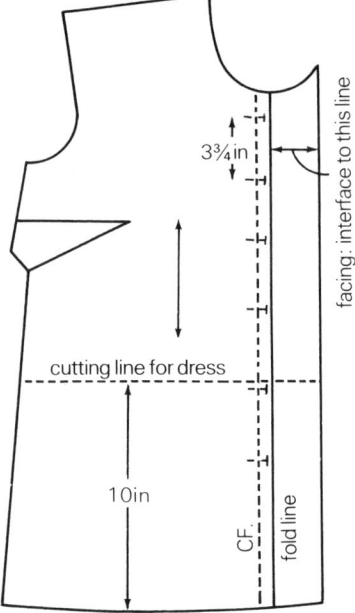

John Hutchinson

3 Mark the position of the first buttonhole with a pin $\frac{5}{8}$in (1.5cm) from the neck seamline on the center front line. Draw the buttonhole horizontally on the pattern, making it $\frac{1}{8}$in (3mm) wider than the button being used, and placing it so that it overlaps the front line by $\frac{1}{8}$in (3mm). Mark the other five buttonholes, leaving a $3\frac{3}{4}$in (9.5cm) space between each buttonhole.

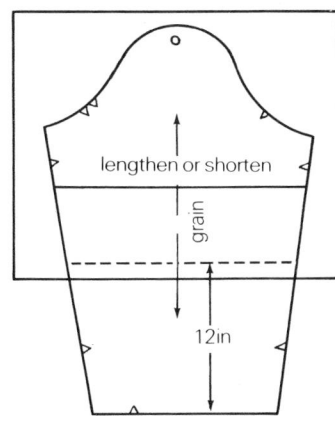

4 On the shirt sleeve pattern measure up 12in (30cm) from the hem edge and draw a line across the pattern at this point, perpendicular to the grain line. Trace this part of the sleeve on paper, marking the grain line and the lengthening and shortening lines.

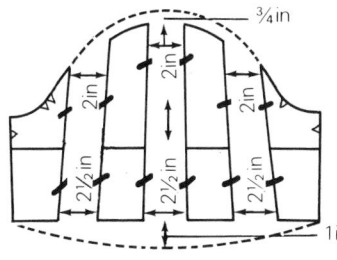

5 Divide the sleeve pattern tracing into four equal parts and draw lines from the sleeve cap to hemline, parallel to straight grain. Slash along these lines and spread the pattern sections apart, placing them on another sheet of paper. At top edge each section is spread 2in (5cm), and at bottom edge 2½in (6.5cm). Tape each section in place. Re-draw the sleeve cap from side sections, raising the center of cap ¾in (2cm). Re-draw lower edge, dropping lower edge 1in (2.5cm) in center, tapering to the side edges. Mark the new grain line through the center of sleeve. The sleeve can be adjusted if necessary on the lengthening and shortening line.

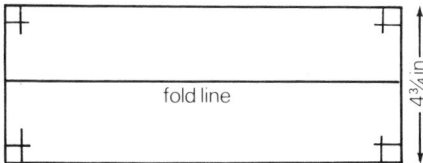

6 For the length of the cuff measure around the upper arm above the elbow. To this measurement add ½in (1.2cm) for ease and 1¼in (3cm) for seam allowance. Draw a rectangle on paper, 4¾in (12cm) wide by the length of the upper arm measurement, plus allowances. The width allows for a ⅝in (1.5cm) seam on each edge. Mark the foldline in the center of the pattern. Cut cuff interfacings 2⅜in (6cm) wide.

7 Trim away the seam allowance around the outer edge of the Peter Pan collar pattern. This edge will be bound.

Dress bodice

The pattern for the Peter Pan blouse is adapted to make the bodice of the dress. For the cutting line for the dress bodice featured on page 74, measure up from the shirt hem at center front 10in (25cm), drawing a line across the pattern to side edge, keeping it parallel to hem edge. Repeat with back pattern, marking line from center back to side edge 10in (25cm) from hem. Adjust length on lengthening or shortening line.

Directions for making

Materials

36in (90cm)- or 45in (115cm)-wide fabric without nap:
  Sizes 10, 12: 2½yd (2.2m)
  Sizes 14-20: 2⅝yd (2.4m)
Lace fabric approx 36in (90cm) wide:
  For all sizes ⅜yd (.4m)
Net fabric approx. 36in (90cm) wide:
  For all sizes ⅜yd (.4m)
Matching thread
Six ⅜in (1cm) buttons
36in (90cm)-wide interfacing:
  ⅜yd (.3m)
36in (90cm)-wide satin fabric for binding: ⅜yd (.4m)

Key to adjusted pattern pieces
1 Shirt front   cut 2
2 Shirt back   cut 1 on fold
3 Sleeve   cut 2
Top collar   cut 1 on fold
Lower collar   cut 1 on fold
A Cuff   cut 2
Interfacing:
Use pieces 1 (cut to foldline only) and A (half width only).

Suggested fabrics
Cottons, cotton blends, synthetics, silk, lightweight woolens.

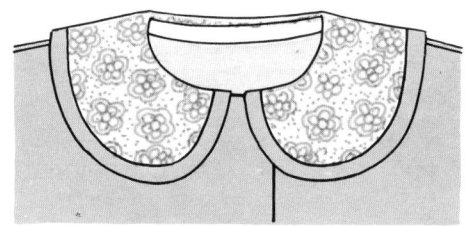

2 Make the lace collar and bind the outer edge. Apply to the neck edge of blouse with binding, as shown on page 64.

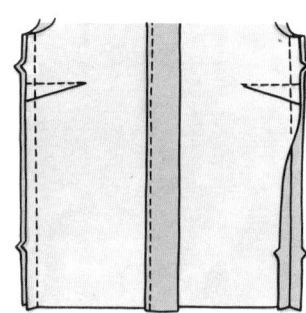

3 With right sides together, baste and stitch the side seams, using a plain seam. Press seams open.

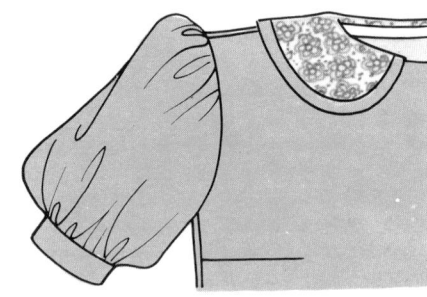

4 Make the sleeves, with cuffs, and gather up to fit armholes as shown on page 65.

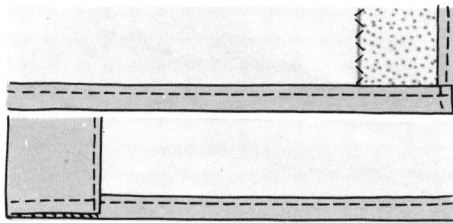

5 Open out the front facing at the hemline. Turn in $\frac{1}{4}$in (6mm) and another fold of $\frac{3}{8}$in (1cm) at the lower edge and stitch in place. Press. Turn the facing back to the inside and slip stitch the bottom edge to the hem. Press.

6 Make buttonholes by hand or machine in positions marked. Sew buttons on the center front of the left front to correspond with buttonholes. Sew a hook and eye on the top edge of the front at the neck—the hook on the inside of the right front and the eye on the upper side of the left front. Position the hook and eye with the blouse buttoned up.

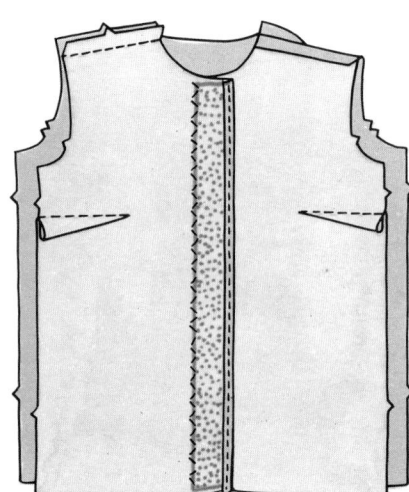

1 Prepare the fabric and cut out. Transfer all pattern markings to the fabric. Baste interfacing to the wrong side of the facing. Catch-stitch to the foldline. Trim $\frac{1}{4}$in (6mm) from the edge of the interfacing. Fold over $\frac{1}{4}$in (6mm) of facing and stitch. Baste and stitch bust darts and press them down. Join the shoulder seams, using a flat seam. Press seams open.

Cutting layout: 36in or 45in-wide fabric

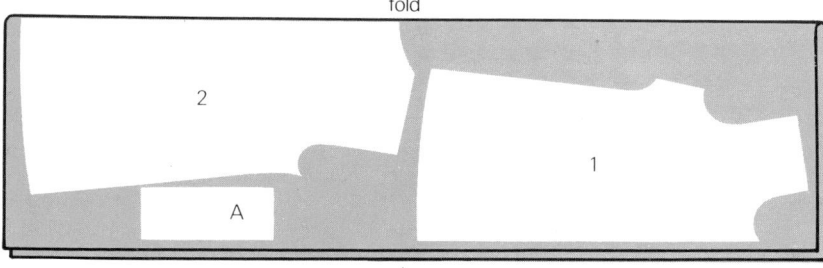

Lace and net: 36in wide or less

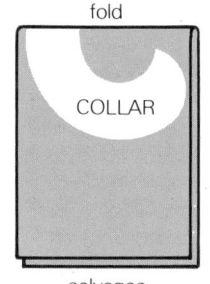

Interfacing: 36in wide

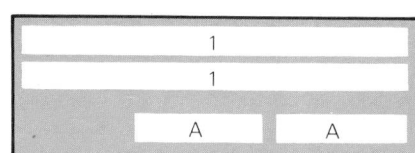

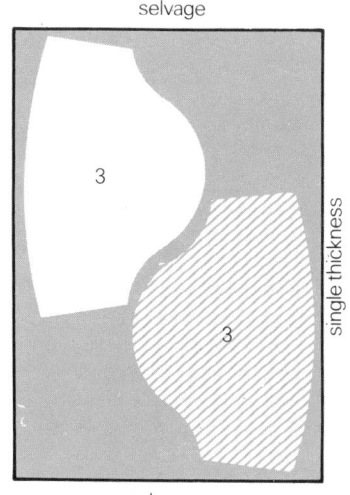

*Bound buttonholes—patch
method
*Attaching a gathered skirt
to a gathered bodice
*Pattern for a buttoned
skirt and a shirtwaist dress
adapting the pattern
directions for making

Bound buttonholes—patch method

A bound buttonhole gives a strong, neat finish to any garment made in medium weight or closely woven fabric. Always attach the interfacing to the main part of the garment, not to the facing, when you are making bound buttonholes.

If you are making several bound buttonholes, finish each step for each buttonhole before proceeding to the next step. Make a test buttonhole on a scrap of the garment fabric first.

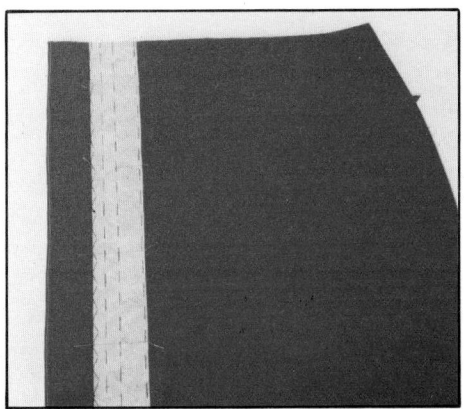

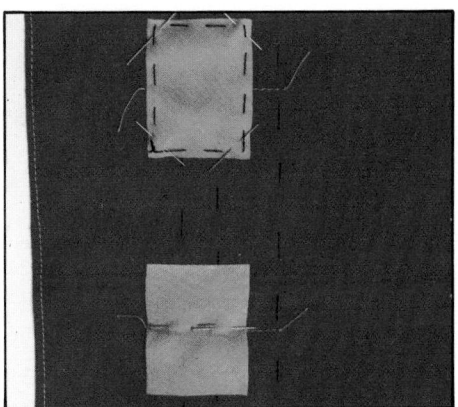

1 Baste interfacing in place on the wrong side and catch-stitch to the foldline. Fold under and stitch $\frac{1}{4}$in (6mm) raw edge of facing to finish. Mark all the guidelines for the position and size of the buttonholes with basting (see Volume 4, page 56). Run a horizontal line of matching stitches through the center of the marked buttonhole, extending the stitches at each end.

2 For each buttonhole, cut a patch of self fabric (we have used a contrasting color for clarity) on the bias 2in (5cm) wide and 1in (2.5cm) longer than the finished buttonhole. Crease lightly through the center, parallel to the long edge. With right sides together, place a patch over the middle of each buttonhole mark. Pin and baste patch in place.

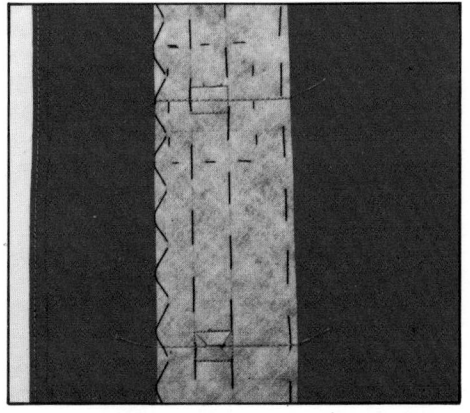

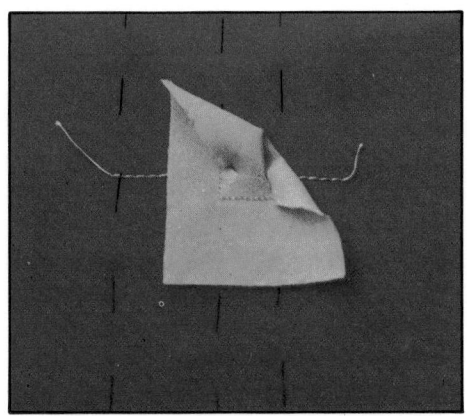

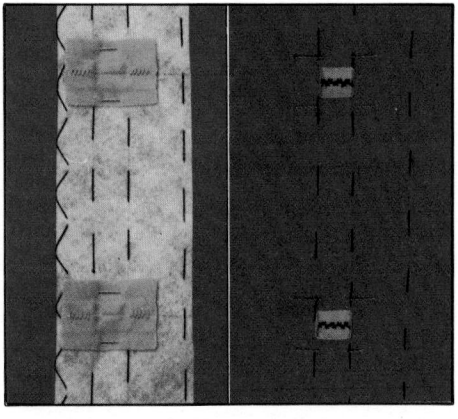

3 Using a very small stitch, sew around buttonhole on the wrong side, $\frac{1}{8}$in (3mm) from center mark. Begin stitching in the middle of one long side and stitch to end. Leaving needle in fabric, raise presser foot and pivot fabric on needle. Lower foot and stitch across end. Stitch around buttonhole, turning corners same way. Press. Remove the basting. Without cutting stitches, cut through center of buttonhole to within $\frac{1}{4}$in (6mm) of each end. Cut diagonally into corners.

4 Pull the patch through the opening to the wrong side and carefully pull out the triangular ends to square the corners.

5 Press ends and side seams away from opening. Fold each side of the patch to form pleats that meet in the center of the opening. A small pleat will also form at each end. Pin and herringbone-stitch the two folds together along center. On the wrong side, overcast the pleat folds together at the ends. Remove basted guidelines and press.

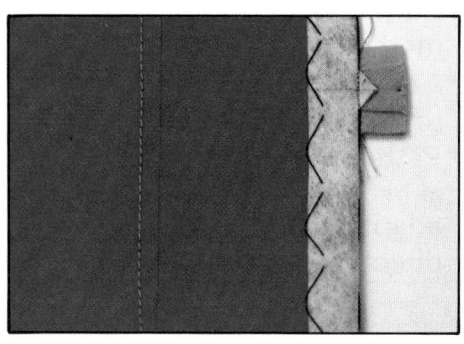

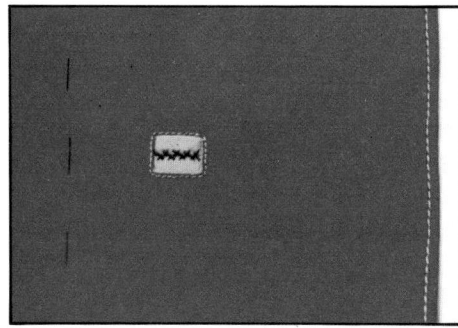

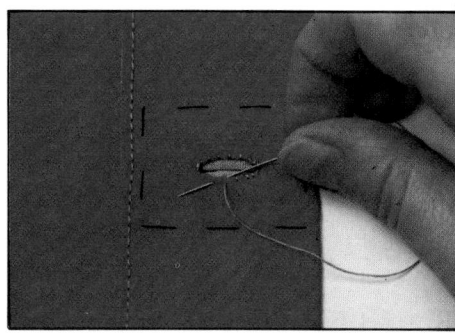

6 With right side of the garment up, fold back the garment fabric and sew across the triangular ends, following the original stitching line. Begin and end the stitches at the outer edge of the patch. Fold garment fabric back and press from the right side.

7 With right side up, sew along sides and ends of buttonhole through previous seamlines. Pull threads to wrong side and tie off, or backstitch by hand around the buttonhole using very small stitches.

8 The back of the buttonhole is finished with the facing. Trim patch to $\frac{3}{8}$in (1cm) from stitching line and remove basting. Fold facing between pins. Turn under the edges with the needle point and slip stitch facing in place, forming an oval shape. Remove basting and press.

Attaching a gathered skirt to a gathered bodice

Seam binding applied to a gathered bodice before it is attached to a gathered skirt will control the fullness around the waistline after the seam is stitched.
Sewing seam binding into the waist seam also provides reinforcement and helps hold the gathering in place permanently.

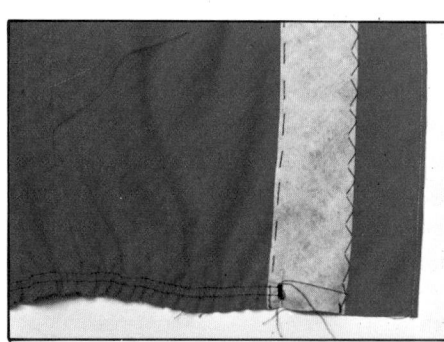

1 After joining side and shoulder seams of bodice, baste interfacing to the wrong side of each front, catch-stitching it to the foldline. Turn under and stitch $\frac{1}{4}$in (6mm) at raw edges of facings to finish. Cut a piece of straight woven seam binding to the length of your waist plus $\frac{1}{2}$in (1.3cm) for ease.

2 Open out the front facing at the lower edge of bodice. Run two rows of gathering stitches around waistline edge to within $1\frac{1}{2}$in (4cm) of center front line. Pull up gathered threads until bodice waistline is $\frac{1}{2}$in (1.3cm) larger than waist measurement. Measure from center front to center front only.

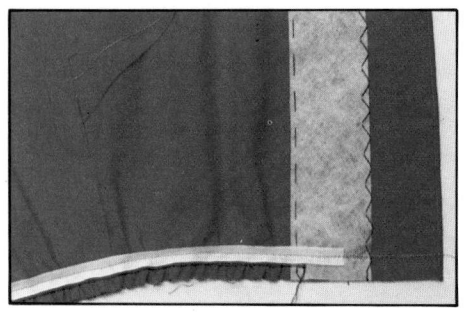

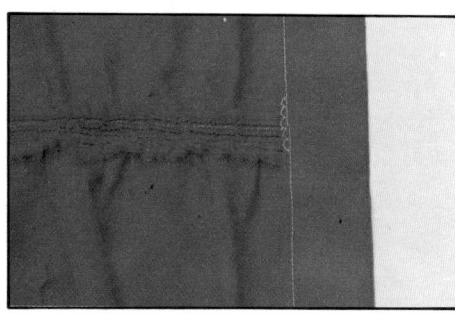

3 Pin seam binding to wrong side of waistline seam, beginning and ending at center front line. Spread gathers evenly along binding—the measurements from center front to side seam should be the same on both sides—and baste in place. The total back measurement should be $1\frac{1}{4}$in (3cm) less than the front (do not include overlap). Sew binding to wrong side of garment. Remove basting.

4 Open out front facing on skirt. Run two rows of gathering stitches around waistline edge to within $1\frac{1}{2}$in (4cm) of center front line. Matching front edges, side seams and center backs, pin skirt to bodice pulling up gathering threads until skirt fits bodice. Baste, spreading gathers evenly. With wrong side of bodice up, sew skirt to bodice, following line of stitches along seam binding.

5 Remove basting and press seam open. Press into seam with point of iron; avoid $1\frac{1}{2}$in (4cm) pressing gathered parts. Turn the front facings to the inside and catch-stitch to the waistline seam. Press.

Buttoned skirt and shirtwaist dress

Combine the skirt in this course with the blouse in the previous course to make a third garment: a simple shirtwaist dress with a blouson top, as illustrated on the next page. Add a pristine white collar for a crisp finish. The dress is suitable for almost any occasion; wear it straight from work to a party.

Skirt

Adapting the pattern

Measurements
The skirt is made by adapting the pattern for the A-line skirt in the Stitch by Stitch Pattern Pack, available in sizes 10-20, which correspond to sizes 8-18 in ready-made clothes.

Materials
2 sheets of tracing paper 24×36in (approx. 60×90cm)
Yardstick

1 Trace the skirt front and back pattern pieces omitting front and back waist darts. This amount will be taken up in the gathering. Leave extra at the center front and back edges.

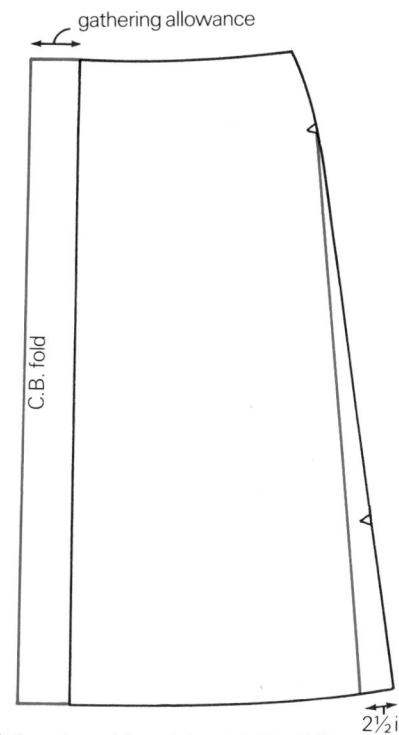
gathering allowance

C.B. fold

2½in

2 For sizes 10 to 14, add 4in (10cm) to center back edge and for sizes 16 to 20 add 5½in (14cm) to center back edge. To make skirt narrower at hemline, mark 2½in (6.5cm) in from side cutting line at lower edge. Using a yardstick, draw the new side cutting line at the lower edge to the original cutting line at the hip, 8in (20.5cm) below waist.

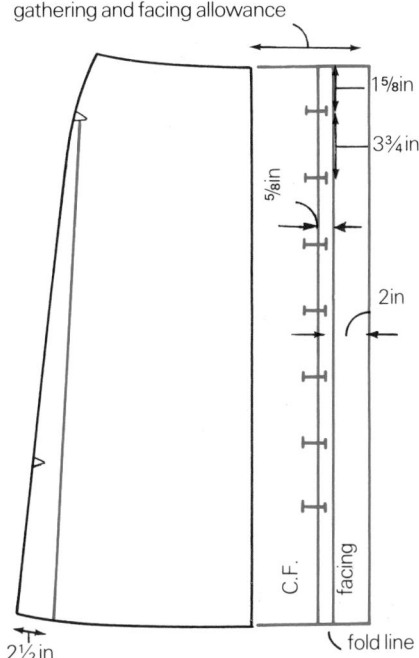
gathering and facing allowance

1⅝in
3¾in
⅝in
2in
C.F.
facing
2½in
fold line

3 On the skirt front adaptation, add the buttonhole extension, the facing allowance and the gathering allowance to the front edge. For sizes 10 to 14, add a total of 6½in (16.5cm) to front edge. For sizes 16 to 20, add a total of 8½in (21.5cm) to front edge. Make the same alteration to side edges as for back, taking off same amount at the hem, 2½in (6.5cm).
4 To mark the foldline for the facing, measure in 2in (5cm) from new front edge. Draw a line from waist to hem. For the buttonhole extension, measure in a further ⅝in (1.5cm) from foldline and draw the center front line from waist to hem. Mark the horizontal buttonhole positions at the front as shown for the blouse (see page 66). The first buttonhole is placed 1⅝in (4cm) from waist seamline and the other six at 3¾in (9.5cm) intervals from the first.

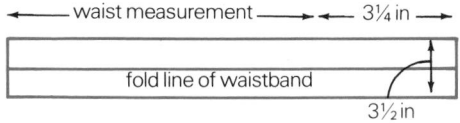
waist measurement
3¼in
fold line of waistband
3½in

5 The waistband is cut to the waist measurment plus ½in (1.3cm) ease,

1⅜in (3.5cm) for button extensions, and 1¼in (3cm) for seam allowances, making a total of 3⅛in (7.8cm) more than the true waist measurement. Cut the waistband 3½in (9cm) wide to make a finished width of 1¼in (3cm) after taking ⅝in (1.5cm) seam allowances on both edges. The interfacing is half this width.

Dress

Adapting the pattern

Measurements
The dress is made by combining the blouse (see page 65) and the skirt (on the left), which are both taken from the Stitch by Stitch Pattern Pack, available in sizes 10-20, which correspond to sizes 8-18 in ready-made clothes.
Note The collar on the dress is the basic Peter Pan collar in the Pattern Pack, but it need not be bound with satin as it was for the blouse, unless you are making a lace collar.

Materials
5 sheets of tracing paper 24×36in (approx. 60×90cm)
Yardstick, flexible curve

1 Adapt and trace skirt pieces from basic skirt pattern as directed for skirt (on the left), omitting waistband. Be sure to add correct allowances to center back and center front for your size.
2 Adapt and trace bodice and sleeve pieces from basic shirt pattern as for blouse (see page 65). Be sure to cut bodice pattern to correct length.
3 Draw pattern for cuffs as directed for blouse (see page 67). Trace basic Peter Pan collar pattern, noting that the collar on the dress does not have a bound edge and will therefore need to include seam allowances on the outer edge.

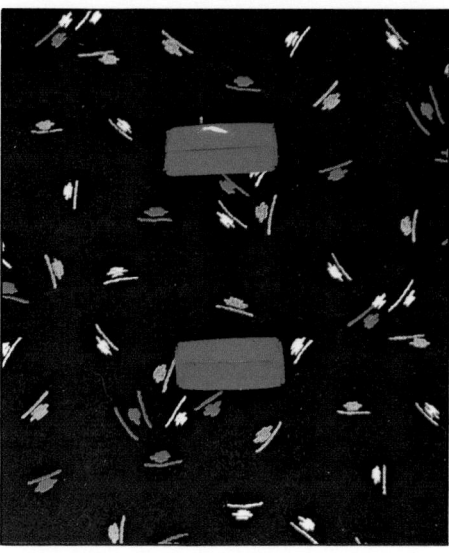

Cutting layout: 45in-wide fabric with or without nap

fold

1

2

WAISTBAND

selvages

54in-wide fabric with or without nap

fold

1

2

WAISTBAND

selvages

Interfacing: 36in-wide fabric Sizes 10/16

selvage

SKIRT FRONT

SKIRT FRONT

WAISTBAND

selvage

Sizes 18/20

SKIRT FRONT

SKIRT FRONT

WAISTBAND

WAISTBAND

John Hutchinson

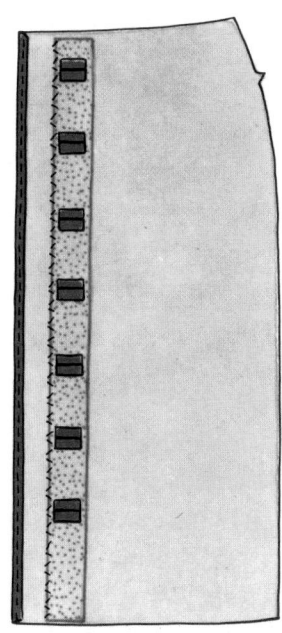

4 Attach interfacing and make bound buttonholes (pages 69 and 70).
Do not complete the buttonholes on the wrong side.

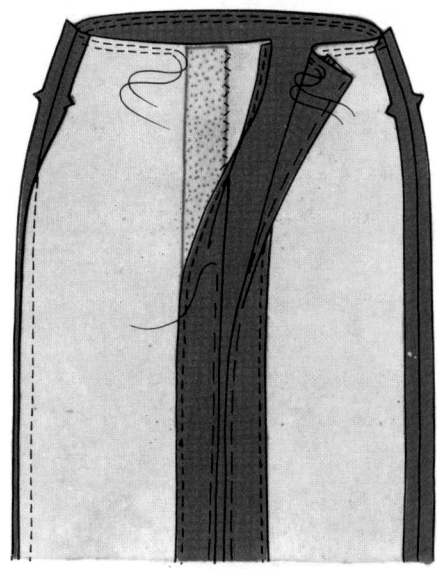

5 With right sides together and notches matching, baste and stitch the side seams of the skirt. Finish and press seams open. Run two rows of gathering stitches around waistline edge to within $1\frac{3}{8}$in (3.5cm) of front line. Fold front facings to the inside and baste close to folded edge. Press.

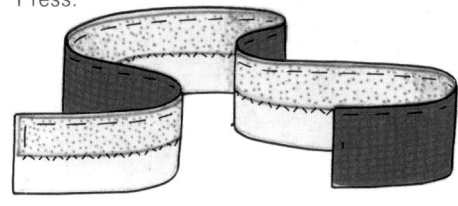

6 To mark the fold on waistband, fold it in half lengthwise with wrong sides together and press the folded edge

Skirt

Directions for making

Suggested fabrics
Cotton or synthetic knits, linen-finish fabrics, pinwale corduroy.

Materials
45in (115cm)-wide fabric with or without nap:
Size 10: $1\frac{7}{8}$yd (1.7m)
Sizes 12, 14, 16: 2yd (1.8m)
Sizes 18, 20: $2\frac{1}{8}$yd (1.9m)
54in (140cm)-wide fabric with or without nap:
Sizes 10, 12: $1\frac{7}{8}$yd (1.7m)
Sizes 14, 16, 18, 20: 2yd (1.8m)
36in (90cm)-wide interfacing:
Sizes 10, 12, 14, 16: $\frac{3}{8}$yd (.3m)
Sizes 18, 20: $\frac{1}{2}$yd (.4m)
Matching thread, hook and bar
7 buttons $\frac{3}{8}$in (1cm) in diameter

Key to adjusted pattern pieces
1 Skirt front   Cut 2
2 Skirt back   Cut 1 on fold
A Waistband   Cut 1
Interfacing   Use piece A (cut 1 to half width only)
Use skirt front (cut facings only)

1 Alter pattern pieces for skirt front and back and cut waistband pattern (see page 71).
2 Prepare the fabric and pin on the pattern pieces as shown in the cutting layout. Make sure that the grain lines on the pattern lie on the straight grain of the fabric. Cut out the pieces.
3 Transfer the markings from the pattern to the fabric before removing pattern pieces. It is best to do this now; the fabric might stretch with handling.

lightly. Open waistband and baste interfacing to wrong side. Catch-stitch to foldline. If piecing waist interfacing, do this before attaching to waistband, overlapping seam for a flat finish.

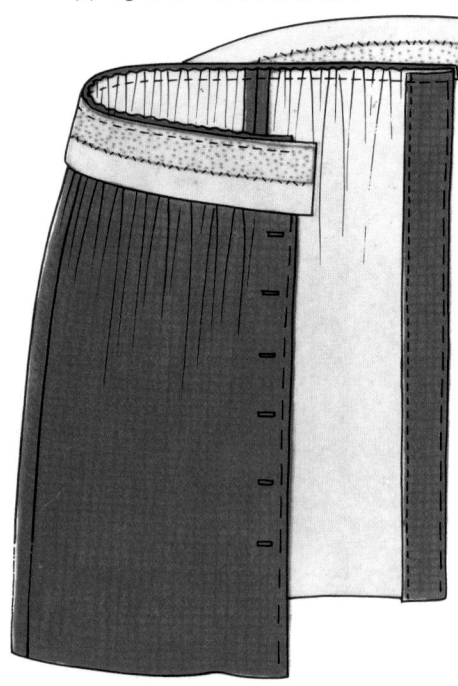

7 Open waistband out. With right sides together and front edges and center backs even, pin skirt to waistband, pulling up gathering threads to fit waistband. Spread gathers evenly along waistband and baste in place. With gathers lying on top, stitch the seam. Trim interfacing close to stitches. Grade seam allowances and press toward waistband.

8 With right sides together, fold waistband along foldline. Baste and stitch across ends. Trim interfacing close to stitches and cut across corners.

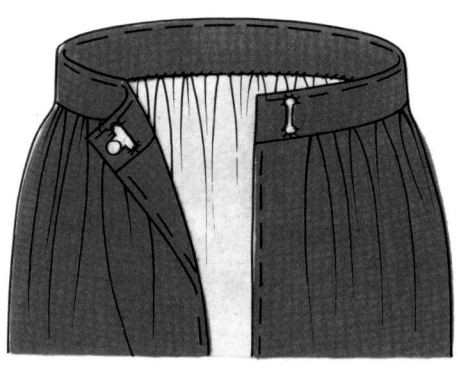

9 Turn the waistband right side out and baste close to folded edge. On the inside, turn under the seam allowance of the waistband and hem to line of stitches. Press. Sew hook and bar to waistband.

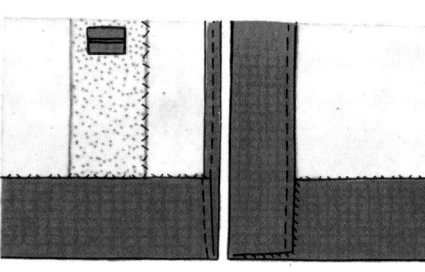

10 Open out the facing at lower edge. Turn up hem using invisible hemming stitch (see Volume 4, page 72). After turning up hem, turn the front facing inside and slip stitch facing to hem allowance. Press folded edge only.
11 Complete the back of buttonholes with the facing (see page 70). Sew buttons on left front to correspond with the buttonholes.

Dress

Directions for making

Suggested fabrics

Light- to medium-weight, easily gathered fabrics, such as cotton or synthetic knits, linen or linen finish fabrics; for evenings: satin or crepe.

Materials

45in (115cm)-wide fabric without nap:
Sizes 10, 12: 3⅜yd (3.1m)
Sizes 14, 16, 18: 3¾yd (3.4m)
Size 20: 3⅞yd (3.5m)
(add ⅜yd [.3m] for a self-fabric collar for all sizes)
54in (140cm)-wide fabric without nap:
Size 10: 2⅝yd (2.4m)
Sizes 12, 14: 2¾yd (2.5m)
Sizes 16, 18, 20: 3yd (2.7m)
For contrasting collar:
36in (90cm)-wide fabric without nap:
⅜yd (.3m) for all sizes
36in (90cm)-wide interfacing:
For all sizes:
(add ⅜yd [.3m] if interfacing collar)
Matching thread, hook and eye
11 buttons ⅜in (1cm) in diameter

Note Bias binding for neck edge is cut from self fabric. If fabric is too bulky, ready-made bias binding can be used.

1 Alter pattern pieces for skirt front and back, bodice front and back and sleeve; trace collar and draw cuff piece as shown on pages 65-67.
2 Prepare the dress fabric and pin the pattern pieces as shown in the cutting layout. Omit collar pieces unless making self fabric collar. Prepare the contrast fabric for collar and pin on pattern as shown in layout. Make sure that the

grain lines on the pattern lie on the straight grain of the fabric. Cut out.
3 Transfer the markings from the pattern to the fabric and remove the pattern pieces.

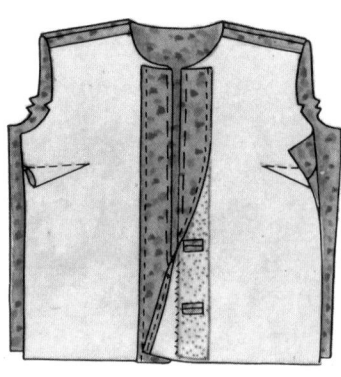

4 On bodice fronts, catch-stitch the interfacings to foldlines. Finish facings. Make bound buttonholes following directions (see page 69) but do not finish the backs. Make bust darts and press down. Join shoulder seams and press open.

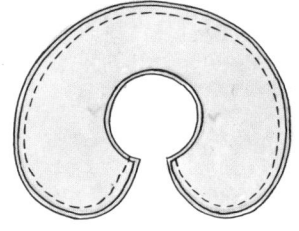

5 When making the Peter Pan collar, try to avoid sheer fabrics, because the seam allowance will show through. If the fabric lacks body, interface the collar before assembling it. Cut the top collar from interfacing and fabric, and attach the interfacing to the wrong side of the top collar. Baste both sections together and treat as one piece.

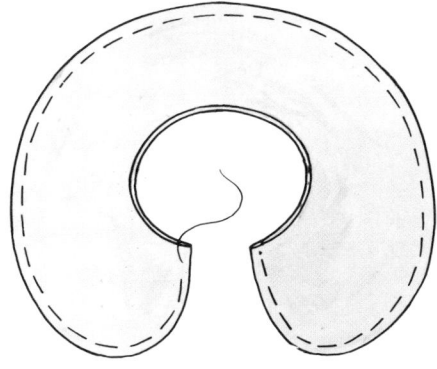

6 Cut out under-collar. With right sides together and outer edges matching, baste and stitch top collar and under-collar together around the outer edges. Trim seam allowances to $\frac{1}{4}$in (6mm). Turn collar right side out and baste close to stitched edge. Press.

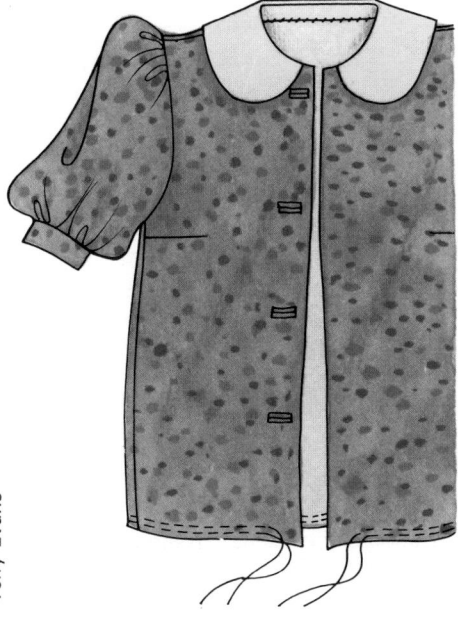

7 Attach collar to neck edge using self-fabric or ready-made bias binding. Baste and stitch side seams and press open. Make sleeves and set in armholes (follow directions for making blouse on page 68). Run two rows of gathering stitches at waist edge, finishing stitches $1\frac{3}{8}$in (3.5cm) from center front on each side, as the front is to be kept flat.

8 On skirt fronts, catch-stitch the interfacings to foldlines. Finish facings. Make skirt with bound buttonholes, omitting the waistband. **Do not** finish backs of buttonholes at this stage; they will be completed later.

9 Attach skirt to bodice at waistline with seam binding as shown on page 70. Turn the front facings to the wrong side and catch-stitch to the waist seam allowance.

Turn up hem as shown for skirt on page 74.

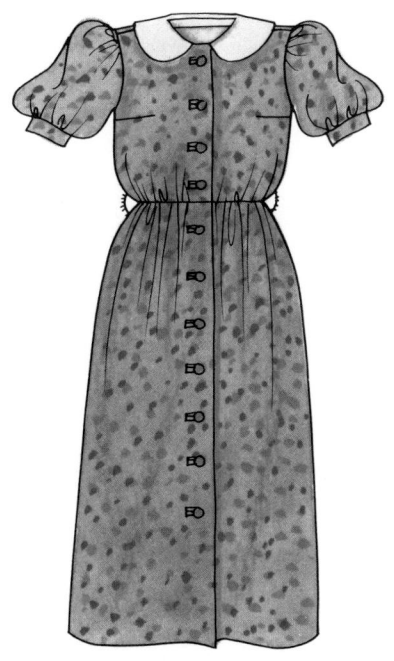

10 Complete the backs of the buttonholes as directed on pages 69 and 70 and sew on buttons to correspond. Attach hook and eye to neckline as for blouse (see page 68). Make thread belt carriers (see Volume 7, pages 66 and 67) at waistline side seams to fit ready-made belt. Or, make fabric belt carriers (see Volume 8, page 67) and a self-fabric belt.

Key to adjusted pattern pieces

1 Skirt front	Cut 2
2 Skirt back	Cut 1 on fold
3 Bodice front	Cut 2
4 Bodice back	Cut 1 on fold
5 Sleeve	Cut 2
Peter Pan collar	Cut 2 on fold
A Cuff	Cut 2
Interfacing	Use piece 1, piece 3 and piece A (cut facings only). Use collar (cut 1 only—optional)

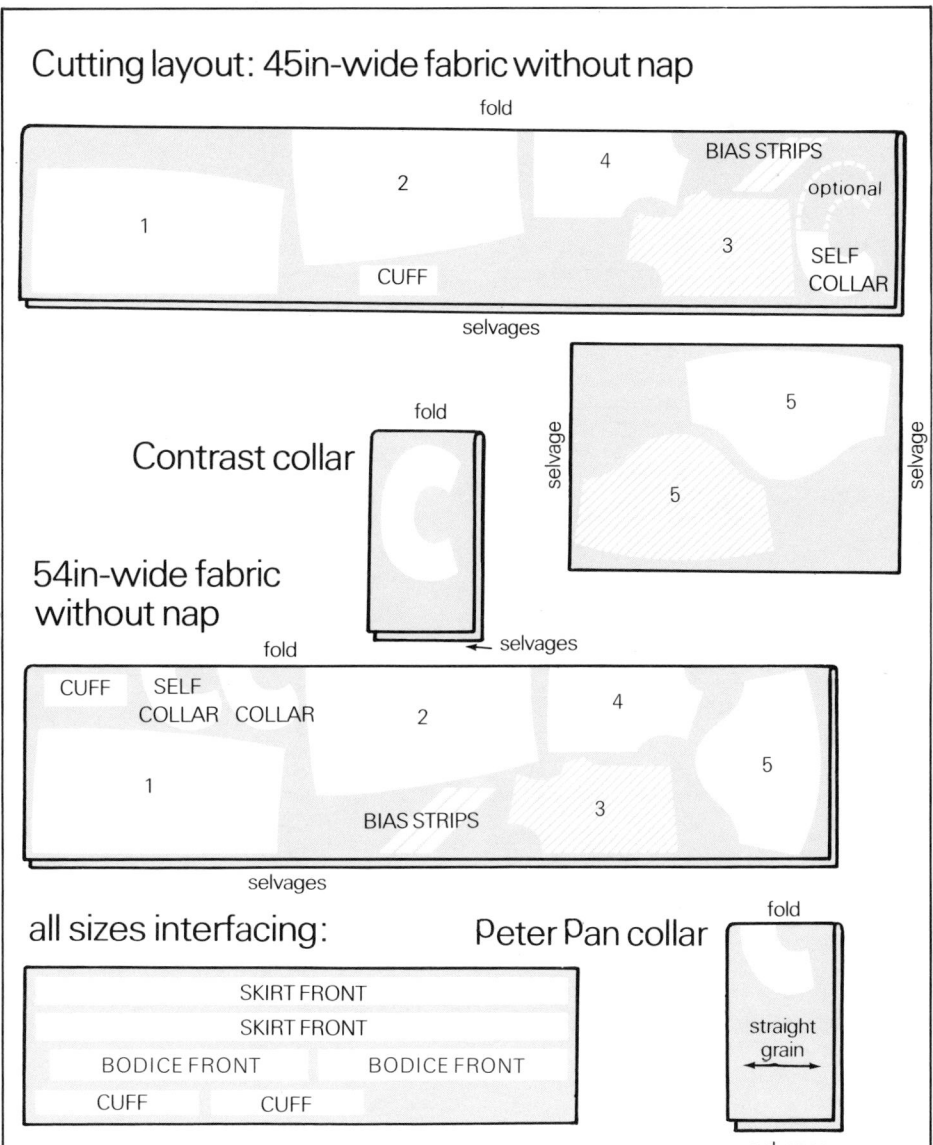

Cutting layout: 45in-wide fabric without nap

Contrast collar

54in-wide fabric without nap

all sizes interfacing:

Peter Pan collar

John Hutchinson

Sewing / COURSE 46

*Applying a sailor collar
*Adding a detachable bib to a sailor collar
*Pressing
*Pattern for a middy blouse; adapting the pattern directions for making

Applying a sailor collar

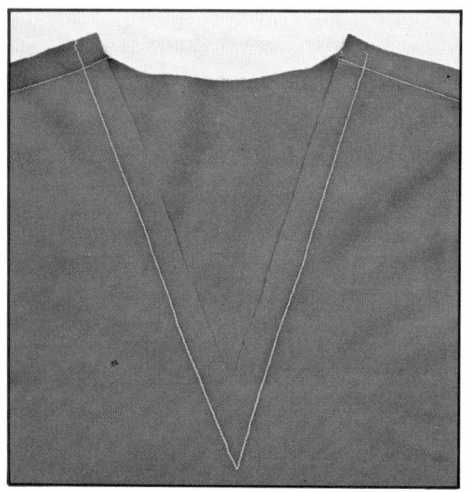

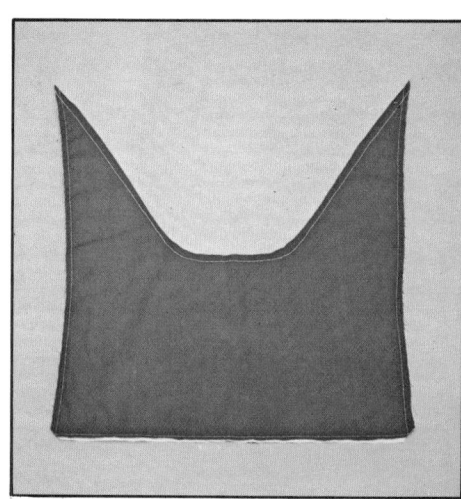

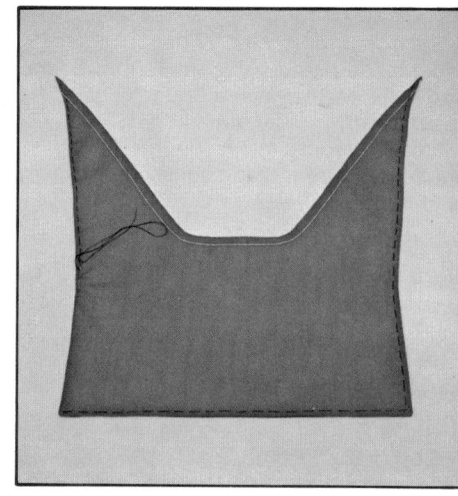

1 To prevent stretching, staystitch the front neck edge of the main front piece, the front facing, and the neck edges of the collar pieces. With right sides together, join the front and back at the shoulder seams. Press seams open.

2 With right sides together, pin, baste and stitch the two collar pieces together around the outer edge. Trim the seam allowances, and cut across corners.

3 Turn collar right side out and baste around outer (stitched) edge. Press. If a lightweight fabric is being used, the collar will need an interfacing. Cut interfacing to collar shape and make collar as shown in Volume 5, page 59.

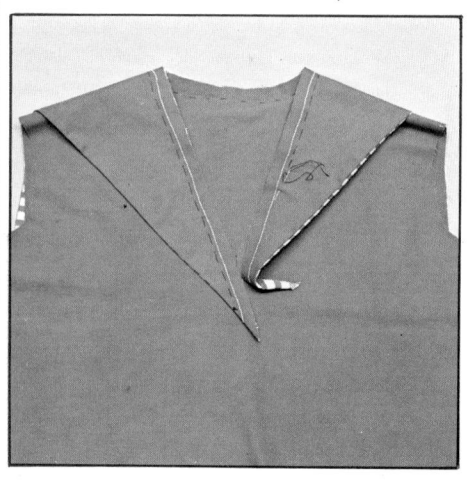

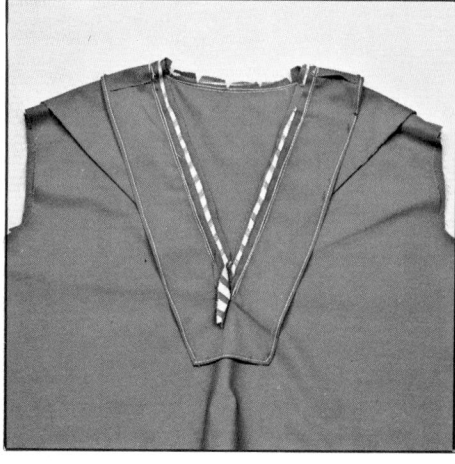

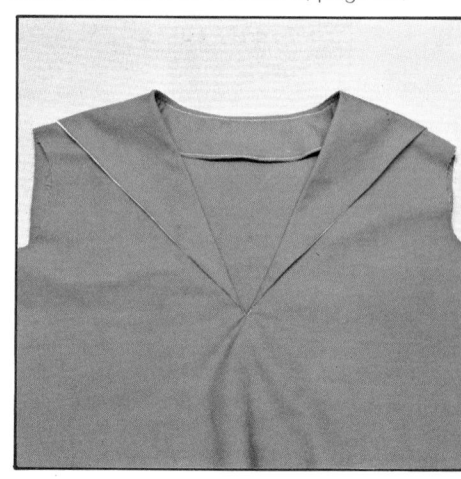

4 Matching center backs and shoulder points, pin and baste the collar to the front and back neck edge, so that the ends of the collar seamline meet at the exact center front and the collar points extend beyond the center front. At the center front clip the shirt seam allowances to the staystitching. This makes it possible for the "V" to be separated and the collar to be attached without catching the ends in the stitches.

5 With right sides together, baste and stitch neck facings together at the shoulders. Press seams open. Finish outer edge of facings. With right sides together, matching center backs, shoulder points and center fronts, pin and baste the neck facings over the collar, keeping the points of the collar free. Starting from the center front, stitch entire neck seam. Grade seam allowances and clip curves.

6 Press seam allowances toward facing and understitch to the facing. Turn facing to the inside of the neck and catch-stitch to the shoulder seam allowances.

Adding a detachable bib to a sailor collar

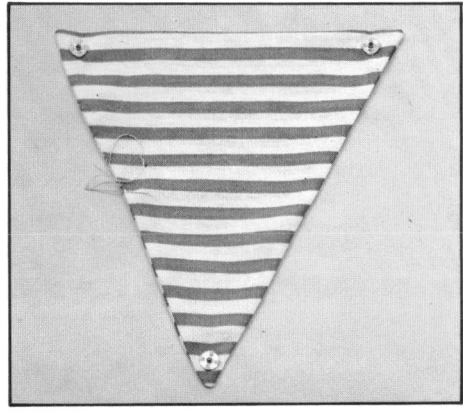

1 To make the bib, fold the piece in half along the foldline with right sides inside. If using striped fabric, make sure the fold is on or parallel to a stripe. Pin and baste around side edges. Stitch seam, leaving 2in (5cm) open at the center of one side. Trim seam allowance to $\frac{1}{4}$in (6mm) and trim across corners. Press.

2 Turn bib right side out. Turn in seam allowance at opening and slip stitch folded edges together. Baste around all edges and press. Remove basting. Stitch one half of a snap to each of the three corners of the bib.

3 When the shirt is complete, try it on and pin the bib to the inside of the shirt front. Position the bib as required. Mark with a pin where each corner of the bib comes on the blouse. Remove bib and sew the other halves of the snaps to the inside of the blouse.

Pressing

To give a professional finish to home-sewn garments it is essential to press the garment well. Pressing should be done at every stage; this intermediate pressing will give the garment a good finish. The final pressing should be done after the garment has been finished.

Pressing should not be confused with ironing. Pressing entails using the iron as a weight, usually with a cloth between it and the fabric. Pressure is applied, then the iron is lifted and moved to the next area to be pressed. This is different from the technique of ironing, in which the iron is pushed along the fabric.

Wet or dry press cloths can be used, depending on the area to be pressed or the type of fabric. A steam iron or water spray gun, such as one used to keep plants moist, may provide enough dampness, particularly on seams or darts. Cloths are used when pressure needs to be applied, and they help to protect the fabric being pressed. It is advisable to use a damp cloth when pressing a section of a garment with many layers, such as faced edges, collars, pockets, etc., followed by dry cloth pressing. A dry cloth should be used when pressing fabrics which might be adversely affected by dampness. The following photographs show basic techniques for pressing cotton fabric such as that used in the middy blouse on page 78. Using a press cloth on seams and darts is not always necessary for this type of fabric. If stubborn wrinkles form, spray them with water; this will usually dampen them enough that you can press them out.

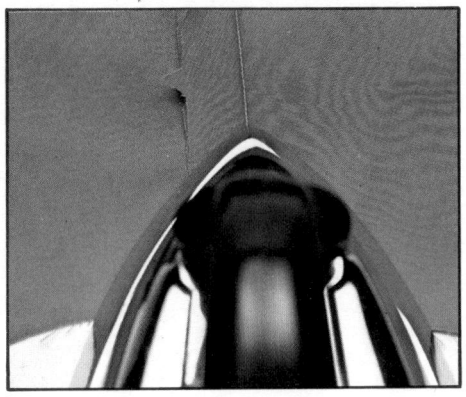

1 When pressing seams, first press the seam to one side along both sides of the stitching line on the wrong side of the fabric. Repeat on the reverse side of the seam, using the point of the iron to press the stitching line only.

2 Press the seams open from the wrong side, using the point of the iron along the seamline. A final press can be given on the right side of the garment along the seam.

3 After the facings are applied to the garment, they are pressed flat before being pressed in place on the garment. It is advisable to use a press cloth, especially if a collar has also been applied.

continued

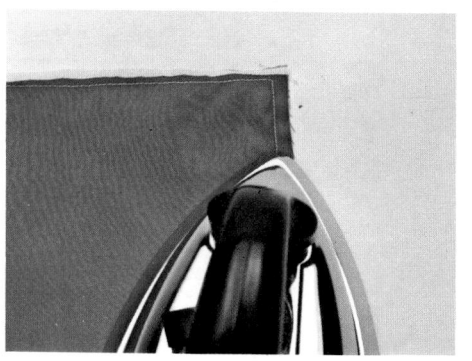

4 When pressing corners of double thickness, first press the corner and seams on the stitching lines from both sides before turning right side out.

5 Turn, pulling out the corners with a pin if necessary, then press carefully using a press cloth and applying pressure for a few seconds.

6 When pressing a decorated surface such as a braid-trimmed one, always press from the wrong side. If the surface is very raised, put a white towel between it and the ironing board.

Far horizons

Set your sights on far horizons with this sporty middy blouse. Made in crisp white cotton, it has a collar trimmed with braid and faced with royal blue to match the detachable bib.

Adapting the pattern

The blouse is made by adapting the pattern for the basic shirt from the Stitch by Stitch Pattern Pack, available in sizes 10-20, which correspond to sizes 8-18 in ready-made clothes.

Materials
3 sheets of tracing paper, approx 16×36in (40×90cm)
Flexible curve; yardstick

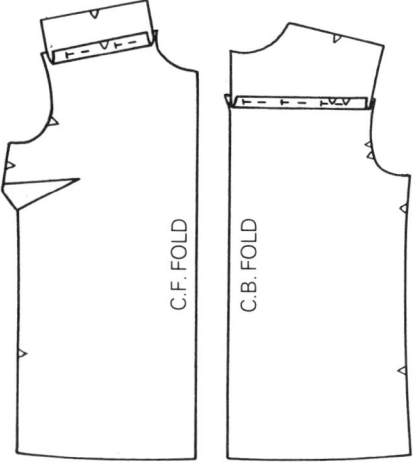

C.F. FOLD

C.B. FOLD

1 Pin the front yoke to the shirt front, and the back yoke to the shirt back, overlapping the ⅝in (1.5cm) seam allowance so that the seamlines match. Trace both complete pieces.

John Hutchinson

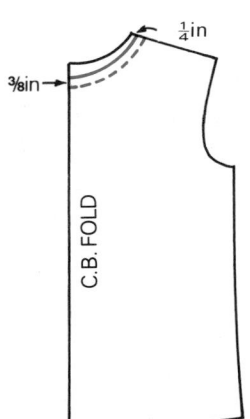

2 On the back tracing, mark a point on the center back 3/8in (1cm) from the neck edge cutting line. Mark a point 1/4in (6mm) from the neck edge cutting line at the shoulder. Using a flexible curve, re-draw the neck edge, following these two points. This is the new cutting line. A 5/8in (1.5cm) seam allowance has been included. Cut out the pattern back following the new cutting lines.

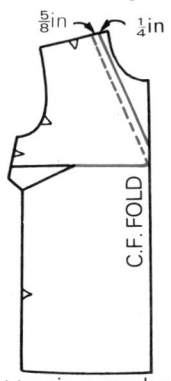

3 On the front tracing, mark a point 1/4in (6mm) in from the neck edge of the shoulder. This will be the new cutting line. Mark another point 5/8in (1.5cm) from the first, along the shoulder line. This will be the new seamline.

4 To mark the depth of the collar at center front, continue the top dart line across the pattern to the center front line. Using a ruler, join this point to the new neck seamline mark. Draw another line parallel to this and 5/8in (1.5cm) away from it, joining the cutting line mark at the shoulder to a point at the center front. Cut the pattern for the front bodice following the new cutting line.

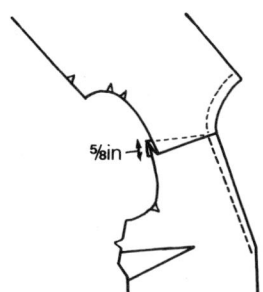

5 To make it easier to cut the collar pattern, fold back the shoulder seam

allowance on the front and back pattern pieces. Place the front and back neck points together at the seamline, and overlap the shoulder seamlines at the armhole edge by 5/8in (1.5cm). Pin pattern pieces together. Cut a piece of tracing paper and place it over this area.

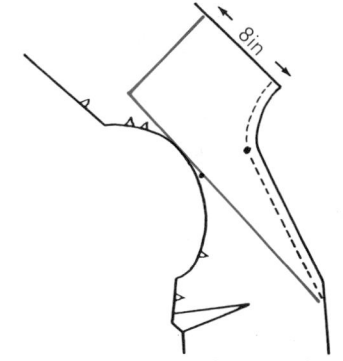

6 Trace center back and front neck edges, and armhole and center point of shoulder overlap. Remove tracing. Mark depth of collar at center back. This is 8in (20cm) down from center back seamline at neck for size 10: add 3/8in (1cm) extra for each larger size. At this point draw a line across from center back toward armhole at right angles to center back line. Make it 7in (17.5cm) long for sizes 10 and 12, 7 1/4in (18.5cm) long for sizes 14 and 16 and 7 5/8in (19.5cm) long for sizes 18 and 20. From this point draw another line at a right angle to first up to shoulder line. From the shoulder draw a line to first seamline point at center front.

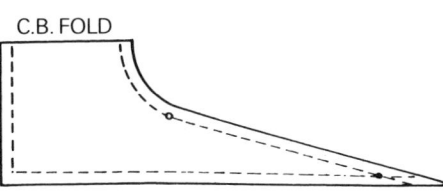

7 Add 5/8in (1.5cm) to the outer edge of collar pattern for seam allowance. The center back is placed on the fold. Mark the neckline shoulder point and cut out the collar pattern. If necessary, smooth out sharp angles at shoulder lines.

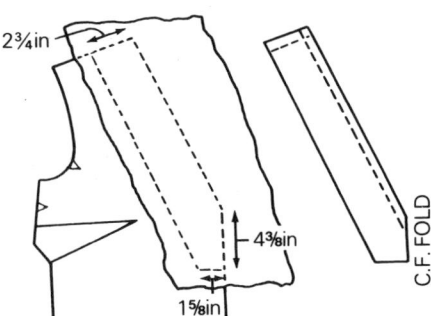

8 Place paper over front and back patterns and trace front and back neck

edge, center front and back and shoulders. On front tracing, measure along shoulder 2 3/4in (7cm) and mark. From the cutting line at neck center front, measure down 4 3/8in (11cm). Draw a line at a right angle to this point, 1 5/8in (4cm) long. Draw a line from the shoulder mark to meet this, parallel to the neck edge. Mark in a 5/8in (1.5cm) seam allowance at neck and shoulder edges. Mark center front to be placed on fold. Cut around facing shape.

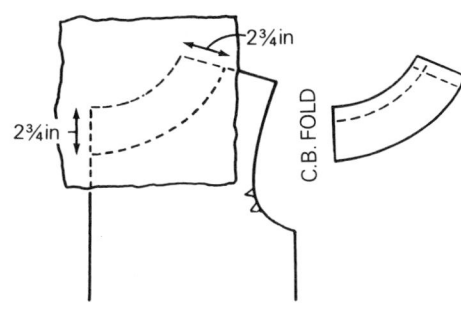

9 Make the back facing the same width as the front facing by measuring 2 3/4in (7cm) down the center back and along the shoulder. Using a flexible curve, draw the facing line connecting the two marked points. Mark the seam allowances. The center back is placed on the fold.

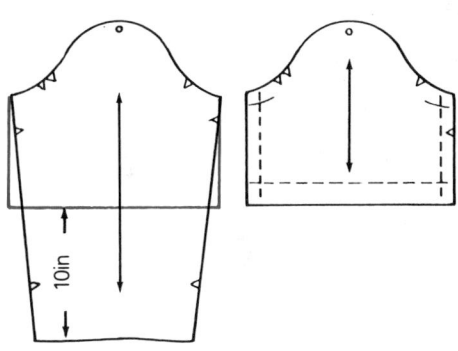

10 For the sleeve, measure up from the lower hem edge 10in (25.5cm). Draw a horizontal line across the pattern at this point. Straighten the side edges of the sleeve, keeping them parallel to the grain line. This length includes a 1 3/8in (3.5cm) hem allowance.

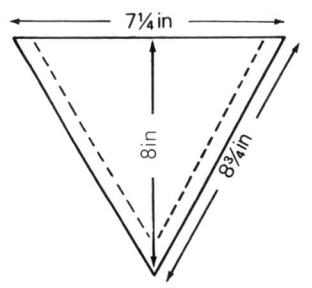

11 Draw the bib pattern piece on tracing paper. Draw a horizontal line 7 1/4in

John Hutchinson

(18.5cm) long. Mark a point at the center of this line and draw a line 8in (20cm) long at a right angle to first. Join sides of triangle, making sure that each side is 8¾in (22cm) long.

12 This triangular piece represents half the pattern and seam allowances have been included. The 7¼in (18.5cm) line will be placed on the fold; if striped fabric is used this line should be placed in the center of a horizontal stripe or parallel to it. The fold line should follow the straight grain.

Directions for making

Suggested fabrics

Crisp fabrics such as piqué, or lightweight sailcloth, poplin or cotton gabardine; for special occasions, satin or crepe.

Materials

36in (90cm)-wide fabric:
　Size 10: 2⅝yd (2.4m)
　Size 12: 2¾yd (2.5m)
　Sizes 14, 16: 2⅞yd (2.6m)
　Sizes 18, 20: 3yd (2.7m)
45in (115cm)-wide fabric without nap:
　Size 10: 2½yd (2.2m)
　Size 12: 2⅝yd (2.3m)
　Size 14: 2⅝yd (2.4m)
　Size 16: 2¾yd (2.5m)
　Sizes 18, 20: 2⅞yd (2.6m)
Contrasting fabric for collar and bib:
　36 or 45in (90 or 115cm)-wide fabric:
　　Sizes 10, 12, 14: ¾yd (.6m)
　　Sizes 16, 18, 20: ¾yd (.7m)
Matching thread
Flat braid 4⅜yd (4m) (optional)
2 decorative buttons (optional)

Cutting layout:
36 in fabric
with or without nap

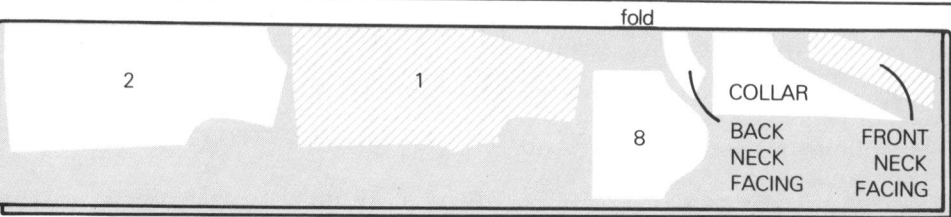

fold

| 2 | 1 | 8 | COLLAR / BACK NECK FACING / FRONT NECK FACING |

selvages

45in-wide fabric
without nap

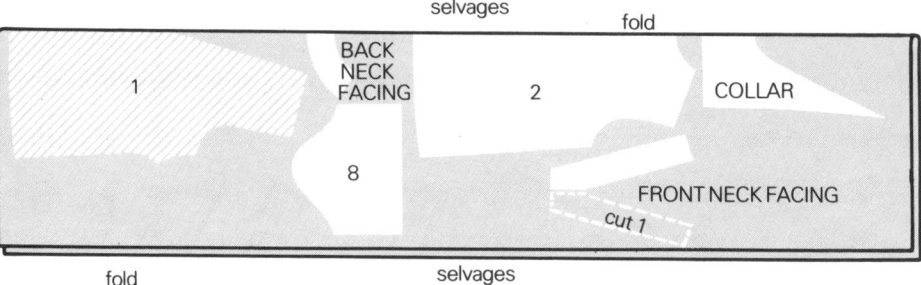

fold

BACK NECK FACING

COLLAR

FRONT NECK FACING
cut 1

1   2   8

selvages

Key to adjusted pattern piece

1 Shirt front	Cut 1 on fold
2 Shirt back	Cut 1 on fold
8 Shirt sleeve	Cut 2
A Collar	Cut 2 on fold (1 of contrast)
B Front neck facing	Cut 1 on fold
C Back neck facing	Cut 1 on fold
D Bib	Cut 1 on fold (of contrast)

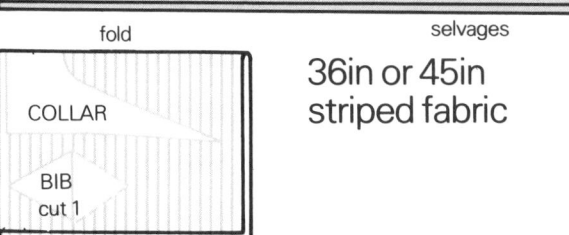

fold

COLLAR

BIB
cut 1

selvages

36in or 45in
striped fabric

COLLAR

BIB

selvage   selvage

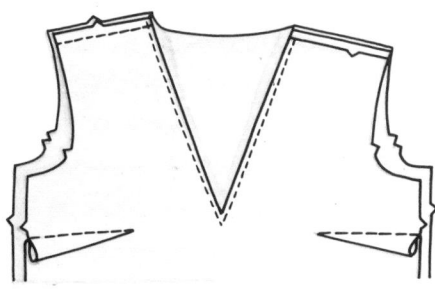

1 Prepare the fabric and cut out. Transfer all pattern markings to the fabric before removing pattern. Staystitch the front neck edge of the garment, front facing and collar. With right sides together, fold, baste and stitch the side bust darts. Press down. With right sides together and notches matching, baste and stitch the shoulder seams. Press seams open.

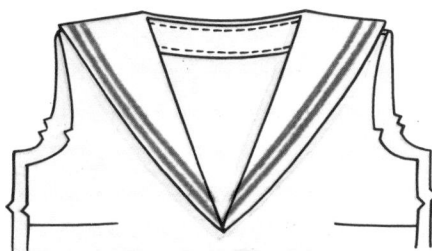

2 Make the sailor collar and apply to the neck edge and complete the neck edge with facings as shown on page 76. If braid is used as a decorative finish, it should be applied before the collar is put on the garment, so that the raw ends of the braid can be caught into the seam.

3 To apply the braid, make the sailor collar as shown in steps 1, 2 and 3 (page 76). Cut two pieces of braid, each long enough to trim the outer edge of the collar. Positioning lines for the braid can be marked on the collar with basting. The first line is $\frac{5}{8}$in (1.5cm) from outer edge and parallel to it all around, and the second is $\frac{1}{2}$in (1.3cm) from and parallel to the first. Baste and sew braid in place along the center channel. Remove basting; press on wrong side.

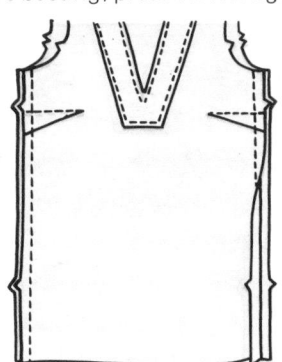

4 With right sides together and notches matching, baste and stitch the side seams. Press seams open.

5 Prepare the sleeve cap for easing by running two rows of gathering stitches between the notches. If braid is to be used on the sleeves, it should be applied before the underarm seam of the sleeve is stitched.

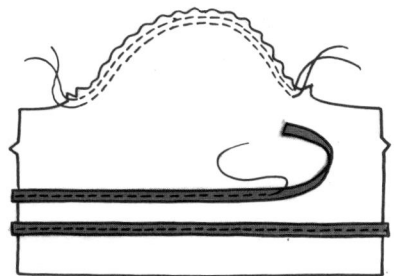

6 Mark the positioning lines for the braid across each sleeve with basting. The first row is $\frac{5}{8}$in (1.5cm) above the hem line and the second row $\frac{1}{2}$in (1.3cm) above the first. Cut four pieces of braid to fit (two to each sleeve); baste and stitch in place. Remove basting and press from wrong side.

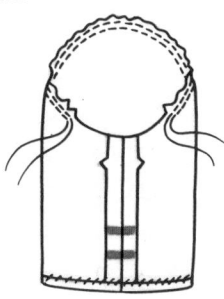

7 With right sides together, baste and stitch underarm seams of sleeves. Press seams open. Finish lower edge of sleeve by turning under $\frac{1}{4}$in (6mm) and machine

stitching. Press. Turn the hem allowance to the inside and baste close to the folded edge. Sew hem to sleeve with invisible hemming stitch. Remove basting and press folded edge only.

8 Set sleeve into armholes as shown in Volume 5, pages 64 and 65. At the lower edge of the shirt, turn hem up to the inside and sew as shown in Volume 5, page 65. Press.

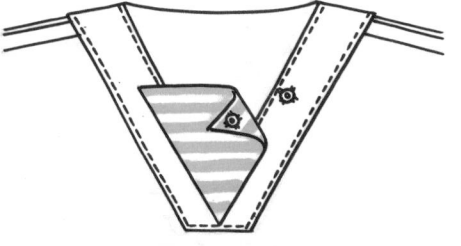

9 Make the bib as shown on page 77 and attach to the inside of the shirt front. On the right side, sew a button to the bottom corners of the outside edge of the collar.

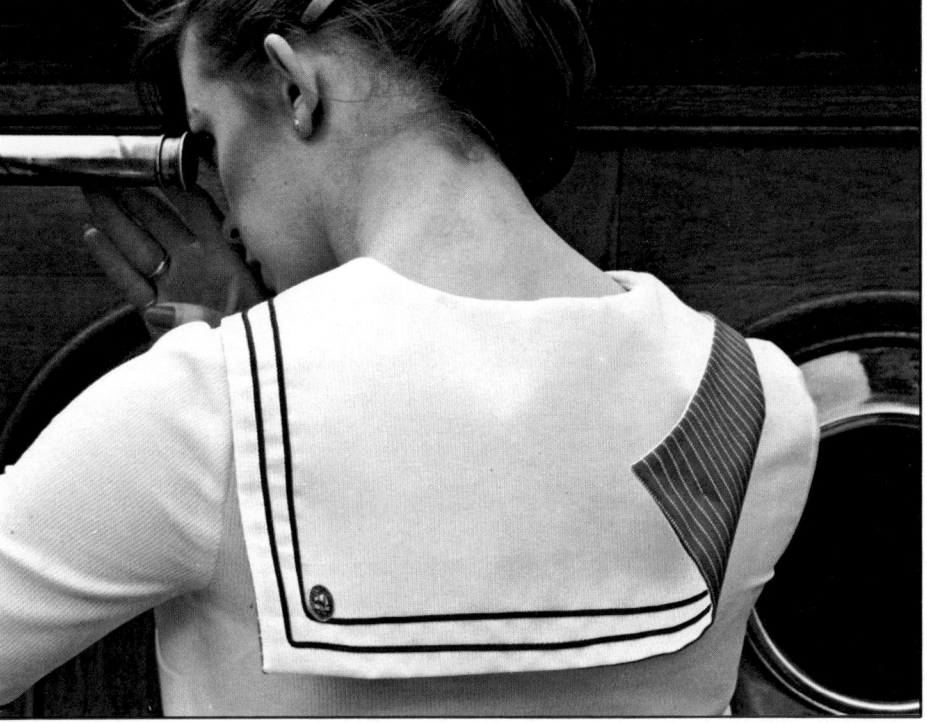

Terry Evans

Rod Delroy

Needlework / COURSE 13

*Free style patchwork—
two methods
*Dress with a patchwork yoke

Free style patchwork

Most patchwork is made up of repeating shapes—either a single shape or combinations of two or more. But you can also make patchwork using all different shapes in a "free," non-repeating design. The "crazy" patchwork so popular in the 19th century is one kind of non-repeating patchwork. A more coherent effect can be achieved by basing the patchwork on a design which may be representational (such as a landscape or still life) or abstract.

The yoke of the dress on page 84 is an example of this free style patchwork using a stylized floral design. The professional designer who created it used her own imagination, but if you want to design your own patchwork you might prefer to base it on a photograph or painting. Or you could make a completely abstract design, using the method described in Needlework course 11, Volume 8, page 87.

An important thing to bear in mind is that the shapes should be simple. Choose a painting or photograph with good strong shapes; a picture by Cézanne, for example, would be suitable, but not one by Monet. Trace the picture, simplifying the lines and omitting details. You will probably need to make several tracings

before you get one that can be successfully translated into patchwork. If you like, you can use embroidery to add detail and textural interest, as in the yoke design.

Once you have achieved a satisfactory design, you may need to enlarge it or reduce it to the correct size. First draw the outline of the area to be filled with patchwork, full size, on graph paper. Then copy the design on the graph paper using the method described in Needlework course 5, Volume 4, page 77. In the meantime you should be thinking about the kinds of fabrics you want to use. If you are still a beginner at patchwork you should stick to closely woven fabrics that don't fray easily, but in any case choose fabrics that will take a crease; those made of natural fibers—cotton, silk, linen, and wool—are best.

Also bear in mind how the patchwork will be used. If it is for a garment all the fabrics should be of similar type so that they can be cleaned or washed in the same way. If it is for a pillow cover or other household item the fabrics should not be too delicate for the wear they will receive. In either case they should be of similar weight. If you want to use very lightweight fabrics, such as China

silks, you can make these easier to handle by applying very lightweight iron-on interfacing to them before cutting out the shapes.

When you've amassed a good collection of fabrics, cut scraps roughly the shape of the patches and arrange them on the design to see how they work together. Experiment in this way until you have a well-balanced arrangement of colors. Number each section of the design and make a note of the fabric chosen for it. A good way to do this is to pin a small sample of each fabric to a slip of paper and label it "A," "B," and so on; then write the letters on the design.

There are several ways to construct free style patchwork. One method is similar to log cabin patchwork: you sew the pieces to a backing fabric, overlapping and turning under the seam allowances so that the patches fit along stitching lines. Another method (Method I below) involves sewing the pieces edge to edge, having first sewn them to pieces of interfacing traced from the design. Method II (shown right) is the one used for the patchwork yoke featured in this chapter. The paper shapes, to which the patches are basted, facilitate accuracy in sewing the patches together.

Free style patchwork—Method I

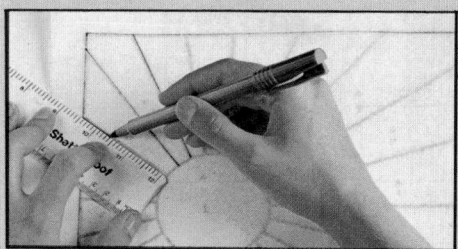
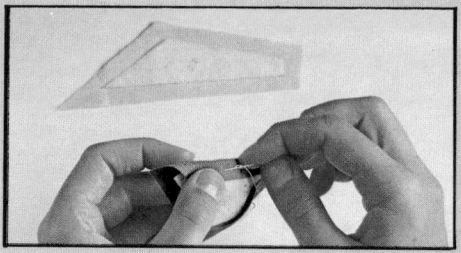
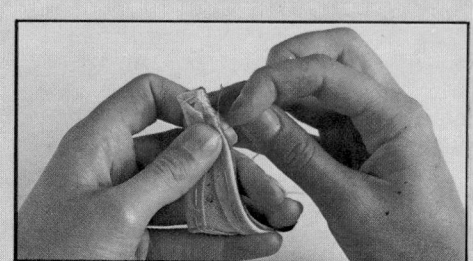

1 Darken the lines of the design (previously enlarged if necessary) with a felt-tip pen. Place a piece of medium-weight interfacing over the design and trace it. Using pencil, draw a short vertical line on each interfacing piece to indicate the straight grain of the fabric when cutting the patches.

2 Cut out the shapes, and number each one on the wrong side. Place each shape on the appropriate fabric, draw around it, adding $\frac{3}{8}$in (1cm) seam allowance all around, and then cut out the fabric patch. Place the interfacing shape on the fabric shape, wrong sides upward. Fold the seam allowance over the interfacing edge and sew it in place with small running stitches, using matching thread, making sure not to sew through the right side. (Contrasting thread is used here.)

3 Sew the patches together, placing them with right sides facing and overcasting the edges with tiny stitches.

Free style patchwork—Method II

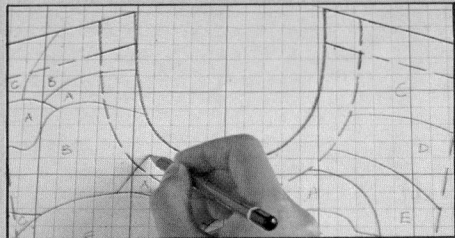

Begin by enlarging or reducing the design to make it the correct size. Select your fabrics and note their arrangement on the design as described on page 82.

1 The edge of the design will be the stitching line of the finished patchwork, so you must add seam allowances to it. Measure and mark ¾in (2cm) around all edges and connect the marks to draw in the cutting line. Extend the lines of the design to the edge, as shown.

2 Now transfer the design onto some medium-weight drawing paper, using dressmaker's carbon. Or, if you prefer, tape the design to a window, tape the drawing paper on top of it, and trace the lines directly. Number all pieces on both drawings.

3 Cut the tracing apart carefully. If you are experienced in using a craft knife, this is preferable to scissors, as it is more accurate. But you can use scissors if you like. Take your time and cut as carefully as possible.

4 When you have cut out all the shapes, number them on the reverse side and add the appropriate color symbols (A, B, etc.), referring to the original full-size drawing. Also on the reverse side, draw a small arrow indicating the lengthwise grain of the fabric, again referring to the drawing.

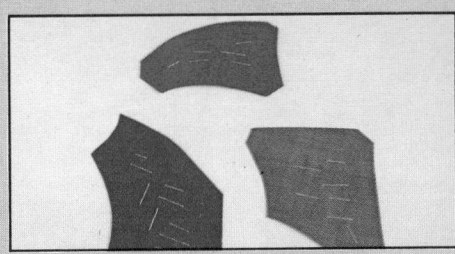

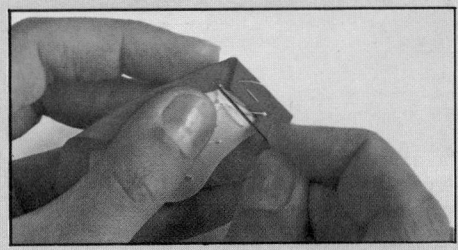

5 Place each shape right side down on the wrong side of the appropriate fabric and draw around it with tailor's chalk or felt-tip pen approximately ⅜in (1cm) from the edge, remembering to align the arrow with the lengthwise grain.

6 Cut out the fabric patches along the marked line. Pin each patch to its paper shape and put it aside until needed.

7 Baste each fabric patch to its corresponding paper shape. Begin in the center and work a few lines of basting outward in different directions.

8 Then fold the seam allowances over the edges of the paper and baste them in place, sewing through all three layers. Clip or gather the edges where necessary and miter the corners as shown.

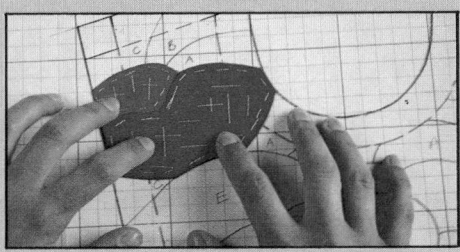

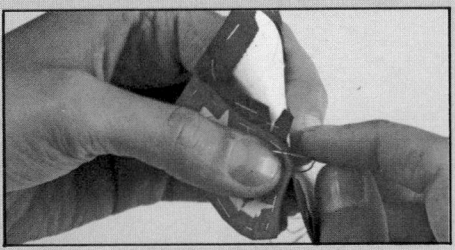

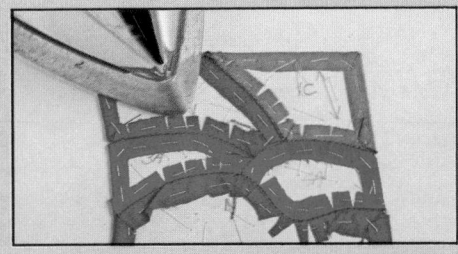

9 When you have covered all the paper shapes, place them on the drawing as you would assemble a jigsaw. Check that the shapes fit and that the colors are correct.

10 Sew the shapes together by hand, using tiny overcasting stitches and stitching through fabric only. It is most important to take pains at this stage and to make sure that the shapes are positioned correctly together. Small inaccuracies will result in badly-fitting patchwork that does not lie flat. Sew several patches together to make one section of the design; repeat to form other sections; then join these sections together.

11 When you have joined all the patches, steam press the work carefully on the wrong side. Remove the basting, press again lightly with a dry iron, and remove paper shapes. The patchwork can then be mounted and embroidered, as described on pages 84-85, lined; and used as required.

Floral fantasy

The glamour of tropical nights is evoked in the rich colors of this patchwork design. We've used it to fill the yoke of the dress given in Sewing course 43, page 59, but you could easily adapt it to fit the yoke of another dress. The main part of the design, adapted to a rectangular shape, would also be suited to an evening bag.

Materials
> Tracing paper for adapting the dress pattern (see page 59).
> Dress fabric and notions as given on page 62 (omit contrasting fabric); we have used wool challis for the dress shown here
> $\frac{1}{8}$yd (.1m) each of five lightweight fabrics for patchwork and sleeve trim: bright pink (fabric A), wine (B), bright blue (C), royal blue (D), and navy blue (E); we have used lightweight silks for the patchwork
> Lightweight iron-on interfacing (optional)
> Piece of lawn at least 14 x 16in (35 x 40cm)
> Silk embroidery thread, or stranded embroidery floss, in deep rose pink, pale pink, cream, and lemon yellow
> Small crewel needle
> Stretcher frame or rectangular embroidery frame at least 14 x 16in (35 x 40cm)
> Tracing paper
> Graph paper ruled in $\frac{1}{2}$in (1.2cm) squares
> Medium-weight drawing paper
> Dressmaker's carbon paper (optional)
> Sharp craft knife (optional)
> Tailor's chalk
> Felt-tip pen (optional)

Peter Pugh-Cook/Designed by Deborah Rowbottom

1 Enlarge the design, right, onto the graph paper. Each square on the page equals $\frac{1}{2}$in (1.2cm) on the graph paper. Do not draw in the stitching lines at this stage. (See Note on design, and if you are using a size other than 12, proceed first to pattern alterations, steps 14 to 17.)
2 Transfer the design to the drawing paper using either of the methods described in step 2, page 83.
3 Number all the pieces on both drawings, referring to the design given.
4 Cut out the individual pieces, using either craft knife or scissors. On the reverse side of each piece write its number and color code (A, B, and so on). Also draw in the grain lines, using the vertical

lines of the graph paper as a guide.
5 If the fabric you are using is very lightweight, you may find it easier to handle if you apply lightweight iron-on interfacing to it.
6 Now draw around the paper shapes on the appropriate fabrics as described in step 5, page 83. Cut out the patches.
7 Baste the fabric patches to the paper shapes as described in steps 7 and 8, page 83

8 Sew the patches together as described in step 10, page 83.
9 Press the completed patchwork as described in step 11, page 83.
10 Pin the patchwork to the piece of lawn, making sure the two layers lie smoothly together and pinning right across the design—through stitching wherever possible. Baste the patchwork to the lawn around the edges, inside the $\frac{3}{4}$in (2cm) seam allowance.

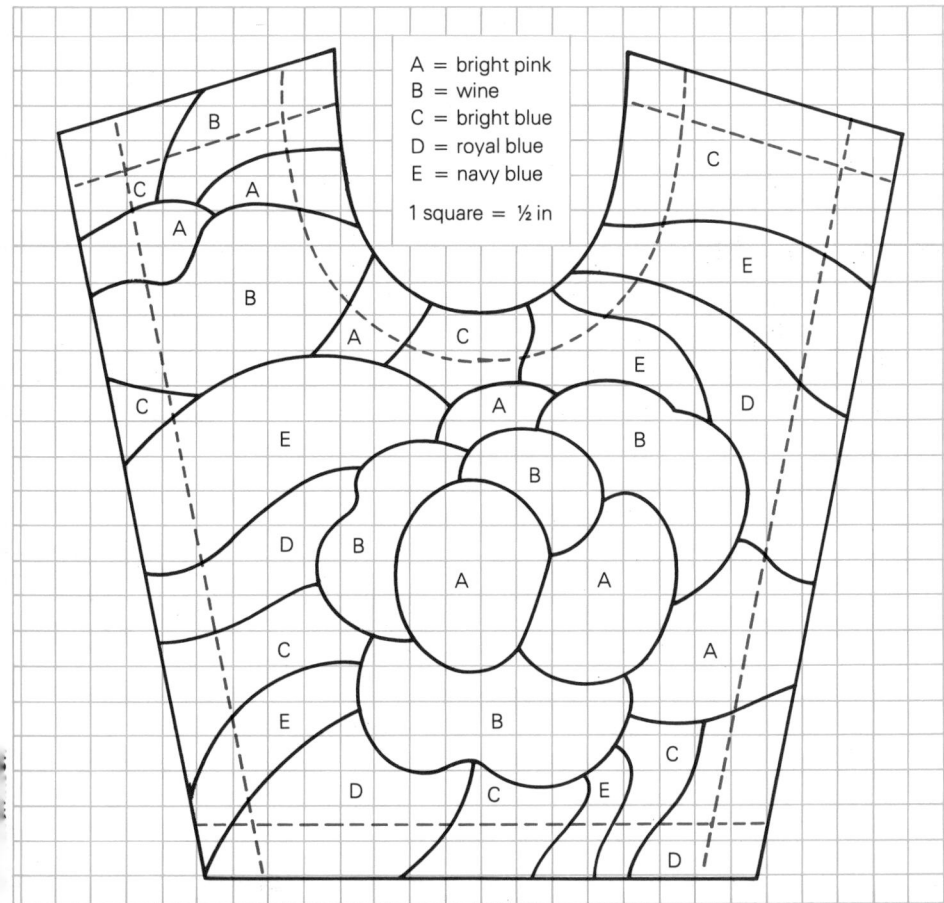

A = bright pink
B = wine
C = bright blue
D = royal blue
E = navy blue

1 square = ½ in

Note: the design as given is based on the size 12 pattern. If you are using a smaller or larger size, cut the dress yoke pattern as instructed on pages 59-60 and lay it on your enlarged design. Draw in the new cutting line, drawing it ⅛ in (3mm) outside the yoke pattern cutting line. Extend patchwork lines as necessary.

11 Attach the lawn to the frame, making sure that it is taut and straight.

12 Work the embroidery, using straight stitches, stem stitch, and French knots as shown in the detail photograph at right. Begin at the center of the blossom and work nine or ten curved, radiating "spokes" of stem stitch in lemon yellow. Use one strand of silk thread or two strands of embroidery floss. Using pale pink, deep rose pink, and cream (one strand of silk or two of cotton), add small straight stitches on the petals. Finally, work French knots in pale pink, cream, and yellow at the center of the blossom. Vary the number of strands to obtain knots of different sizes.

13 Remove the work from the frame and trim away excess lawn. If necessary, press it carefully on the wrong side with a warm iron, first placing it on a thick, folded bath towel to avoid crushing the embroidery.

14 Alter the dress pattern (from the Pattern Pack), following the instructions in Sewing course 43, pages 59-60. but modifying them as instructed below.

15 Ignore the instruction in step 1 to cut away the seam allowance at the neckline.

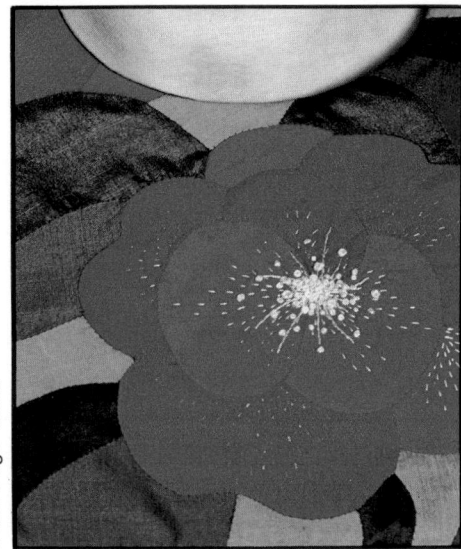

Peter Pugh-Cook

16 On the skirt of the dress omit the extra allowance for the side slit.

17 In adapting the sleeve pattern do not mark in additional seamlines for contrasting trim (that is, omit step 9).

18 In cutting out the dress, cut a yoke facing (piece A) on the fold (position occupied by pocket [B] on the layout given). Move pocket to another part of the fabric, and omit bias strips. Also cut a back neck facing (piece 5 from basic dress pattern).

19 Trim away the seam allowance from the enlarged graph paper yoke design, place it over the patchwork, and carefully and accurately mark in the seamline using tailor's chalk.

20 Join the yoke to the dress front, **not** as shown in Sewing course 43 but by placing them together with right sides facing and pinning, basting, and stitching along the stitching line. Note that seam allowances are unequal—⅝in (1.5cm) on dress and ¾in (2cm) on patchwork yoke. Grade seam allowances, clip at corners and press toward yoke.

21 Continue with step 2, page 62.

22 Baste and stitch the shoulder seams. Finish them and press them open.

23 Baste and stitch the shoulder seams on yoke facing and back neck facing and press them open. Turn under the seam allowance on the outer edge, baste, and topstitch.

24 Place the facing on the dress, right sides together, and baste around the neck edge (note again that patchwork seam allowance is deeper than others). Stitch the neck seam, trim seam allowances, and turn facing to wrong side. Press carefully on wrong side, working the stitching to the edge. Turn under the center back edges on back neck facing and slip stitch them in place on zipper tape.

25 Baste the yoke facing to the dress on the wrong side, so that the facing edge just covers the yoke stitching line. Slip stitch it in place along all three edges.

26 Continue with step 4, page 63.

27 From one of the patchwork fabrics cut contrasting trim for the sleeve (first applying iron-on interfacing if necessary). Cut two pieces on the straight of grain, each measuring 3¼in (8.5cm) × the width of lower edge of sleeve.

28 Trim away hem allowance on sleeve. Place contrasting strip on sleeve, right sides facing, with lower edge of strip ⅜in (1cm) up from lower edge of sleeve. Stitch the two pieces together, ⅝in (1.5cm) from lower edge of strip. Trim strip seam allowance close to stitching, turn strip down over stitching, press, and topstitch close to stitched edge. Baste strip and sleeve together, close to sleeve edge.

29 Placing right sides together, baste and stitch sleeve seam, continuing along strip. Finish and press seam open.

30 Fold strip to wrong side and press. Fold under raw edge of strip along upper stitching line; baste and slip stitch in place. Topstitch close to lower edge of sleeve. Repeat steps 28-30 for other sleeve.

31 Continue with step 9, page 63.

32 Turn up the dress along the desired hem line; hand-hem.

33 Sew a hook and eye at back neck edge.

Cuddly cow

This daisy-munching cow will bring a touch of whimsy to a room, and she's soft and cuddly too.

Size
About 20×15in (50×38cm).

Materials
$\frac{7}{8}$yd (.8m) of 36in (90cm)-wide printed cotton fabric
7in (18cm) square of white cotton fabric
Piece of white felt $3\frac{1}{2}×2\frac{3}{4}$in (9×7cm)
Piece of black felt 5×2in (12×5cm)
2in (5cm) square of yellow felt
Scrap of brown felt
Stranded embroidery floss in green and black
Thick white yarn; suitable stuffing
Matching sewing thread

Spike Powell

1 From printed fabric cut out two triangles, with $3\frac{1}{2}$in (9cm) long sides and a 3in (7.5cm) base, for outer ears. From white fabric cut two triangles the same size for inner ears.
2 Place a printed ear and a white ear together with right sides facing. Pin, baste and stitch all around, taking $\frac{1}{4}$in (5mm) seam allowance and leaving base edges open. Trim seam and turn ear right side out.
3 Pin the base edges together. Baste in place and run a line of gathering stitches along the edges.
4 Repeat steps 2 and 3 to make the other ear in the same way.
5 For the horns, cut out four triangles of white fabric, each one with $3\frac{1}{4}$in (8.5cm) sides and a 2in (5cm) base.
6 Place the horn pieces together in pairs with right sides facing. Pin, baste and stitch around each pair, curving the seam inward on one side. Trim seam and turn horns right side out. Stuff the horns lightly and sew across the open edges to close.
7 For the head, cut two pieces of printed fabric, each $10\frac{1}{2}×10$in (27×26cm).
8 Pin the head pieces together. Round off all four corners. Curve up center of one $10\frac{1}{2}$in (27cm) edge for the mouth (see photo).
9 From white felt, cut out two $2\frac{3}{4}×1\frac{1}{2}$in (7×4cm) ovals for outer eyes and two $\frac{3}{4}×\frac{3}{8}$in (2×1cm) ovals for pupils. For irises cut two $2×1\frac{1}{4}$in (5×3cm) ovals from black felt.
10 Assemble the eyes—pupils on irises,

irises on the outer eyes. Pin, baste and blanket stitch the eyes together.
11 Position the completed eyes on the right side of one head piece as shown, about $2\frac{1}{2}$in (6.5cm) down from top edge. Pin, baste and blanket stitch the eyes in place.
12 For nostrils cut two $1\frac{1}{4}×1$in (3.5×2.5cm) ovals from black felt. Position nostrils on right side of head piece, underneath eyes, as shown. Pin, baste and blanket stitch nostrils in place.
13 For flower, cut one flower shape about 2in (5cm) in diameter from yellow felt. For flower center cut out a $\frac{5}{8}$in (1.5cm)-diameter circle from brown felt. Using yellow sewing thread sew flower center to flower.
14 Position flower on head, beside nostrils, about $1\frac{1}{2}$in (4cm) up from lower edge, as shown. Pin, baste and blanket stitch the flower in place.
15 Using six strands of green embroidery floss, work a $3\frac{3}{8}$in (9.5cm)-long curved line of stem stitch from flower around to mouth.
16 Place the ears and horns on the right side of the face, positioning them with the points facing inward and pulling up the gathering along lower edges of ears slightly. Pin and baste.
17 Place back of head and face together with right sides facing, sandwiching in

ears and horns. Pin, baste and stitch all around, taking $\frac{3}{8}$in (1cm) seam allowance and leaving 3in (7.5cm) open along lower edge. Turn head right side out.
18 For body, cut out two pieces of printed fabric, each $21×15\frac{1}{2}$in (53×40cm). Place body pieces together with the longer sides horizontal. Round off the two top corners for the head and tail.
19 Position the head on the right side of one body at top left-hand corner. Place other body piece, right side down, on top. Pin, baste and stitch all around, taking $\frac{3}{8}$in (1cm) seam allowance and leaving an 8in (20cm) opening in tail end of body. Trim seam and turn body right side out.
20 Using six strands of black embroidery floss, work feet, udders and underbody in stem stitch along lower edge of body.
21 Stuff head lightly. Turn in opening edges and slip stitch together to close.
22 Stuff body. Turn in opening edges and pin together.
23 For tail cut eighteen 14in (36cm) lengths of thick white yarn. Knot the strands together at one end. Divide them into three equal groups and braid them together for $8\frac{1}{2}$in (22cm). Knot again and brush out the ends.
24 Tuck top of tail into body opening. Slip stitch the opening edges together to close, catching in the tail.

EXTRA SPECIAL CROCHET

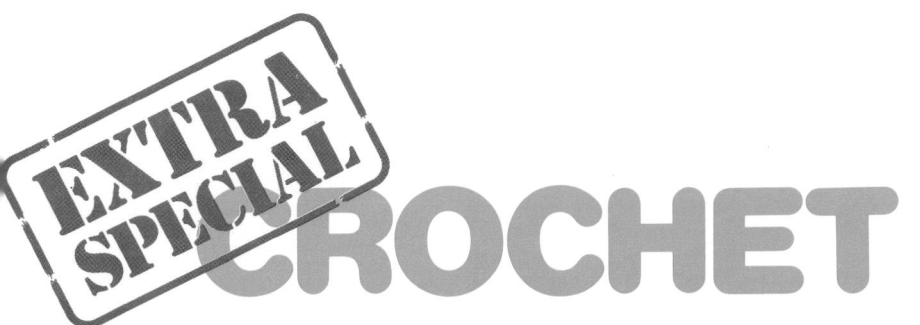

Baby's first layette (1)

Crochet this blanket, jacket and cardigan for a young baby.

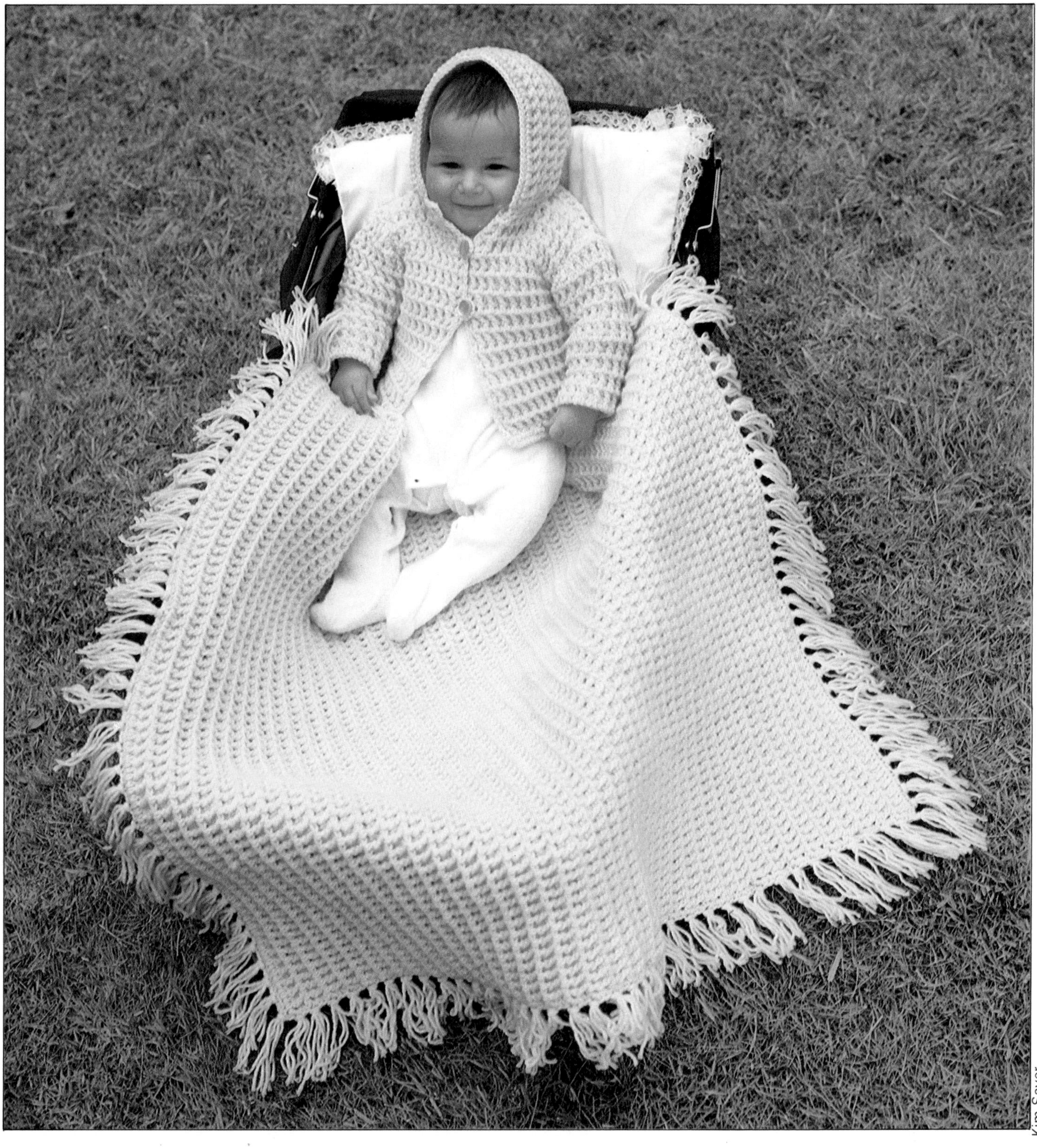

Kim Sayer

Sizes
Blanket 30in (74cm) square excluding fringe.
Jacket To fit birth to 3 months.
Length, 9in (23cm).
Sleeve seam, 5¼in (13.5cm).
Cardigan To fit birth to 3 months.
Length, 8in (20cm).
Sleeve seam, 5in (13cm).

Materials
Blanket *24oz (680g) of a sport-weight yarn*
Sizes C and F (3.00 and 4.00mm) crochet hooks
Jacket *8oz (200g) of a sport-weight yarn*
Sizes C and F (3.00 and 4.00mm) crochet hooks
Three buttons
Cardigan *3oz (80g) of a sport-weight yarn main color (A)*
1oz (20g) in contrasting color (B)
Sizes B and E (2.50 and 3.50mm) crochet hooks; six buttons

Gauge
Blanket and jacket 20 sts and 12 rows to 4in (10cm) patt on size F (4.00mm) hook.
Cardigan 20dc and 11 rows to 4in (10cm) on size E (3.50mm) hook.

Blanket
Using size F (4.00mm) hook make 151ch.
Base row 1dc into 4th ch from hook, 1dc into each ch to end. Turn. 149 sts.
Beg patt.
1st row 3 ch to count as first dc, work around next dc by working yo, insert hook from front to back between next 2dc, around dc at left and through work from back to front, draw yarn through and complete dc in usual way—called 1 double around front or dc around ft—, 1dc into next dc in the normal way, rep from * to end, ending with 1dc into top of ch. Turn.
2nd row 3ch, *1dc into top of next dc in the normal way, 1dc around ft rep from * to last 2sts, 1dc into each of last 2dc. Turn. Cont in patt until a total of 88 rows has been worked. Fasten off.

Edging
Using size C (3.00mm) hook rejoin yarn to first of foundation ch, working along foundation ch work 1sc into each ch to corner, 3sc into corner, working along row ends work (2sc into next row end, 1sc into next row end) to corner, 3sc into corner, 1sc into each dc, 3sc into corner, (2sc into next row end, 1sc into next row end) to corner, 2sc into corner, sl st into first sc. Fasten off.

Fringe
Using three 6¼in (16cm) pieces of yarn tog knot fringe into every 3rd sc all around outer edge.

Jacket
Back
Using size F (4.00mm) hook make 50ch

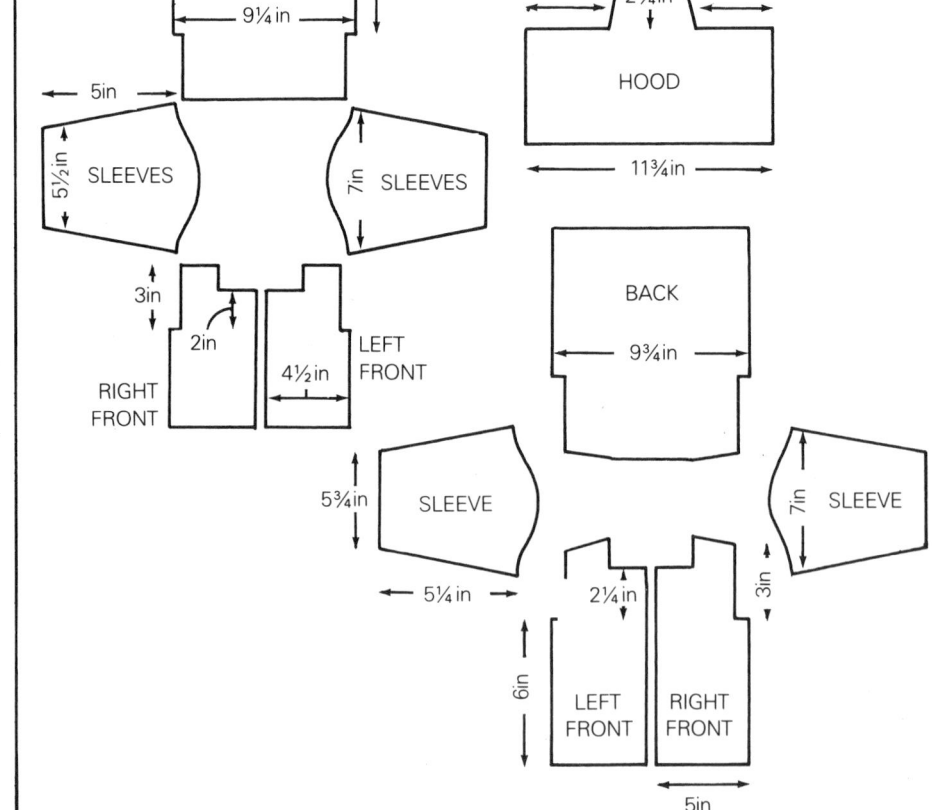

and work base row and 2 patt rows as for blanket. 49 sts. Cont in patt until 18 rows have been worked from beg.
Shape armholes
Next row Sl st over first 4sts, 3ch, patt to within last 3sts, turn.
Cont in patt until 27 rows have been worked from beg.
Shape shoulders
Next row Sl st over first 4sts, 3ch, patt to within last 3sts. Turn.
Rep last row once more.
Next row Sl st over first 6sts, 3ch, patt to within last 5sts.
Fasten off.

Right front
Using size F (4.00mm) hook make 27ch and work base row and 2 patt rows as for blanket. 25sts. Cont in patt until 18 rows have been worked from beg.
Shape armhole
Next row Sl st over first 4sts, 3ch, patt to end. Turn. Patt 6 rows.
Shape neck
Next row Sl st over first 12sts, 3ch, patt to end. Turn. Patt 1 row.
Shape shoulder
Next row Patt to within last 3sts. Turn.
Next row Sl st over first 4sts, 3ch, patt to end.
Fasten off.

Left front
Work as for right front, reversing shaping.

Sleeves
Using size F (4.00mm) hook make 31ch and work base row and 2 patt rows as for blanket, inc one st at each of 2nd patt row. 29 sts.
Cont in patt, inc one st at each end of every 3rd row until there are 35sts.
Cont without shaping until 16 rows have been worked from beg.
Shape top
Next row Sl st over first 4sts, 3ch, patt to within last 3sts. Turn.
Rep last row twice more. Fasten off.
Hood
Using size F (4.00mm) hook make 61ch and work base row and 2 patt rows as for blanket. Cont in patt until 14 rows have been worked from beg.
Fasten off.
Shape back
Skip first 20sts, rejoin yarn to next st with a sl st, 3ch, patt across next 18sts, turn.
Patt 1 row.
Dec one st at each end of next row. Work 2 rows without shaping.
Rep last 3 rows once more. Fasten off.
Join back seams.
Edging
Using size C (3.00mm) hook join on yarn and work (1sc into next row end, 2sc into next row end) to seam, then work 7sc along center back neck, (1sc into next row end, 2sc into next row end) to face edge. Fasten off.

Kim Sayer

Shape armhole
Next row Sl st over first 4sts, 3ch, work to end. Turn.
Work 4 rows without shaping.
Shape neck
Next row Sl st over first 11sts, 3ch, work to end. Turn.
Work 2 rows. Fasten off.

Right front
Work as for left front, reversing shaping.

Sleeves
Using size B (2.50mm) hook and A, make 28ch and work base row as for back. 27sts.
Next row 1ch to count as first sc, 1sc into each sc to end. Turn.
Rep last row 4 times more.
Change to size E (3.50mm) hook and work 1 row dc. 27 sts.
Cont in dc, inc one st at each end of every 3rd row until there are 35 sts, ending with an inc row.
Shape top
Next row Sl st over first 4sts, 3ch, 1dc into each dc to within last 3dc. Turn.
Rep last row twice more. Fasten off.

To finish
Press or block, according to yarn used. Join shoulder seams. Set in sleeves, then join side and sleeve seams.
Neck edging
With RS facing, using size B (2.50mm) hook and A, rejoin yarn to first st of right front neck and work 1sc into each st along neck edge, 1sc into next row end, 2sc into next row end, 1sc into next row end, 1sc into each st along back neck, 1sc into next row end, 2sc into next row end, 1sc into next row end, 1sc into each st along left front neck, turn.
Next row 1ch, 1sc into each st to end. Turn.
Rep last row once more. Fasten off.

Left front band
With RS facing, using size B (2.50mm) hook join on yarn and work 1sc into each of the row ends of neck edging, then (1sc into next row end, 2sc into next row end) along front edge, turn.
Next row 1ch, 1sc into each sc to end. Turn.
Rep last row once more. Fasten off.

Right front band
With RS facing using size B (2.50mm) hook join on yarn and work (1sc into next row end, 2sc into next row end) along front edge, turn.
Buttonhole row 1ch, 1sc into first sc, *1ch, skip next sc, 1sc into each of next 5sc, rep from * 5 times more, ending with 1sc into each of last 2sc. Turn. 6 buttonholes.
Next row 1ch, 1sc into each sc and 1sc into each sp to end. Fasten off.
Sew on buttons.

To finish
Join shoulder seams. Set in sleeves, then join side and sleeve seams. Using size C (3.00mm) hook join yarn to lower edge at center back and working along foundation ch work 1sc into each ch to right front edge, 3sc into corner, up right front work (1sc into next row end, 2sc into next row end) to neck, 3sc into corner, 1sc into each st along neck edge, (1sc into next row end, 2sc into next row end, 1sc into next row end) up side neck, 1sc into each st across back neck, (1sc into next row end, 2sc into next row end, 1sc into next row end) down side neck, 1sc into each st along front neck, (1sc into next row end, 2sc into next row end) along left front edge, 3sc into corner, 1sc into each ch along lower edge to center back, sl st into first sc. Fasten off.
With RS together join hood to neck edge, leaving 4sc free at each front edge. Using size C (3.00mm) hook work a row of sc evenly around face edge of hood and lower edge of sleeves.
Make 3 button loops on one side of front edge and sew buttons to other front edge to correspond with button loops.

Cardigan

Back
Using size B (2.50mm) hook and A, make 47ch.

Base row 1sc into 2nd ch from hook, 1sc into each ch to end. Turn. 46sc.
Next row 1ch to count as first sc, 1sc into each sc to end.
Turn.
Rep last row 4 times more.
Bobble row 1ch, 1sc into each of first 3sc, *omitting the last stage of last sc, drop A and draw through B, using B, work 5dc into next sc, remove hook from loop, insert hook from front to back into first of the 5dc, then draw dropped loop through—bobble made or MB—, now draw A through loop on hook and using A work 1sc into each of next 3sc, rep from * to last 2sc, 1sc into each of last 2sc. Turn. Cut off B. Change to size E (3.50mm) hook.
Next row 3ch, 1dc into each st to end, 1dc into top of 3ch.
Turn.
Next row 3ch, 1dc into each dc to end.
Turn.
Rep last row 9 times more.
Shape armholes
Next row Sl st over first 4sts, 3ch, 1dc into each dc to within last 3sts, turn.
Cont straight until 8 rows have been worked from beg of armhole shaping. Fasten off.

Left front
Using size B (2.50mm) hook and A, make 24ch and work base row and up to beg of armhole as for back. 23sts.

EXTRA SPECIAL CROCHET

Baby's first layette (2)

Complete the layette begun on page 87 just in time for the christening.

Sizes
To fit birth to 3 months.
Dress Length, $12\frac{1}{4}$in (31cm).
Sleeve, $5\frac{1}{2}$in (14cm).
Sweater Length, 9in (23cm).
Sleeve, $5\frac{1}{2}$in (14cm).
Leggings Inner leg seam, 8in (20cm).

Materials
Sport-weight yarn
Dress *6oz (160g) in main color (A)*
Sweater *3oz (80g) in main color (A)*
Leggings *5oz (120g) in main color (A)*
Bonnet *2oz (40g) in main color (A)*
Bootees and mittens *2oz (40g) in main color (A)*
3oz (60g) in contrasting color for set (B)
Sizes B and E (2.50 and 3.50mm) crochet hooks
4 small buttons for dress
2 small buttons for leggings

Gauge
20dc and 11 rows to 4in (10cm) on size E (3.50mm) hook.

Dress
Front yoke
Using size E (3.50mm) hook and A, make 47ch.

Base row 1sc into 3rd ch from hook, 1sc into each ch to end. Turn. 46 sts.
Bobble row 2ch to count as first sc, 1sc into each of next 2sc, *omitting the last stage of last sc, drop A and draw through B, using B, work 5dc into next sc, remove hook from loop, insert hook from front to back into first of the 5dc, then draw dropped loop through—bobble made or MB—now draw A through loop on hook and using A work 1sc into each of next 3sc, rep from * to end, finishing with 1sc into each of last 2sc. Turn. Cut off B.
Next row 2ch to count as first sc, skip first sc, 1sc into each st to end. Turn.
Shape armholes
Next row Sl st over first 4 sts, 3ch, 1dc into each sc to within last 3 sts. Turn. 40 sts.
Next row 3ch to count as first dc, 1dc into each dc to end. Turn.
Rep last row 3 times more.
Shape neck
Next row Work across first 10 sts, turn. Work 2 rows dc on these 10 sts. Fasten off. Skip center 20dc, rejoin yarn to next dc, 3ch, 1dc into each dc to end. Turn. Work 2 rows dc on these 10 sts. Fasten off.

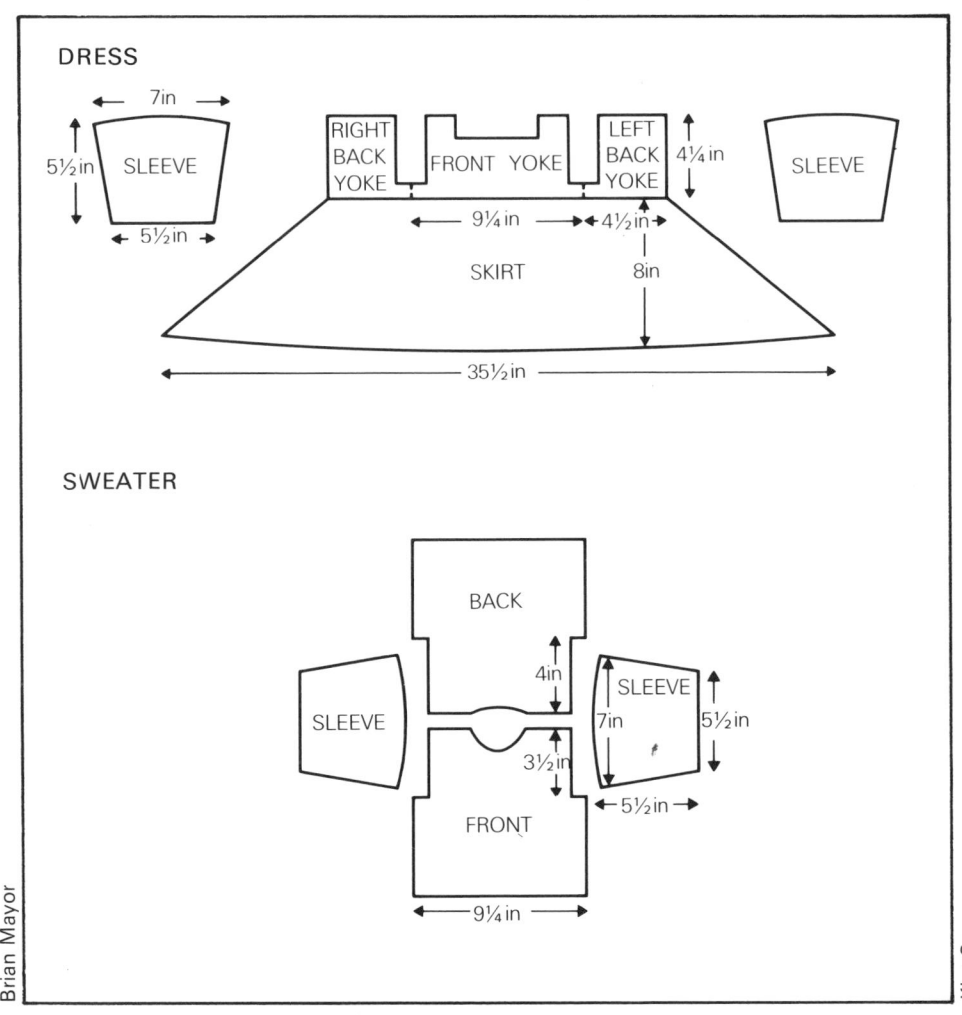

DRESS

SLEEVE 7in, $5\frac{1}{2}$in, $5\frac{1}{2}$in

RIGHT BACK YOKE | FRONT YOKE | LEFT BACK YOKE $4\frac{1}{4}$in

$9\frac{1}{4}$in | $4\frac{1}{2}$in

SKIRT 8in

SLEEVE

$35\frac{1}{2}$in

SWEATER

BACK

SLEEVE 4in

SLEEVE 7in $5\frac{1}{2}$in

$3\frac{1}{2}$in

$5\frac{1}{2}$in

FRONT

$9\frac{1}{4}$in

Right back yoke

Using size E (3.50mm) hook and A, make 23ch and work base row and bobble row as for front yoke. 22 sts.

Next row 1ch, 1sc into each st to end. Turn.

Shape armhole

Next row Sl st over first 4 sts, 3ch, 1dc into each sc to end. Turn. 19 sts. Work 7 rows dc. Fasten off.

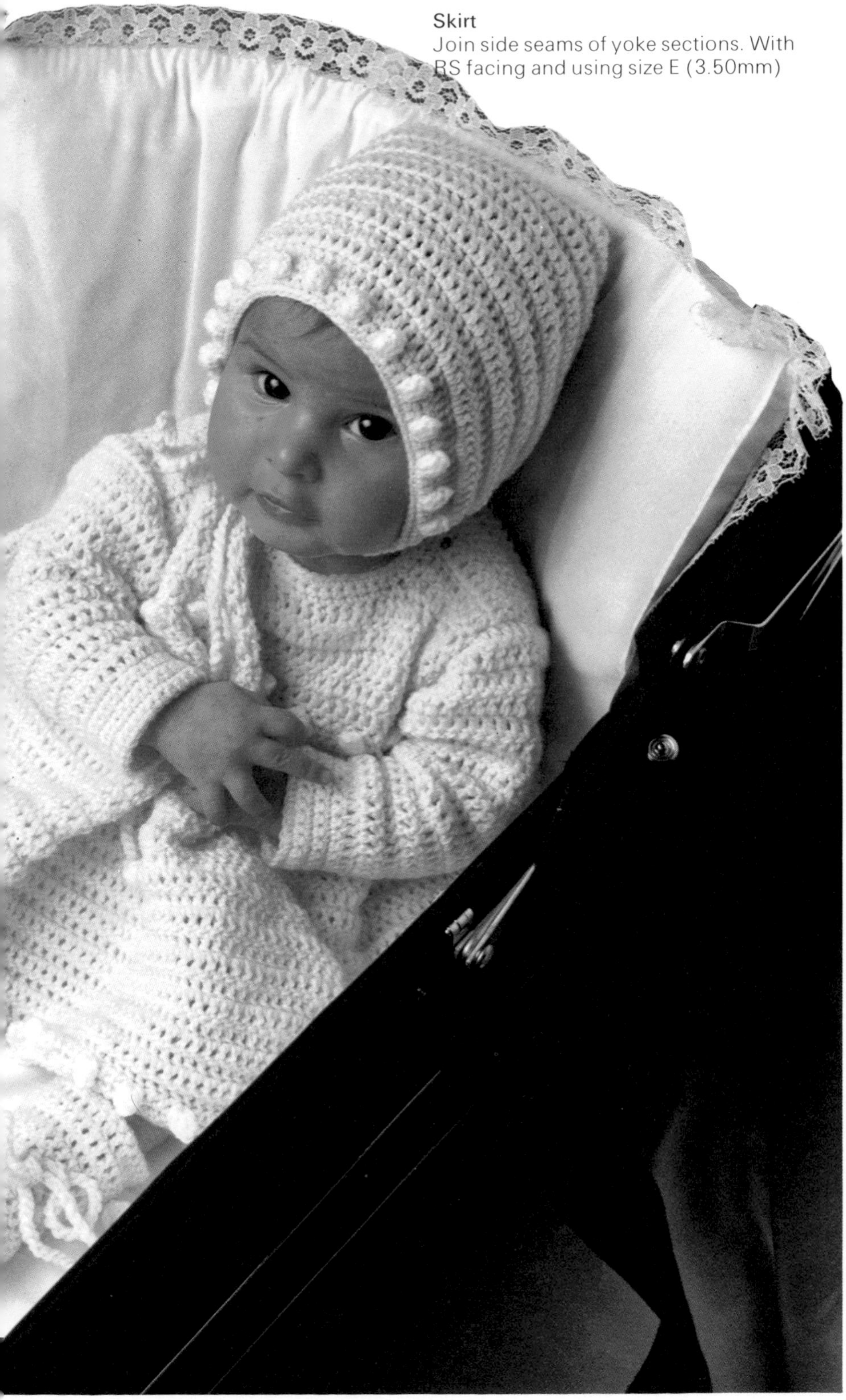

Left back yoke

Using size E (3.50mm) hook and A, make 23ch and work base row and bobble row as for front yoke.

Next row 1ch, 1sc into each st to end. Turn.

Shape armhole

Next row 3ch to count as first dc, 1dc into each dc to within last 3 sts. Turn.19 sts. Work 7 rows dc. Fasten off.

Skirt

Join side seams of yoke sections. With RS facing and using size E (3.50mm) hook join yarn to right back yoke with a sl st, 3ch, now work 2dc into each of the foundation ch to within last ch, 1dc into last ch. Turn. 178 sts.

Next row 3ch, skip first dc, 1dc into each dc to end. Turn.

Rep last row until skirt measures 8in (20cm); end with a RS row.

Next row 1ch, 1sc into each dc to end. Turn.

Bobble row Work as for bobble row of front yoke.

Next row 1ch, 1sc into each st to end. Turn.

Rep last row once more. Fasten off.

Sleeves

Using size B (2.50mm) hook and A, make 28ch and work base row as for back yoke. 27 sts.

Next row 2ch to count as first sc, skip first sc, 1sc into each sc to end. Turn. Rep last row 4 times more.

Change to size E (3.50mm) hook and work 1 row dc. 27dc.

Cont in dc, inc one st at each end of every 3rd row until there are 35 sts; end with an inc row.

Next row Sl st over first 4 sts, 3ch, 1dc into each dc to within last 3dc. Turn. Rep last row twice more. Fasten off.

Neck border

Join shoulder seams. With RS facing, using size B (2.50mm) hook and A, work 1sc into each of 9 sts on left back yoke, then (2sc into next row end, 1sc into next row end, 2sc into next row end) down side of neck, 1sc into each sc across front neck, (2sc into next row end, 1sc into next row end, 2sc into next row end) up side of neck, then 1sc into each of the 9 sts on right back yoke. Turn. 50sc.

Next row 1ch, 1sc into each sc to end. Turn.

Rep last row once more. Fasten off.

Button border

With RS of work facing join yarn to first row end of right neck and work 1sc into this row end, then 1sc into each of next 2 row ends, (2sc into next row end, 1sc into next row end) down dc row ends, 1sc into each of the sc row ends and (2sc into next row end, 1sc into next row end) twice on the first 4 dc rows of skirt. Turn.

Next row 1ch, 1sc into each sc to end. Turn.

Rep last row once more. Fasten off.

Buttonhole border

Join yarn to 4th row end of dc on skirt, work 1sc into this row end, 2sc into next row end, 1sc into next row end, 2sc into next row end, 1sc into each of the sc row ends, then (1sc into next row end, 2sc into next row end) of dc row ends on yoke, then 1sc into each of the 3sc row ends of neck border. Turn.

Buttonhole row *2ch, skip next 2sc, 1sc into each of next 3sc, rep from * 3 times more, 1sc into each sc to end. Turn.
Next row 1ch, 1sc into each sc and 2sc into each ch sp to end. Fasten off.

To finish
Join sleeve seams to within 2 rows ot top shaping. Set in sleeves. Join center back skirt seam. Lap buttonhole border over button border and sew in place. Sew on buttons to correspond with buttonholes.

Sweater

Back

Using size B (2.50mm) hook and A, make 47ch.
Base row 1sc into 3rd ch from hook, 1sc into each ch to end. Turn. 46 sts.
Next row 2ch, 1sc into each st to end. Turn. Rep last row 4 times more.
Bobble row 2ch, to count as first sc, 1sc into each of next 2sc, *MB with B, 1sc into each of next 3sc with A, rep from * to end, finishing with 1sc into each of last 2sc. Turn. Cut off B.
Change to size E (3.50mm) hook.
Next row 3ch to count as first dc, 1dc into each st to end, 1dc into top of 3ch. Turn.
Next row 3ch, 1dc into each dc to end. Turn. Rep last row 9 times more.

Shape armholes
Next row Sl st over first 4 sts, 3ch, 1dc into each dc to within last 3 sts. Turn.
Cont straight until 8 rows have been worked from beg of armhole shaping.

Kim Sayer

Shape neck
Next row Work across first 13 sts, 1hdc into next st, 1sc into next st, sl st into next st. Fasten off.
Next row Skip sl st, sc and hdc, sl st into next st, 1sc into next sc, 1hdc into next st, 1dc into each of rem 10 sts. Fasten off. Skip center 8dc, sl st into next st, 1sc into next st, 1hdc into next st, then work 1dc into each of the rem 13dc. Turn.

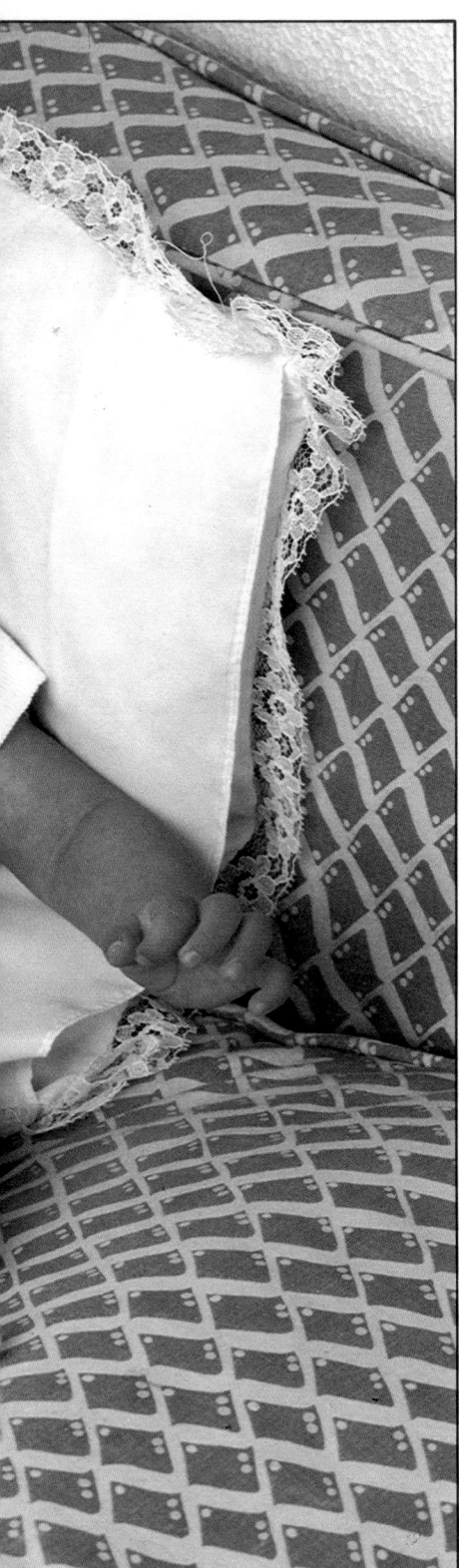

armhole shaping. Cont straight until 5 rows have been worked from beg of armhole shaping.

Shape neck

Next row Work across first 13 sts, 1 hdc into next st, 1 sc into next st, sl st into next st. Fasten off.

Next row Skip the sl st, sc and hdc, sl st into next st, 1 sc into next sc, 1 hdc into next st, 1 dc into each of rem 10 sts. Turn.

Next row Work across first 7 dc, then work 1 hdc into next st, 1 sc into next st, sl st into next st. Fasten off.

Skip center 8 sts, sl st into next st, 1 sc into next st, 1 hdc into next st, then work 1 dc into each of rem 13 dc. Turn.

Next row Work across first 10 dc, 1 hdc into next st, 1 sc into next st, sl st into next st. Fasten off.

Next row Skip sl st, sc and hdc, sl st into next st, 1 sc into next st, 1 hdc into next st, then work 1 dc into each of rem 7 sts. Fasten off.

Next row Working across all sts, work 1 sc into each st to end. Turn.
Rep last row once more. Fasten off.

Sleeves

Work as for sleeves of dress.

To finish

Count up to the 8th row of armhole on back and mark with a pin. Match points of front to markers. Fold remainder of back armhole over front and sew down along armhole edge so that back overlaps front at shoulder on right side of work. Join side seams. Join sleeve seams to within last 2 rows before shaping, then set in sleeves, taking the double thickness at shoulder into the seam of sleeve inset.

Leggings

Front

Using size E (3.50mm) hook and A, make 23 ch for top edge of bib.
Base row 1 sc into 3rd ch from hook, 1 sc into each ch to end. Turn. 22 sts.
Next row 3 ch to count as first dc, 1 dc into each sc to end. Turn. 22 dc.
Work 8 rows dc. Fasten off.
Next row Make 12 ch, then work 1 dc into each dc of bib, make 14 ch. Turn.
Next row 1 dc into 4th ch from hook, 1 dc into each of the 9 ch, 1 dc into each dc of bib, then 1 dc into each of the 12 ch. Turn. 46 sts. Work 17 rows dc.

Divide for legs

Next row Work across first 23 sts for first leg, make 5 ch. Turn.
Next row 1 dc into 4th ch from hook, 1 dc into next ch, then 1 dc into each dc to end. Turn. 26 sts.
** Cont in dc, dec one st at inside leg edge on next 2 rows, then work 1 row without shaping. Rep last 3 rows until 14 sts rem, ending with 1 row worked straight.
Eyelet hole row 3 ch, 1 dc into next dc, *1 ch, skip next dc, 1 dc into next dc, rep from * to end. Turn.

Next row Work across first 10 dc, then work 1 hdc into next st, 1 sc into next st, sl st into next st.
Fasten off.
Work a row of bobbles across all sts.
Next row 1 ch, 1 sc into each st to end.
Fasten off.

Front

Work as for back to completion of

Next row 3 ch, *1 dc into next sp, 1 dc into next dc, rep from * to end, 1 dc into top of 3 ch. Turn. 14 sts.

Shape instep

Dec one st at inside edge of next and foll 2 alternate rows, then dec one st at each end of next row. Fasten off.**
Next row Make 3 ch, then work 1 dc into each of the rem 23 dc for 2nd leg. Turn.
Next row Work to end, then work 1 dc into each of the 3 ch. Turn. 26 dc.
Now work as first leg from ** to **.

Back

Using size E (3.50mm) hook and A, make 48 ch.
Base row 1 dc into 4th ch from hook, 1 dc into each ch to end. Turn. 46 sts.

Shape back

Next row Work in dc to within last 7 sts, 1 hdc into next st, 1 hdc into next st. Turn.
Next row 1 sc into first st, 1 hdc into next st, work in dc to within last 7 sts, 1 hdc into next st, 1 sc into next st. Turn.
Rep last row 4 times more.
Next row 1 sc into next st, 1 hdc into next st, 1 dc into each dc, then 1 dc into each st to end. Turn.
Next row 3 ch, 1 dc into each st to end. Turn. 46 sts.
Cont in dc without shaping until back measures same as front measured at side edges.
Now divide for legs and work legs as for front to completion of eyelet hole row.
Next row 3 ch, *1 dc into next sp, 1 dc into next dc, rep from * to end, 1 dc in top of 3 ch. 14 sts. Fasten off.

Left leg

Rejoin yarn to first dec row end on front and work 3 ch, 1 dc into same row end as joining, (1 dc into next row end, 2 dc into next row end) twice, 1 dc into each of the 6 sts along toe edge, (2 dc into next row end, 1 dc into next row end) 3 times, then 1 dc into each of the 14 dc on back. Turn. Work 2 rows straight on these dc. Fasten off.

Right leg

Join yarn to first of 14 dc on back, 3 ch, 1 dc into each of next 13 dc, (1 dc into next row end, 2 dc into next row end) 3 times, 1 dc into each of the 6 sts along toe edge, (2 dc into next row end, 1 dc into next row end) twice, 2 dc into next row end. Turn. Work 2 rows straight on these dc. Fasten off. Join inner leg, side seams and foot seams.

Ties (make 2)

Using size E (3.50mm) hook and A double, make a ch approx 22in (56cm) long. Fasten off. Thread ties through eyelet holes.

Bobbles (make 4)

Using size E (3.50mm) hook and B, make 4 ch, sl st into first ch to form a ring.
Next round 3 ch, 11 dc into ring, sl st into top of 3 ch. Fasten off, leaving a long end. Thread end around top of dc, pull up tightly and secure. Attach one bobble to each end of ties.

Straps

Using size B (2.50mm) hook and A, make 60ch, then working along left side edge of bib, with RS facing, work (2sc into next row end, 1sc into next row end) along edge of bib, 1sc into each foundation ch along back, then (2sc into next row end, 1sc into next row end) along other side of bib, make 61 ch. Turn.

Next row 1sc into 3rd ch from hook, 1sc into each ch, 1sc into each sc all around, then 1sc into each ch to end. Turn.

Buttonhole row 1ch, 1sc into each of first 2sc, *2ch, skip next 2sc, 1sc into each of next 3sc, rep from * twice more, then cont working 1sc into each sc to within last 14 sts, (2ch, skip next 2sc, 1sc into each of next 3sc) twice, 2ch, 1sc into each of last 2sc. Turn.

Next row 1ch, 1sc into each sc and 2sc into each sp all around. Fasten off.

With RS of work facing rejoin yarn to first of foundation ch on left strap and work 1sc into each of the 60ch, then work 1sc into each of the foundation ch across top of bib, 1sc into each of the foundation ch on other strap. Fasten off. Sew 2 buttons inside back waist.

Bonnet

Using size B (2.50mm) hook and A, make 61ch.

Base row 1sc into 3rd ch from hook, 1sc into each ch to end. Turn. 60 sts.

Bobble row 2ch to count as first sc, 1sc into each of next 3sc, *MB with B, 1sc into each of next 3sc with A, rep from * to end. Turn. Cut off B.

Next row 2ch to count as first sc, 1sc into each sc to end. Turn. Change to size E (3.50mm) hook.

Next row 3ch to count as first dc, 1dc into each sc to end. Turn.

Cont in dc until 13dc rows have been worked. Fasten off.

Next row Skip first 20 sts, rejoin yarn to next st with a sl st, 3ch, 1dc into each of next 19dc. Turn.

Now work 10 rows in dc, dec one st at each end of every 3rd row. Fasten off.

To finish

Join side back seams. Using size B (2.50mm) hook, A and with RS facing work 1sc into each of the foundation ch all around face edge working 3sc into last ch, then work (1sc into next row end, 2sc into next row end) to seam, 1sc into each dc along back neck edge, then (1sc into next row end, 2sc into next row end) along to face edge, sl st into first sc. Turn.

Eyelet hole row 4ch, skip first 2sc, *1hdc into next sc, 1ch, skip next sc, rep from * to end, finishing 1sc into last sc. Fasten off.

Tie

Using size E (3.50mm) hook and A double, make a ch approx 45in (114cm)

long. Fasten off. Thread through eyelet holes. Make 2 bobbles as for leggings and sew one to each end of tie.

Bootees

1st bootee

Using size E (3.50mm) hook and A, make 30ch.

Base row 1 sc into 3rd ch from hook, 1 sc into each ch to end. Turn. 29 sts.

Next row 3ch to count as first dc, 1dc into each sc to end. Turn.

Next row 3ch, 1 dc into each dc to end. Turn. Rep last row 3 times more.

Eyelet hole row 4ch, skip first 2dc, 1dc into next dc, *1ch, skip next dc, 1dc into next dc, rep from * to end. Turn.

Next row 3ch, *1dc into next sp, 1dc into next dc, rep from * to last sp, 1dc into sp. Turn. 28dc.

Next row 3ch, dec over next 2dc, 1dc into each of next 8dc, dec 1dc, 1dc into next dc, turn. Mark the point between the 7th and 8th dc of the rem 14dc for back heel. ****Next row** 3ch, 1dc into each dc to end. Turn.

Now dec one st at each end of next and foll alternate row, then dec one st at each end of next row. Fasten off.**

Rejoin yarn to first dec row end on edge farthest away from the 14 unworked dc, 3ch, 1dc into same row end as joining (1dc into next row end, 2dc into next row end) twice, then 1dc into each of the 6 sts along toe, then (2dc into next row end, 1dc into next row end) 3 times, 1dc into each of the 14 unworked dc. Turn. Work 2 rows straight on these dc. Fasten off.

2nd bootee

Work as for first bootee until eyelet hole row and foll row have been completed. Fasten off.

Next row Skip first 14 sts, (mark the point between the 7th and 8th sts),

rejoin yarn to next st, 3ch, dec over next 2dc, 1dc into each of next 8dc, dec 1dc, 1dc into top of the 3ch. Turn.

Now work as instep of first bootee from ** to **.

Rejoin yarn to fasten-off point of the 14 unworked sts, 3ch, 1dc into each of next 13dc, (1dc into next row end, 2dc into next row end) 3 times, 1dc into each of the 6 sts along toe edge, (2dc into next row end, 1dc into next row end) twice, 2dc into next row end. Turn. Work 2 rows straight on these dc. Fasten off.

To finish

Join side leg seam. Fold each bootee in half, taking the marked point between the 7th and 8th dc for back heel, then join foot seam.

Ties (make 2)

Using size E (3.50mm) hook and A double, make a ch approx 22in (56cm) long. Fasten off. Thread through eyelet holes. Make 4 bobbles as for leggings. Sew to each end of ties.

Mittens

Work as for bootees until the eyelet hole row has been completed.

Next row 3ch, *1dc into next sp, 1dc into next dc, rep from * to end, working last dc into 3rd of the 4ch. Turn. 29dc. Work 4 rows dc.

Dec row 3ch, dec 1dc, 1dc into each of next 9dc, dec 1dc, 1dc into next dc, dec 1dc, 1dc into each of next 9dc, dec 1dc, 1dc into top of 3ch. Turn. Cont to dec in this way, on next two rows working 2dc less between dec on each row. Fasten off.

To finish

Fold mittens in half and join side seam. Make ties and bobbles as for bootees.

EXTRA SPECIAL KNITTING

Boys and girls come out to play

Keep them warm in this patterned sweater vest and cardigan, which can be worn either together or separately. We knitted ours in soft muted shades of yellow, cream and brown, but bright, vibrant colors would be just as attractive.

Victor Yuan

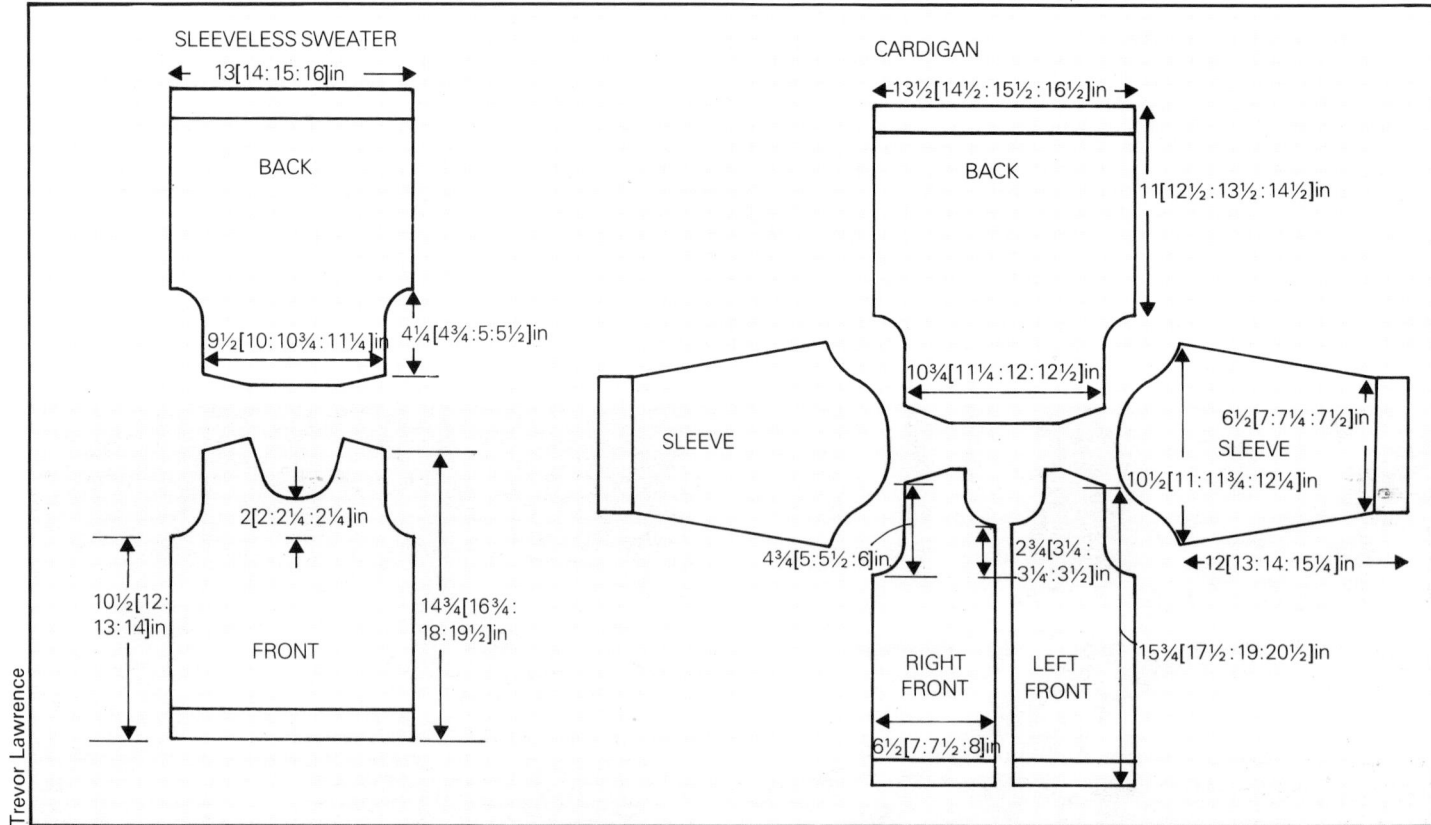

SLEEVELESS SWEATER

BACK

13[14:15:16]in

9½[10:10¾:11¼]in 4¼[4¾:5:5½]in

2[2:2¼:2¼]in

10½[12:13:14]in FRONT 14¾[16¾:18:19½]in

CARDIGAN

BACK

13½[14½:15½:16½]in

11[12½:13½:14½]in

10¾[11¼:12:12½]in

SLEEVE

4¾[5:5½:6]in

6½[7:7¼:7½]in SLEEVE

10½[11:11¾:12¼]in

2¾[3¼:3¼:3½]in

12[13:14:15¼]in

RIGHT FRONT   LEFT FRONT   15¾[17½:19:20½]in

6½[7:7½:8]in

Trevor Lawrence

Sizes

To fit 24[26:28:30]in (61[66:71:76]cm) chest.
Sweater vest Length 14¾[16¾:18:19½]in (38[42:46:50]cm).
Cardigan Length 15¾[17½:19:20½]in (40[44:48:52]cm).
Sleeve seam, 12[13:14:15¼]in (30[33:36:39]cm).
Note: Directions for larger sizes are in brackets []; if there is only one set of figures it applies to all sizes.

Materials

Sweater vest *4[4:6:6]oz (100[100:150:150]g) of a sport yarn in main color (A)*
2oz (50g) in each of 2 contrasting colors (B and C)
Cardigan *6[6:8:8]oz (150[150:200:200]g) in main color (A)*
2oz (50g) in each of 2 contrasting colors (B and C)
1 pair each Nos. 2 and 4 (2¾ and 3¼mm) knitting needles
1 set of four No. 2 (2¾mm) double-pointed knitting needles
6 buttons

Gauge

25 sts to 4in (10cm) in stockinette st on No. 4 (3¼mm) needles.

Sleeveless sweater

Back

Using No. 2 (2¾mm) needles and A, cast on 81[87:93:99] sts.

1st ribbing row K1, (P1, K1) to end.
2nd ribbing row P1, (K1, P1) to end.
Rep these 2 rows 4 times more.
Change to No. 4 (3¼mm) needles and beg with a K row, cont in stockinette st until work measures 10½[12:13:14]in (27[30:33:36]cm); end with a P row.
Shape armholes
Bind off 6 sts at beg of next 2 rows, 2 sts at beg of next 2 rows, then dec one st at each of next and foll 2[3:4:5] alternate rows. 59[63:67:71] sts. Cont straight until armhole measures 4¼[4¾:5:5½]in (11[12:13:14]cm); end with a P row.
Shape shoulders
Bind off 4 sts at beg of next 6 rows and 3[4:5:6] sts at beg of foll 2 rows. Cut yarn, leave rem 29[31:33:35] sts on holder.

Front

Using No. 2 (2¾mm) needles and A, cast on 81[87:93:99] sts and work 2 ribbing rows of back 5 times. Change to No. 4 (3¼mm) needles. Reading RS rows from right to left and WS rows from left to right, beg with a K row cont in stockinette st working from chart, until work measures the same as back to armholes; end with a P row.
Shape armholes
Bind off 6 sts at beg of next 2 rows, 2 sts at beg of next 2 rows, then dec one st at each end of next and foll 2[3:4:5] alternate rows. 59[63:67:71] sts. Cont straight until armhole measures 2[2:2¼:2¼]in (5[5:6:6]cm); end with a P row.

Shape neck

Next row K25[27:28:30], turn and leave rem sts on a spare needle. Bind off 2 sts at beg of next and foll alternate row. Dec one st at end of next and foll 5[6:6:7] alternate rows. 15[16:17:18] sts. Cont straight until armhole measures same as back armhole up to beg of shoulder shaping; end at armhole edge.
Shape shoulder
Bind off 4 sts at beg of foll 2 alternate rows. Work 1 row. Bind off. Return to sts on spare needle. With RS of work facing place next 9[9:11:11] sts on a holder, join yarn to next st and K to end of row. Complete to match first side, reversing shaping.

Neckband

Join shoulder seams. Using 3 of set of four needles as required and A, with RS facing K back neck sts from holder, pick up and K 35[38:38:41] sts down left front neck, K front neck sts from holder, then pick up and K 35[38:38:41] sts up right front neck. 108[116:120:128] sts. Using 4th needle, work 7 rounds K1, P1 ribbing, then bind off in ribbing.

Armhole borders (alike)

Using No. 2 (2¾mm) needles, A and with RS facing pick up and K 83[89:95:101] sts evenly along armhole edge. Beg with a 2nd ribbing row, work 2 ribbing rows of back 3 times, then work the first row again. Bind off in ribbing.

96

To finish
Press or block. Join side seams and press.

Cardigan

Back
Using No. 2 (2¾mm) needles and B, cast on 85[91:97:103] sts.
1st ribbing row K1, (P1, K1) to end.
2nd ribbing row P1, (K1, P1) to end.
Rep these 2 rows 4 times more. Change to No. 4 (3¼mm) needles and beg with a K row, cont in stockinette st until work measures 11[12½:13½:14½]in (28[31:34:37]cm); end with a P row.

Shape armholes
Bind off 6 sts at beg of next 2 rows, then dec one st at each end of next and foll 2[3:4:5] alternate rows. 67[71:75:79] sts. Cont straight until armhole measures 4¾[5:5½:6]in (12[13:14:15]cm); end with a P row.

Shape shoulders
Bind off 5 sts at beg of next 6 rows and 3[4:5:6] sts at beg of foll 2 rows. Cut off yarn and leave rem 31[33:35:37] sts on a holder.

Left front
Using No. 2 (2¾mm) needles and B, cast on 39[43:45:49] sts and work 2 ribbing rows of back 5 times inc one st at end of last row on first and 3rd sizes. 40[43:46:49] sts. Change to No. 4 (3¼mm) needles. Reading RS rows from right to left and WS rows from left to right, beg with a K row cont in stockinette st working from chart, until work measures same as back to armholes; end with a P row.

Shape armhole
Bind off 6 sts at beg of next row, then dec one st at beg of foll 3[4:5:6] alternate rows. 31[33:35:37] sts. Cont straight until armhole measures 2¾[3¼:3¼:3½]in (7[8:8:9]cm); end at front edge.

Shape neck
Bind off 3[3:3:4] sts at beg of next row, 3 sts at beg of foll 2 alternate rows. Dec one st at neck edge on next and foll 3[4:5:5] alternate rows. 18[19:20:21] sts. Cont straight until armhole measures same as back armhole up to beg of shoulder shaping; end at armhole edge.

Shape shoulder
Bind off 5 sts at beg of next and foll 2 alternate rows. Work 1 row. Bind off.

Right front
Work to match left front, reversing all shaping.

Sleeves
Using No. 2 (2¾mm) needles and B, cast on 41[43:45:47] sts and work 2 ribbing rows of back 5 times. Change to No. 4 (3¼mm) needles and beg with a K row cont in stockinette st, inc one at each end of next and every foll 8th row until there are 65[69:73:77] sts. Cont straight until work measures 12[13:14:15¼]in (30[33:36:39]cm); end with a P row.

Shape top
Bind off 6 sts at beg of next 2 rows. Dec one st at each end of next and foll 7[8:9:10] alternate rows; end with a P row. Bind off 2 sts at beg of next 8[8:10:10] rows, 3 sts at beg of next 4 rows, then bind off.

Button band
Using No. 2 (2¾mm) needles and B, cast on 9 sts.
1st ribbing row K1, (P1, K1) to end.
2nd ribbing row P1, (K1, P1) to end.
Rep these 2 rows until band, slightly stretched, fits along front edge to neck; end with a 2nd ribbing row. Cut off yarn and leave sts on a holder. Baste band in position and mark 5 button positions on this band, the first on 5th row from cast-on edge, the last 4 rows below sts on holder and the others evenly spaced between.

Buttonhole band
Work as for button band, but make buttonholes to correspond with markers thus: **Buttonhole row** K1, P1, K1, P2 tog, yo, (P1, K1) twice.

Neckband
Join shoulder seams. Rib 9 sts of buttonhole band, pick up and K 30[30:32:32] sts to shoulder, K back neck sts from holder, pick up and K 30[30:32:32] sts down left front neck, then rib sts from holder. 109[111:117:119] sts. Cont in ribbing, work 7 rows making buttonhole as before on 4th of these rows. Bind off in ribbing.

To finish
Press or block according to yarn used. Set in sleeves, then join side and sleeve seams. Sew on front bands, then buttons. Press seams.

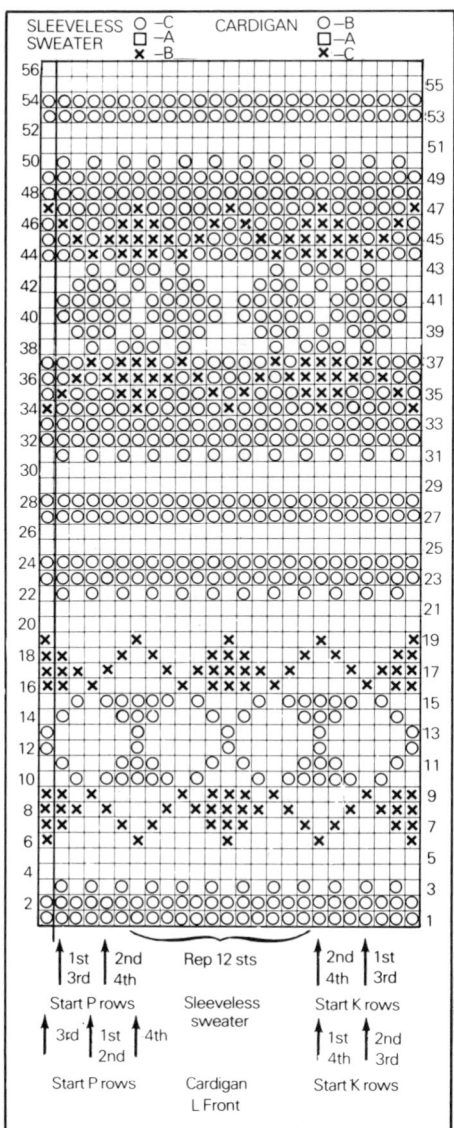

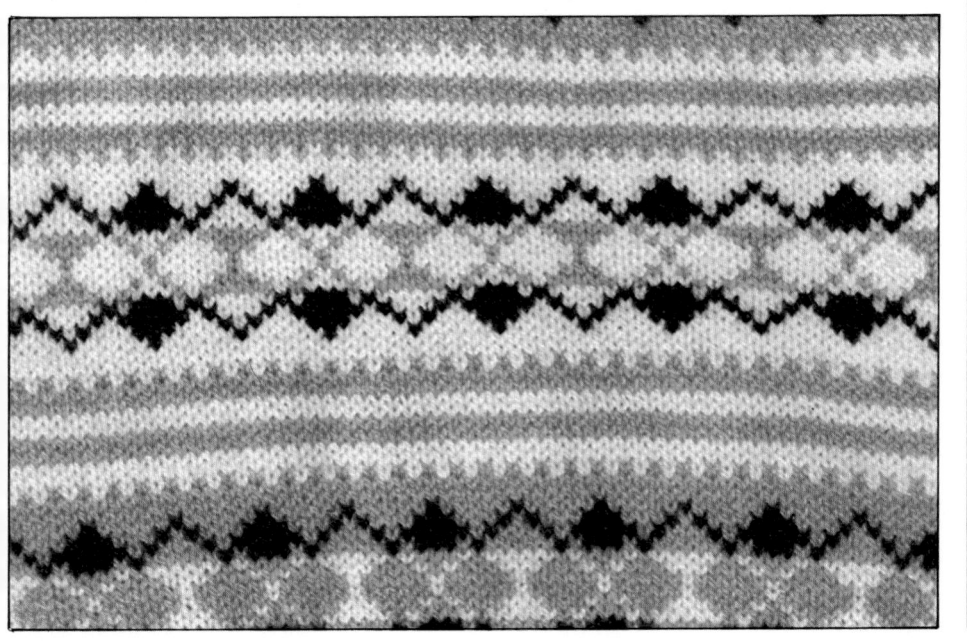

Jean-Claude Volpelière

Tubular tops

Take a few balls of yarn. Knit one or two pieces in simple stitches. The result? Four high-fashion summer tops.

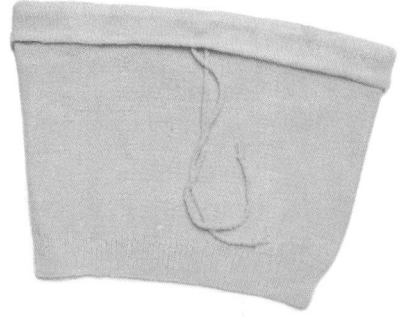

Sizes

To fit 32[34:36]in (83[87:92]cm) bust. Length, 11½[11½:12]in (29[29:30]cm).
Note Directions for larger sizes are in brackets []; if there is only one set of figures it applies to all sizes.

Materials

4[4:5]oz (100[100:120]g) of a sport yarn
1 pair each Nos. 2 and 3 (2¾ and 3¼mm) knitting needles

Gauge

28 sts to 4in (10cm) in reverse stockinette st on No. 3 (3¼mm) needles.

Back and front (alike)

Using No. 2 (2¾mm) needles cast on 108[114:122] sts. Work 18 rows K1, P1 ribbing. Change to No. 3 (3¼mm) needles and cont in reverse stockinette st until work measures 11[11:11½]in (28[28:29]cm); end with a P row.
Eyelet hole row K1, *yo, K2 tog, rep from * to last st, K1.
Beg with a P row, work 4 rows reverse stockinette st.
Next row K to mark hemline for cuff.
Beg with a K row, work 17 rows stockinette st. K 4 rows. Bind off.

To finish

Press, omitting ribbing, or block. Join side seams. Turn under last 4 rows and slip stitch to P side of cuff. Using five 4¾yd (4.25m) pieces of yarn tog, make a twisted cord. Thread cord through eyelet holes to tie at front. Fold back cuff.

  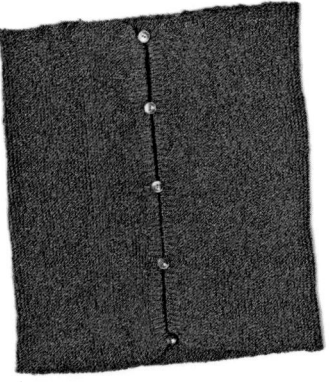

Sizes

To fit 32[34:36:38]in (38[87:92:97]cm) bust. Length, 14½in (36cm).

Note: Directions for larger sizes are in brackets []; if there is only one set of figures it applies to all sizes.

Materials

6[6:7:7]oz (150[150:175:175]g) of a lightweight mercerized cotton yarn
1 pair each Nos. 0 and 2 (2¼ and 2¾mm) knitting needles
Five buttons

Gauge

32 sts and 36 rows to 4in (10cm) with garter st slightly stretched.

To make

Using No. 0 (2¼mm) needles cast on 115 sts.

1st ribbing row K1, (P1, K1) to end.
2nd ribbing row P1, (K1, P1) to end.
Rep these 2 rows for 1¼in (3cm); end with a 2nd ribbing row. Change to No. 2 (2¾mm) needles. Cont in garter st (every row K) until work measures 32[34:36: 38]in (83[87:92:97]cm) when slightly stretched. Change to No. 0 (2¼mm) needles and rep 2 ribbing rows for 1¼in (3cm). Bind off in ribbing. Fold ribbing at each end in half and slip stitch in place to form hems. Catch hems tog at top and lower edges and at three evenly spaced positions between. Sew on buttons where hems are joined.

Straps

Make 2 twisted cords each 20in (50cm) long. Sew to front and back.

Sizes

To fit 32[34:36:38]in (83[87:92]cm) bust.

Length, 11½[11½:12]in (29[29:30]cm).

Note: Directions for larger sizes are in brackets []; if there is only one set of figures it applies to all sizes.

Materials

5[5:6]oz (125[125:150]g) of a medium weight mohair
1 pair each Nos. 6 and 8 (4½ and 5½mm) needles

Gauge

18 sts to 5in (12cm) in reverse stockinette st on No. 8 (5½mm) needles.

Back and front (alike)

Using No. 6 (4½mm) needles cast on 56[60:64] sts. Work 10 rows K1, P1 ribbing. Change to No. 8 (5½mm) needles and cont in reverse stockinette st until work measures 11[11:11½]in (28[28:29]cm); end with a P row.

Eyelet hole row K1, *yo, K2 tog, rep from * to last st, K1.
P 1 row and K 1 row.

Next row K to mark hemline for cuff. Beg with a K row, work 9 rows stockinette st. K 3 rows. Bind off.

To finish

Join side seams. Turn under last 3 rows and slip stitch to P side of cuff. Using two 4¾yd (4.25m) pieces of yarn tog, make a twisted cord. Thread cord through eyelet holes to tie at center front. Turn back cuff.

Sizes

To fit 32[34:36:38]in (83[87:92:97]cm) bust. Length, 14½in (36cm).

Note: Directions for larger sizes are in brackets []; if there is only one set of figures it applies to all sizes.

Materials

6[7:8:9]oz (150[175:200:225]g) of a fingering yarn with Lurex®
1 pair each Nos. 1 and 2 (2¾ and 3mm) knitting needles
Five buttons

Gauge

32 sts and 36 rows to 4in (10cm) with garter st slightly stretched.

To make

Using No. 1 (2¾mm) needles cast on 115 sts.

1st ribbing row K1, (P1, K1) to end.
2nd ribbing row P1, (K1, P1) to end.
Rep these 2 rows for 1¼in (3cm); end with a 2nd ribbing row. Change to No. 2 (3mm) needles. Cont in garter st (every row K) until work measures 32[34:36: 38]in (83[92:97]cm) when slightly stretched. Change to No. 1 (2¾mm) needles and rep 2 ribbing rows for 1¼in (3cm). Bind off in ribbing.

To finish

Fold ribbing at each end in half and slip stitch in place to form hems. Catch hems tog at top and lower edges and at three evenly spaced positions between. Sew on buttons where hems are joined.

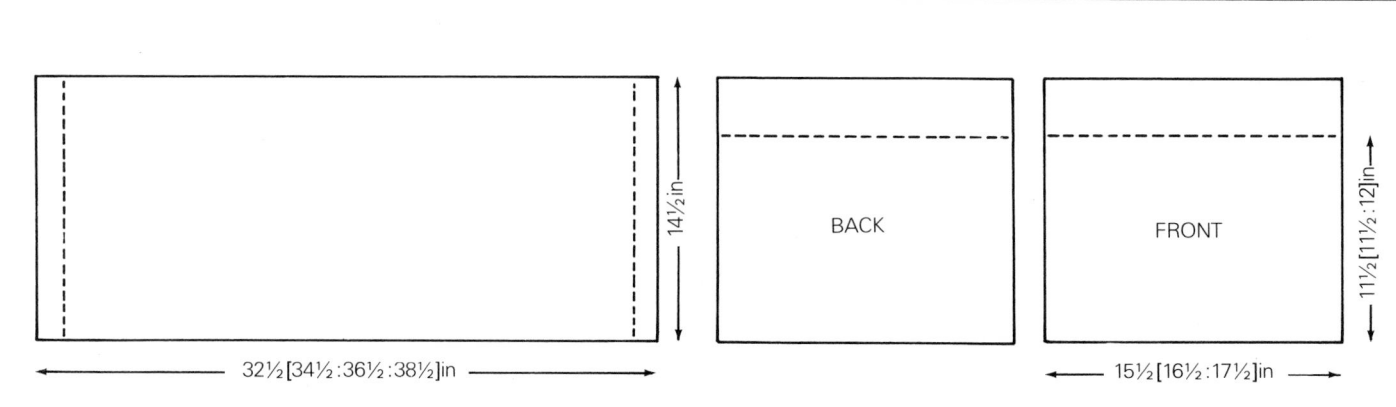

32½[34½:36½:38½]in   14½in

BACK   FRONT   11½[11½:12]in   15½[16½:17½]in

EXTRA SPECIAL SEWING

Sunshine

Pretty and cool, this sundress can be made in two versions. One is trimmed with a panel of drawn thread work; the other features contrasting bands of appliquéd lace.

Stuart Macleod

Cutting layout: 60in-wide fabric

fold

BACK YOKE		
FRONT AND BACK		FRONT AND BACK
FRONT YOKE cut 1		
BIAS STRIPS		RUFFLE

Front yoke: cut 2 on dotted lines for appliquéd version

selvages

36 in-wide fabric

| BIAS STRIPS | RUFFLE | FRONT YOKE | FRONT AND BACK | FRONT AND BACK |
| | FRONT AND BACK | FRONT AND BACK | RUFFLE | BACK YOKE |

single thickness

Measurement diagram

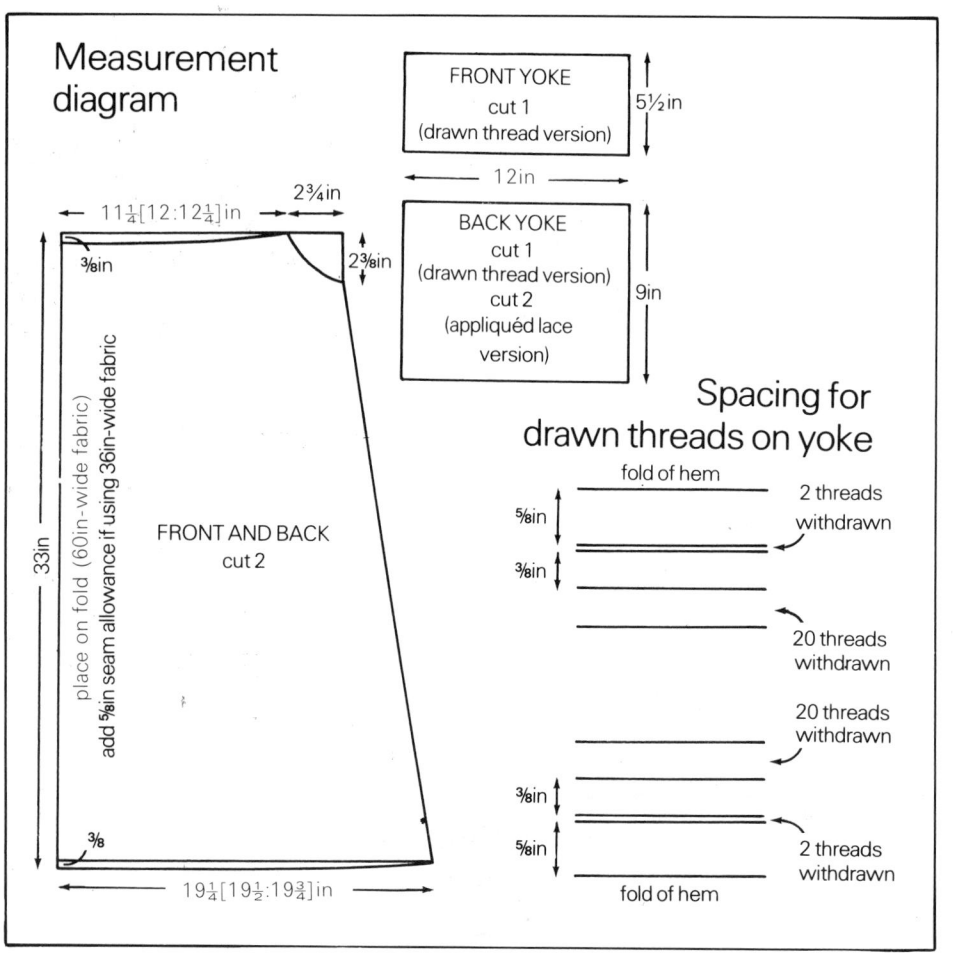

FRONT YOKE
cut 1
(drawn thread version)

5½in

12in

BACK YOKE
cut 1
(drawn thread version)
cut 2
(appliquéd lace version)

2¾in

2⅜in

9in

11¼[12:12¼]in

2¾in

⅜in

33in

place on fold (60in-wide fabric)
add ⅝in seam allowance if using 36in-wide fabric

FRONT AND BACK
cut 2

⅜

19¼[19½:19¾]in

Spacing for drawn threads on yoke

fold of hem

⅝in — 2 threads withdrawn

⅜in

— 20 threads withdrawn

20 threads withdrawn

⅜in

⅜in — 2 threads withdrawn

⅝in — 2 threads withdrawn

fold of hem

Measurements
To fit sizes 10 to 14. Finished length, from yoke to hem, 45in (1.14m).

Note The dress length includes an 8in (20cm)-deep ruffle. If you want to adjust the length, make your calculations before buying fabric.

Note Measurements are given for size 10 (size 8 in ready-made clothes). Figures in brackets [] are for larger sizes. When only one figure is given, this applies to all sizes. Seam allowances of ⅝in (1.5cm) have been included, unless otherwise stated.

Suggested fabrics
Cotton, gingham, seersucker, lightweight linen. For the drawn thread work version, choose an evenweave fabric.

Materials
2¼yd (2m) of 60in (150cm)-wide fabric or 4yd (3.8m) of 36in (90cm)-wide fabric
Matching thread
Flexible curve
Yardstick
Tailor's chalk
For drawn thread version:
    Matching embroidery floss
    Tapestry needle
For appliquéd version:
    3yd (2.7m) of 4in (10cm)-wide cotton lace

Drawn thread work version

1 Using tailor's chalk, yardstick and flexible curve, cut out back and front sections, following the measurement diagram and appropriate cutting layout. If you are using 36in (90cm)-wide fabric, add a ⅝in (1.5cm) seam allowance to center front and center back.
Cut two strips, each 9×55in (23×140cm), for the ruffles.
Cut out front and back yokes.
Cut out 1⅝in (4cm)-wide bias strips to a total length of 2¼yd (2m).

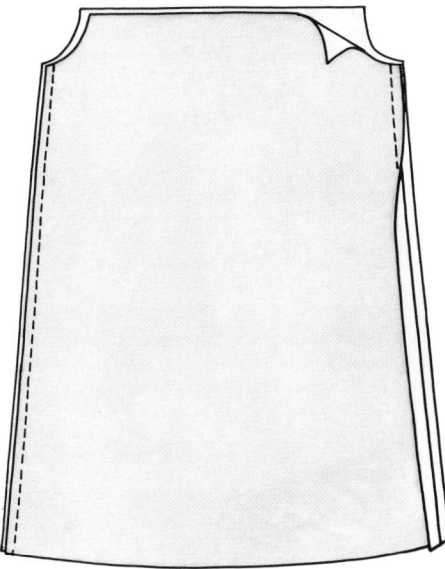

2 With right sides together and raw edges even, stitch center front and back seams (for 36in [90cm] fabric only). Stitch side seams. Press seams open and finish raw edges.

3 Embroider front yoke (see Technique tip), first overcasting edges to prevent raveling.

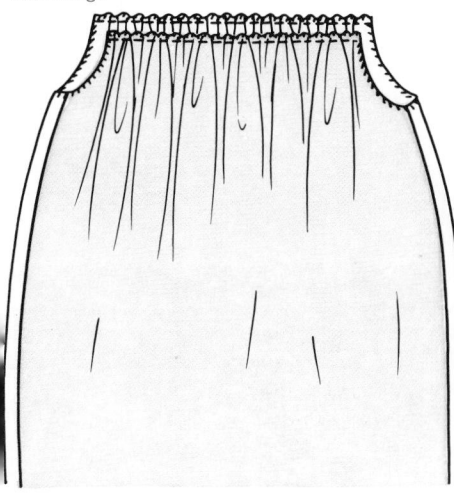

4 Overcast top and underarm edges of dress to prevent raveling. Sew two lines of running stitches in seam allowances at top of back and front dress sections. Draw up gathers to fit lower edges of yoke sections.

Technique tip

Drawn thread work

This is a method of creating a lacy fabric from a plain one by removing threads in one direction and grouping the remaining threads with special stitches. In the samples shown here, we have withdrawn the horizontal (weft) threads and stitched the vertical (warp) threads. When selecting fabric for drawn thread work, be sure to get evenweave fabric—one containing the same number of warp and weft threads per inch (centimeter) in a plain, fairly loose weave, so they can be counted and withdrawn easily. The fabric used here has about 50 threads per inch (20 per cm).
The embroidery floss used should be the same color as the fabric. Two strands have been used for the hem stitch and four for the fagot openwork. The needle should be a tapestry or yarn needle; its rounded point separates the threads.

To embroider the yoke

Following the diagram shown opposite, measure up ¾in (2cm) from the lower edge of the front yoke section, then withdraw 2 weft threads. On the lower edge, turn up ¼in (6mm) and then another ⅝in (1.5cm) and baste. Top of hem should lie within one thread of the drawn threads. Work hemstitching as described below. Repeat for the upper edge of the yoke.
Measure up ⅜in (1cm) from the hemstitching at the lower edge. Withdraw 20 threads. Work hemstitching along upper and lower edges of withdrawn section, turning the fabric so that the stitches at the top run in the opposite way from the stitches at the bottom. Using four threads of stranded embroidery floss, work fagot openwork as described here.
Measure down ⅜in (1cm) from the hemstitching along the upper edge, withdraw 20 threads and repeat the hemstitching and fagot openwork.

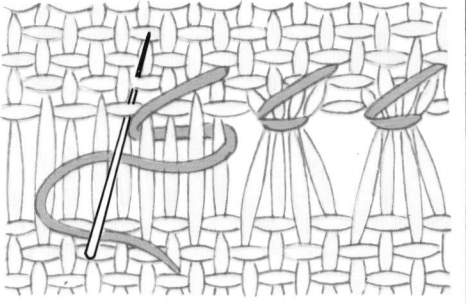

Hemstitch

This is the best known of the traditional drawn thread stitches. It can be used by itself to form a hem, or worked along both sides of bands of openwork to strengthen the fabric.
The hem must be turned up and basted to within one thread of the withdrawn band before the hemstitching is started. Working from left to right, on either side of the fabric, take the needle from right to left around four of the warp threads. Pull the needle through, re-insert it at the same point as before and pick up two threads of the hem. Start and finish the stitching within fold of the hem.

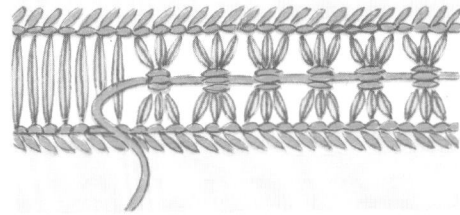

Fagot openwork

Hemstitch has the effect of dividing the weft threads into groups of four. Fagot openwork draws the threads together in groups of three.
Working from right to left, make three back stitches around every three threads, slipping the needle under the first two stitches as you make the third stitch to anchor the thread.

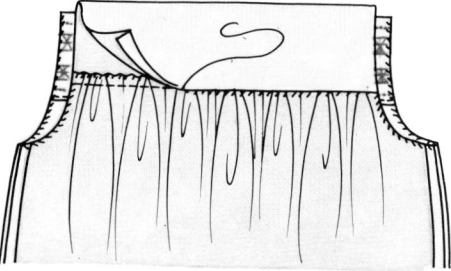

7 Slip stitch inside of yoke to inside of dress as shown, over the seamline. Press, avoiding gathers.

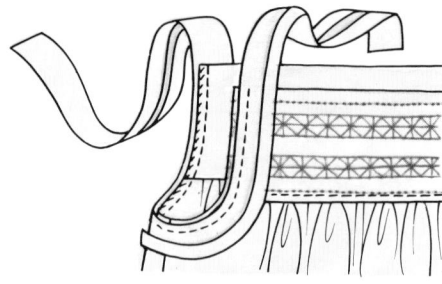

8 Join bias strips to make two 1⅛yd (1m) pieces. Mark center of strips. Press under ¼in (6mm) along each side of strip. With center of strip matching underarm seam, right sides together and raw edges matching, pin, baste and stitch strip to armhole, ¼in (6mm) from edges.

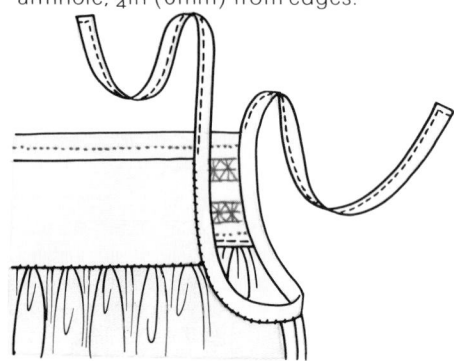

9 Fold strip to inside and slip stitch folded edge to inside of dress. Above the yoke section, press the bias strip so that it is folded in half, and topstitch folded edges together to form straps. Tuck in ends and slip stitch.

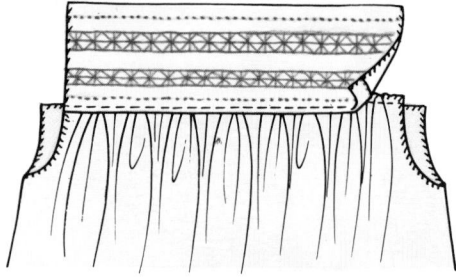

5 Pin front yoke over dress front section, wrong side of yoke to right side of dress, distributing gathers evenly. Baste and topstitch in place close to lower edge of yoke.

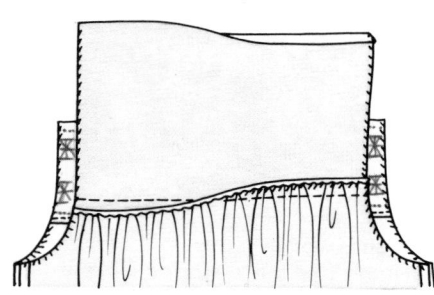

6 Place back yoke on dress back section, right sides together and raw edges matching. Pin in place, distributing gathers evenly. Baste and stitch in place; press seam up. Turn under and press along free edge of yoke. Fold yoke in half and press.

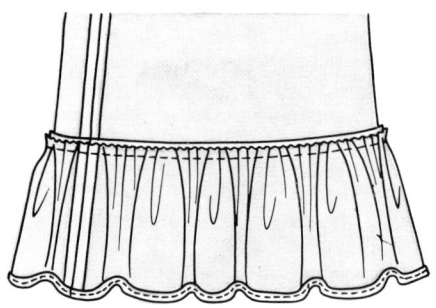

10 Stitch ruffle sections together along short edges to form a circle. Stitch a ⅜in (1cm)-deep double hem along one long edge. Apply ruffle to lower edge of dress.

Appliquéd lace version

1 Cut out as for drawn thread version, cutting the front yoke the same size as the back yoke, as shown in measurement diagram and cutting layout.
2 Make the dress as described in steps 2 and 4. Apply both front and back yokes as described for back yoke in steps 6 and 7 for drawn thread version.

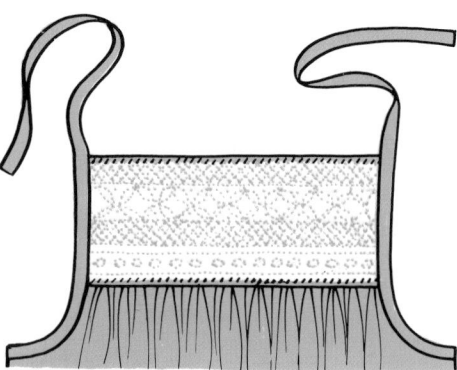

3 Cut a strip of lace to yoke width and slip stitch it to front yoke along upper and lower edges.
4 Apply armhole binding and finish straps as described in steps 8 and 9.
5 Apply ruffle as shown in step 10.

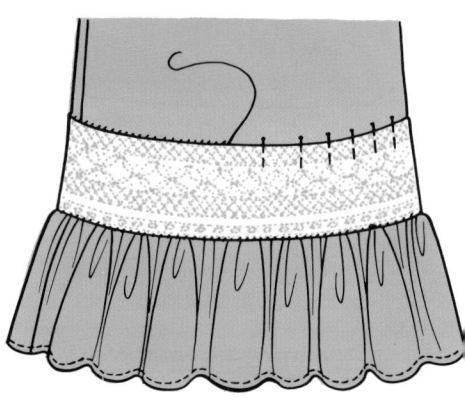

6 Pin remaining piece of lace around dress, just above ruffle, starting at one side seam. Make tiny darts in upper edge of lace to fit curve of skirt. Slip stitch in place along both edges, turning under and slip stitching raw edges at ends.

Stuart Macleod

Take a piece of fabric . . .

Elasticize it, edge it with braid, or simply tie it around you, and you will have a flexible addition to your wardrobe.

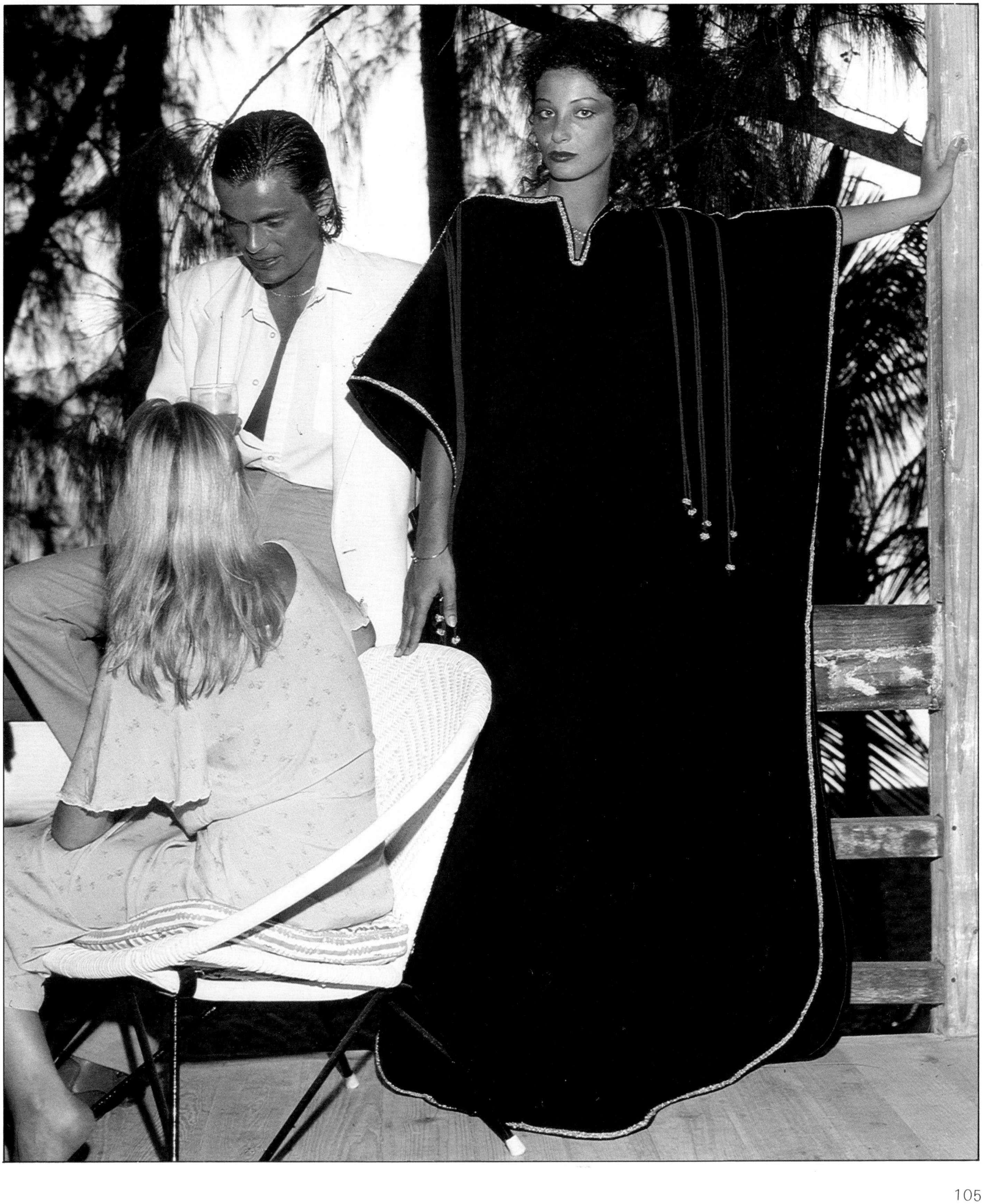

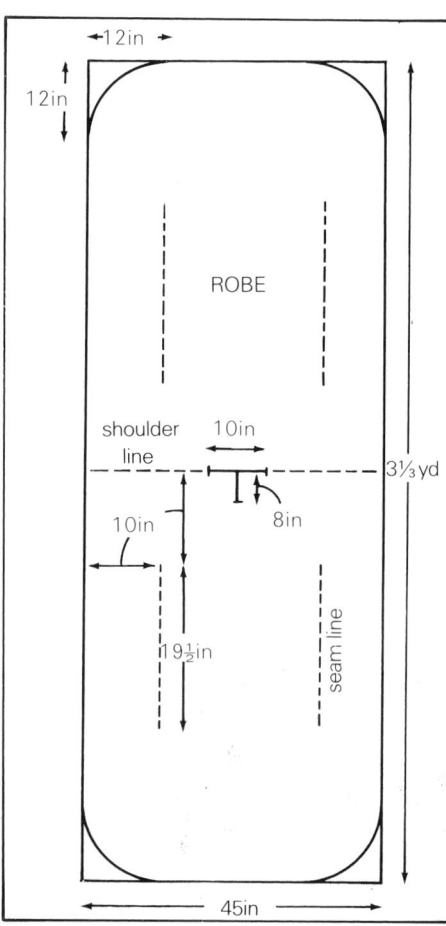

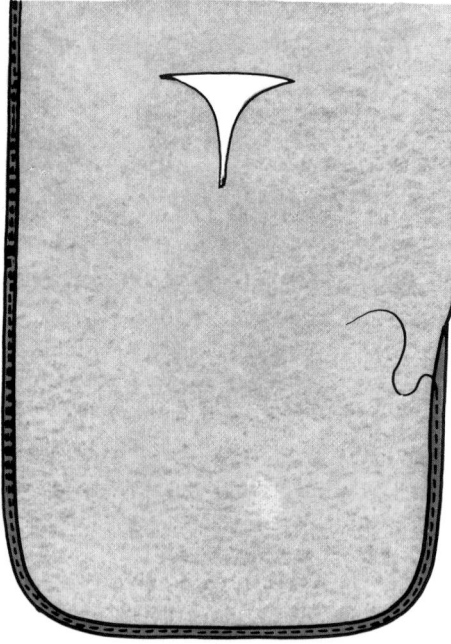

to finish the triangles left by the longer pieces of binding. Turn in binding and slip stitch in place, turning in raw edges. This will square off the opening at these points.

6 Baste and topstitch the braid in place around the outer edge of the robe and around the neck edge.

7 For shoulder decorations, cut 12 pieces of cord $1\frac{2}{3}$yd (1.5m) long. Knot a bead at each end of the cords. Pin the cords along the shoulder line in pairs, $2\frac{3}{4}$in (7cm) apart, positioning three pairs on each shoulder.

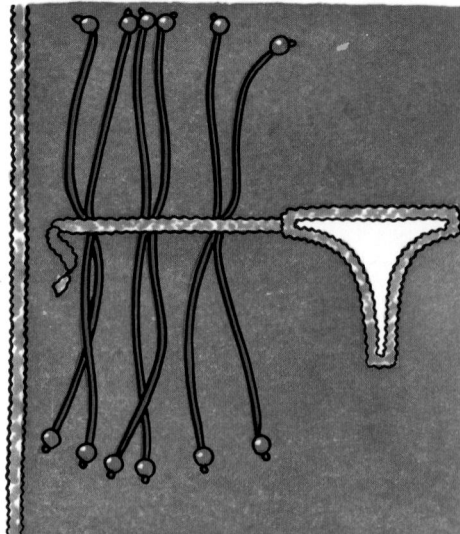

2 Turn under a $\frac{3}{8}$in (1cm)-wide double hem all around the outer edge of the fabric. Pin, baste and stitch in place.

3 To finish the neck edge of the garment, cut a piece of bias binding $10\frac{5}{8}$in (27cm) long for back neck edge, two pieces $11\frac{3}{8}$in (29cm) long for front neck edges and opening and three pieces 2in (5cm) long to finish points of opening.

8 Pin the braid in place along the shoulder line from the neck edge to the outer edge. Baste and stitch in place.

Caftan

This simple garment may be worn as a robe, as a cover-up on the beach or as a comfortable evening outfit as shown here. The decorative shoulder trims are optional.

Size
Finished length, 59in (150cm).

Suggested fabrics
Cottons, particularly heavy cottons or furnishing fabrics, terrycloth.
Strong one-way designs are not suitable, as there are no shoulder seams, the design would run upside-down on the back of the robe.

Materials
- $3\frac{3}{8}$yd (3m) of 45in (115cm)-wide fabric
- $10\frac{3}{8}$yd (9.5m) braid for edging, plus $1\frac{1}{8}$yd (1m) extra for optional shoulder trim
- $19\frac{5}{8}$yd (18m) thin cord (optional)
- Thread to match braid and fabric
- 24 beads (optional); bias binding

1 Curve the corners of the fabric as shown in the measurement diagram. Cut a T-shaped slit to form the neck and front opening. Trim the fabric away slightly around the corners at the centerfront neck edge.

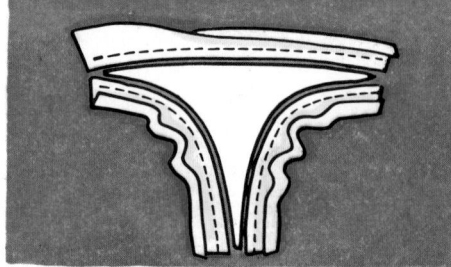

4 Stitch each of the long pieces in place to the right side of the opening, positioning the binding with the fold line $\frac{1}{4}$in (6mm) from the raw edge of the fabric. Stitch $\frac{1}{4}$in (6mm) past the end of the opening at each point. Turn the binding inside, so that it does not show on the right side. Clip diagonally from the point of the fabric to the end of the stitching. Slip stitch the free folded edge of binding in place, turning under all raw edges.

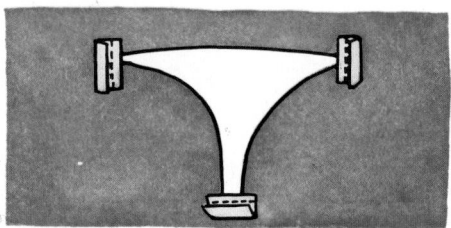

5 Position the three short pieces of binding across the ends of the opening

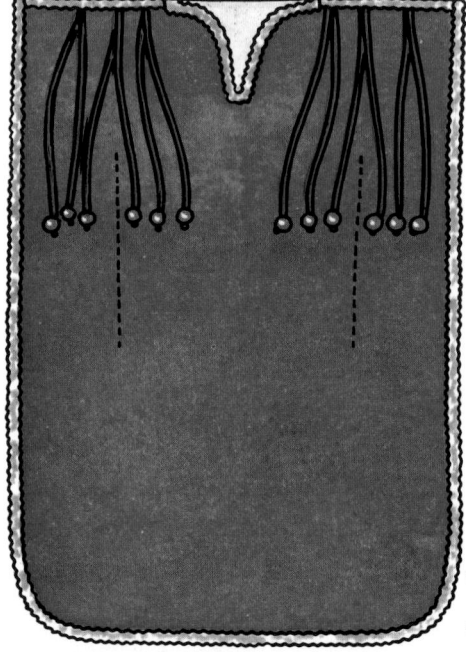

9 Pin, baste and stitch the side seams as indicated on measurement diagram, making seams $19\frac{1}{2}$in (50cm) long, starting 10in (25cm) from shoulder edge. Stitch with wrong sides of fabric together.

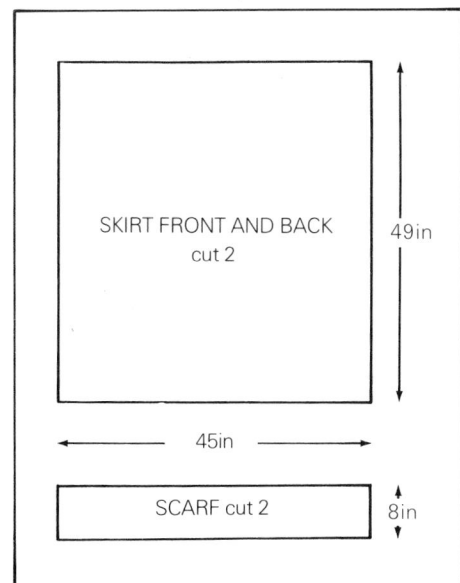

SKIRT FRONT AND BACK cut 2	49in
45in	
SCARF cut 2	8in

Skirt and scarf

This simple wrap can be worn as a long skirt with the scarf as a bikini top, or as a strapless sundress with the scarf tied around the waist.

Size
The skirt has an elasticized waist, to fit sizes 10–16, with a finished length of about 44in (112cm). The scarf is 88in (224cm) long and $6\frac{1}{4}$in (16cm) wide.

Suggested fabrics
Poplin, cheesecloth, crepe (but not for the scarf, as it is cut across the width of the fabric), gingham, etc.

Materials
$2\frac{3}{4}$yd (2.5m) of 45in (115cm)-wide patterned fabric
$\frac{1}{2}$yd (.4m) of 45in (115cm)-wide plain fabric
$1\frac{1}{8}$yd (1m) elastic, matching thread

1 Prepare the fabric and cut in half across the width, following the crosswise grain of the fabric.

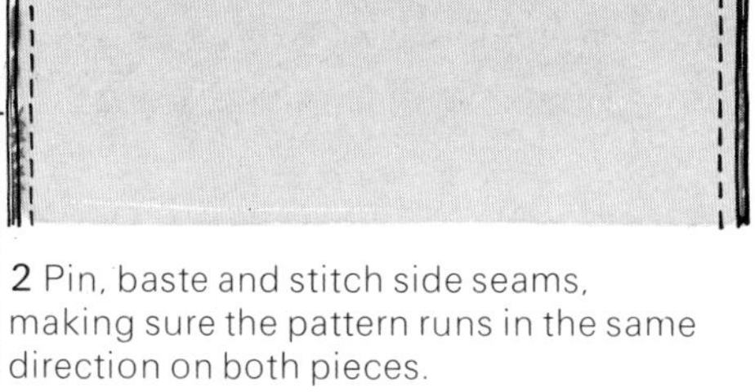

2 Pin, baste and stitch side seams, making sure the pattern runs in the same direction on both pieces.

Jean-Claude Volpelière

Terry Evans

3 Turn under and baste a 1⅝in (4cm)-wide double hem all around the top of the skirt. To form a casing, stitch around the skirt twice, positioning lines of stitching 1in (2.5cm) and 1⅜in (3.5cm) from top fold of skirt. Leave a short opening at one side of the skirt in the bottom row of stitching for threading the elastic through.

4 Turn up, baste and stitch a ⅜in (1cm) hem all around lower edge of skirt. Turn up a 1⅝in (4cm) hem and sew in place.

5 Thread elastic through the casing at the top of the skirt. Try on and trim off excess elastic. Sew ends together firmly. Slip stitch openings to close.

6 Cut the plain fabric for the scarf in half across the width of the fabric to form two strips as shown in the diagram.

7 Join two short ends (selvages) to make a narrow flat seam. Press open. Turn under and stitch a ⅜in (1cm)-wide double hem all around scarf. Press.

Sarong

This outfit is just a rectangle—use it as a beach towel, fasten it around your waist or tie it in a halter around your neck.

Size
72×45in (180×115cm).

Materials
Panel of printed fabric, 72×45in (180×115cm), or 2yd (1.8m) plain or patterned 45in (115cm)-wide fabric

1 Trim raw edges if necessary. Unless the fabric is loosely woven, there is no need to hem the raw edges.

Homemaker

Soft gathers and ruffles make these Austrian shades a pretty way to add a touch of femininity to a bedroom.

Austrian shades

Spike Powell

Materials

Lightweight printed cotton fabric
Coordinating printed cotton fabric
for ruffle
Shirring tape for Austrian shades
Plain double shirring tape
A wooden batten (1×2in [2.5×5cm])
the same length as the width of
the finished shade; nylon cord
Curtain hooks and weights
$\frac{7}{8}$in (2.2cm) fence staples and
hammer
Screw eyes and cleat
Fabric glue; matching thread

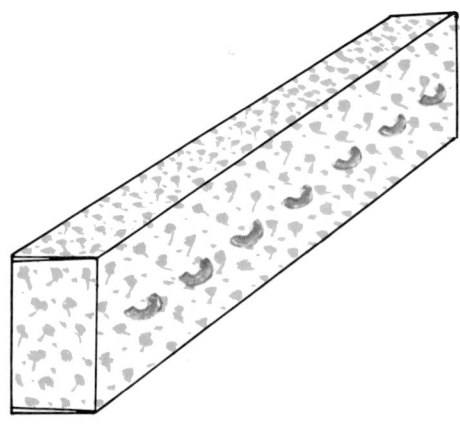

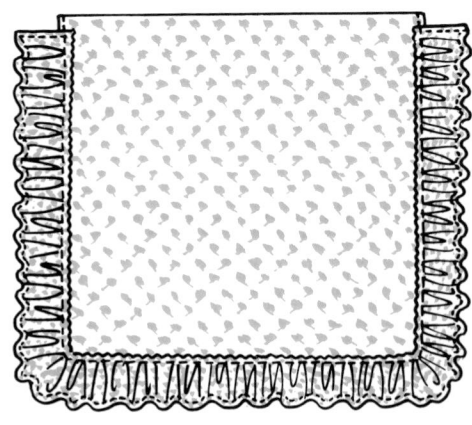

Calculating the amount of materials

1 Measure the area to be covered, using a yardstick or steel tapemeasure for accuracy. For a shade hung inside the frame, measure the inside width; for one outside the frame, add 2in (5cm) to the width to allow for complete window coverage.
2 Decide on the number of sections for the shade. These should measure— when hanging—between 8 and 10in (20 and 25cm) in width. To the window width measurement add 2-3in (5-7.5cm) for **each section** for fullness. Add another $\frac{3}{4}$in (2cm) for each side hem to get the total width of fabric needed. (If fabric must be joined to make up the width, seams should be placed on section lines, i.e. where tape is placed.)
3 For the length of fabric needed, multiply the length to be covered by $1\frac{1}{2}$ or 2. Add $1\frac{1}{4}$in (3cm) for upper and lower hems (combined). Buy enough fabric to cover the wooden batten also.
4 Buy enough contrasting fabric for a strip measuring twice the distance around the side and lower edges and 4in (10cm) in depth.
5 You will need enough plain shirring tape to go across the width of the shade. For the amount of Austrian shade tape, count the number of sections, add 1, multiply this by the fabric length and add about $\frac{1}{2}$yd (.5m). Multiply the amount of Austrian shade tape by $2\frac{1}{2}$ to get the amount of nylon cord needed.

Making the shade

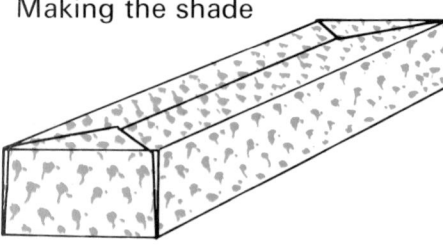

1 Cut the wooden batten to the correct size. Cut a piece of the shade fabric to cover it. Fold the fabric around the batten as if wrapping a package, with the raw edges meeting on one long side; glue the edges in place.

2 Hammer staples to the covered batten, centering them on the long side opposite the fabric edges. Space the staples at 1in (2.5cm) intervals.
3 Cut out the shade fabric, making sure that it is cut exactly on the straight grain. If necessary, join the lengths of fabric with French seams to get the correct width.
4 Turn in a $\frac{3}{8}$in (1cm) double hem along both side edges of shade. Pin, baste and stitch in place.

5 Turn up a $\frac{3}{8}$in (1cm) double hem along bottom edge of shade. Pin, baste and stitch in place.
6 Cut the coordinating ruffle fabric into 4in (10cm) strips and join them to make one long strip twice the distance around the side and bottom edges. Finish the seams and press.

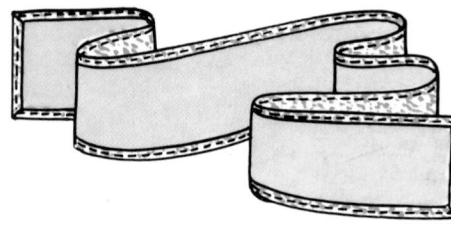

7 Turn under a $\frac{3}{8}$in (1cm)-wide double hem along all four edges of ruffle. Pin, baste and stitch in place.
8 Run a line of gathering stitches along one long edge of ruffle.

9 Leaving a $\frac{3}{8}$in (1cm) margin at top edge of shade, pin wrong side of ruffle to right side of shade down each side and along bottom edge, pulling up the gathers evenly. Pin, baste and stitch, close to finished edge of ruffle.
10 Turn $\frac{3}{8}$in (1cm) to wrong side on top edge of shade piece; pin and baste.

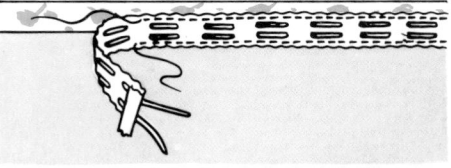

11 Cut a piece of shirring tape the width of the shade, plus $\frac{3}{4}$in (2cm). Place the tape across top edge of shade, covering the raw edge of fabric. Turn under $\frac{3}{8}$in (1cm) at each end of tape; in place, close to both long edges, leaving cord ends free on each side.
12 On the right side of the shade, mark the positions of the Austrian shade tape with rows of pins. Leave a $1\frac{1}{2}$in (4cm) margin (not including ruffle) at each side edge, and divide the remaining width by the number of sections.
13 Cut pieces of tape about 2in (5cm) longer than the shade.

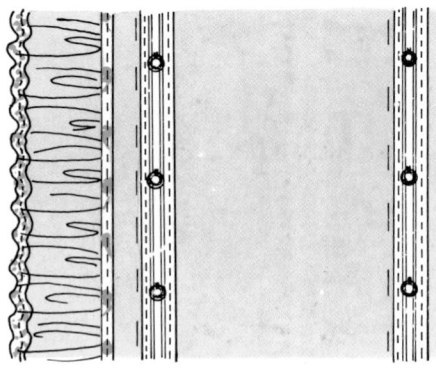

14 Pin the tape in place, with the first ring positioned about $2\frac{1}{2}$in (6cm) from the bottom. Trim ends, leaving $\frac{3}{8}$ (1cm) for turning under. Baste and stitch the tape in place. Do not stitch top edge. Repeat with the remaining tape, aligning rings horizontally.

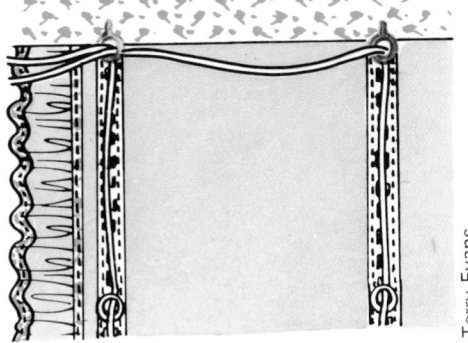

15 Pull up the cords on the plain shirring tape, pulling from both ends, until the shade is the width of the batten. Knot the ends of the cord, but do not cut off excess. Adjust the gathers evenly across the shade.

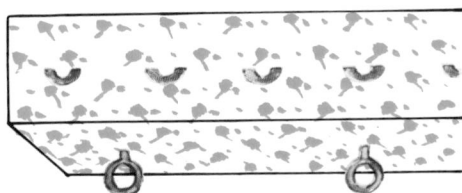

16 Fix a screw eye into the base of the batten, correspondingly to the position of each vertical tape.
17 Pull up the vertical tapes evenly until the shade is the right length. Knot cord ends, but do not cut off excess.

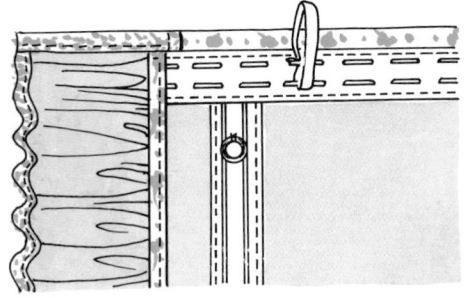

18 Insert curtain hooks into the plain shirring tape, corresponding to the position of the staples. Slot the hooks into the staples to hold up the shade.
19 Tie one end of the nylon cord to the left-hand bottom ring. Thread the cord through each ring on the left-hand side tape, then through the row of screw eyes at the top. Let this cord hang loose down the opposite side of the blind, and cut it off at the base.

20 Repeat step 19 for each vertical tape.
21 Make small bags in matching fabric to hold curtain weights. Assess the number of weights needed. Sew a bag to the base of each vertical tape.
22 Fix the batten to the window frame.
23 Fix the cleat at the side of the window Tie the lengths of cord together and wind them round the cleat.

Homemaker

Home, sweet home

Children will love to play in this make-believe house that fits neatly over a kitchen table. There are roses growing up the back wall and a roll-up front door for easy entry.

Size Fits a 29in (74cm)-high table, 54 × 30in (137×76cm). Seams of $\frac{3}{4}$in (2cm) have been allowed on walls and roof; $\frac{3}{8}$in (1cm) on all other seams.

Materials

5yd (4.5m) of 36in (90cm)-wide white sailcloth or other firm fabric

$2\frac{7}{8}$yd (2.6m) of 36in (90cm)-wide red fabric

$1\frac{1}{8}$yd (1m) of 36in (90cm)-wide blue fabric

$\frac{3}{4}$yd (.7m) of 36in (90cm)-wide brick-red fabric

Di Lewis

112

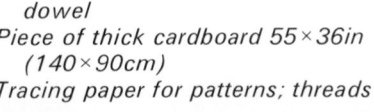

$4\frac{3}{8}$yd (4m) of $1\frac{1}{2}$in (4cm)-wide blue
  woven tape
$6\frac{1}{2}$yd (6m) of $\frac{1}{2}$in (1.2cm)-wide bias
  binding in assorted greens
Scraps of fabrics in yellow, mauve,
  orange, pink, crimson and greens
Yellow embroidery thread
Two $\frac{5}{8}$in (1.5cm) diameter buttons
12in (30.5cm) of $\frac{3}{8}$in (1cm)-diameter
  dowel
Piece of thick cardboard 55×36in
  (140×90cm)
Tracing paper for patterns; threads

1 For front and back walls, from white fabric cut out two pieces each $55\frac{1}{2} \times 31\frac{1}{2}$in (141×80cm). For side walls cut out two pieces each $31\frac{1}{2}$in (80cm) square.

2 For door frame, from blue fabric cut out two pieces each $26\frac{1}{2} \times 2\frac{3}{4}$in (67×7cm) and one piece $16 \times 2\frac{3}{4}$in (41×7cm). Place the short piece at right angles to the other two; overlapping and mitering the two corners, trimming away excess fabric. Pin, baste and stitch across the miters.
3 Pin the right side of the door frame in the center of wrong side of front wall, matching the bottom edges.

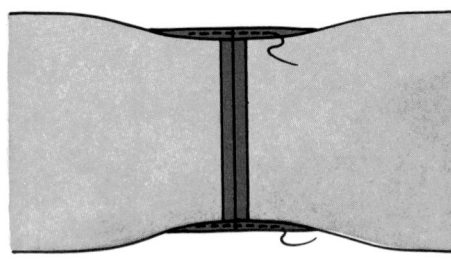

4 For the door, from red fabric cut two pieces 23×12in (58×30.5cm). Pin, baste and stitch door pieces together along one short edge (the bottom). Open the doors out flat. Turn in $\frac{3}{8}$in (1cm) on each side of the base seam for $1\frac{1}{4}$in (3cm). Pin, baste and stitch the edges down for $1\frac{1}{4}$in (3cm) on each side of the seam.
5 Place doors together with right sides facing; pin, baste and stitch side seams to within $\frac{3}{4}$in (2cm) of bottom edge. Turn door right side out. Pin, baste and stitch across bottom edge of door, $\frac{3}{4}$in (2cm) from edge, to form casing.

6 Pin and baste top edges of the door together. Place top edge of door under the top of door frame.
7 Pin, baste and stitch around inner edge of door frame through all thicknesses. Cut away excess fabric. Clip into corners. Bring door frame completely around to the right side of the front wall. Turn under outer edge of door frame. Pin, baste and topstitch door frame to front wall, close to outer edge of door frame.

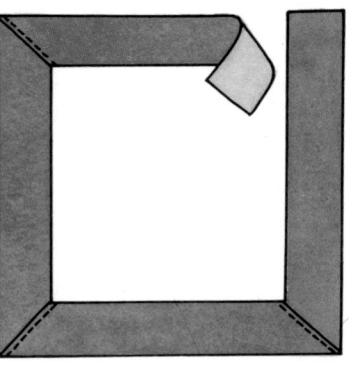

8 For window frames, from blue fabric cut 24 pieces each $12\frac{1}{2} \times 2\frac{3}{4}$in (32×7cm). For each window frame, place four frame pieces together forming a square. Fold under one end of each strip diagonally, and pin, baste and stitch it over the adjacent strip. Trim away excess fabric.

 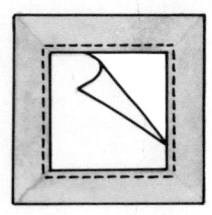

9 Fix two window frames to the front wall on each side of the door. Place right side of one window frame on wrong side of front wall, 5in (13cm) down from top edge and 2in (5cm) from door frame. Pin, baste and stitch around inner edge of window frame. Cut out center of window and clip into corners. Turn window frame through to right side of wall. Turn under outer edge of frame. Pin, baste and topstitch frame to front wall, close to outer edge of frame.
10 Repeat step 9 to stitch the second window frame to front wall in the same position but on the other side of the door.
11 Repeat step 9 to stitch two window frames to the back wall, 5in (13cm) down from top edge and 8in (20cm) in from each side edge.
12 Repeat step 9 to stitch one window frame in the center of each side wall, 5in (13cm) down from top edge.

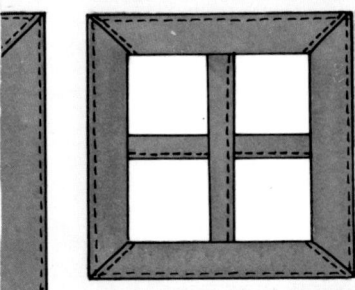

13 For window bars cut blue tape into twelve 9in (23cm)-long pieces. Fold in half lengthwise; pin, baste and stitch

Terry Evans

down each length, close to edges. Place two pieces in a cross to form window bars with short edges behind window frame. Turn under short edges; pin, baste and stitch in place. Catch-stitch bars together in the center. Repeat at each window.

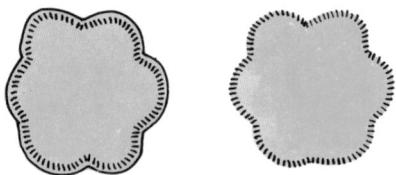

14 Trace patterns for rose and small rose leaf. Cut out ten pink roses and nine dark green leaves. Place the roses together in pairs. Pin, baste and close zig-zag stitch around the edges of each pair. Trim off excess fabric. Pin and baste roses to back wall between two windows. Attach the roses to the wall by the centers, with a few French knots worked in yellow embroidery thread.

15 Fold dark green bias binding in half lengthwise. Pin and baste folded binding between roses for stems. Topstitch in place down center of binding. Pin and baste leaves to each side of stem. Close zig-zag stitch each leaf in place around outer edge.
16 Trace patterns of flowers, centers and leaves. Cut out seven daisies, seven centers and seven tulips in assorted colors and fabrics. Cut out 11 rounded leaves and 14 pointed leaves, all in different green fabrics. Pin and baste flowers and leaves to the walls of the house. Place a tulip and a daisy on each side of the front door and on each side of the roses. Place a tulip between the two daisies on one side wall and a daisy between the two tulips on the other side wall.
17 Add bias binding stems as for roses.

18 Pin and baste one or two leaves at the base of each stem, placing them at

different angles and overlapping them in some cases.
19 Close zig-zag stitch all the flowers, centers and leaves in place. Leave the leaves that overlap the side edges of the walls unsewn.

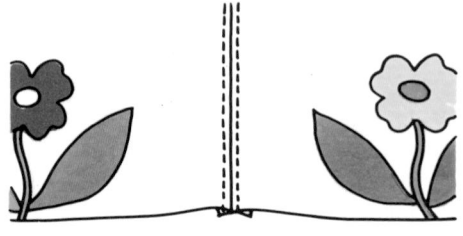

20 Pin, baste and stitch side walls to front wall, with right sides together. Press seams open. Stitch down each side of each seam again through seam allowances.
21 Repeat step 20 to stitch back wall to each side wall.

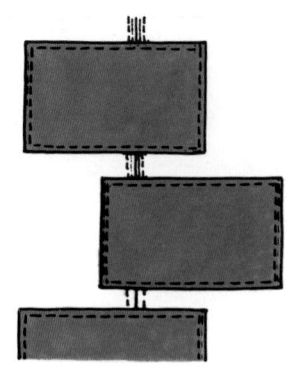

22 For bricks, cut out 20 pieces each 7 × 5½in (18 × 14in) from brick-red fabric. Turn under ⅜in (1cm) around each brick; pin and baste. Pin five bricks in place over one corner seam, about ¾in (2cm) apart spacing them alternately. Baste and topstitch each brick in place.

23 Repeat step 22, stitching five bricks over each corner seam.
24 Pin, baste and close zig-zag stitch any leaves that overlap the corner bricks.

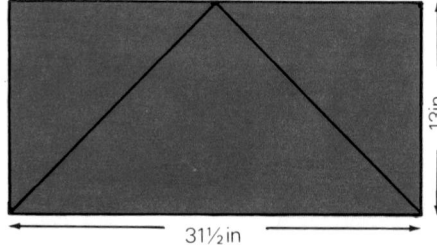

31½in   13in

25 For the roof, from red fabric cut out two pieces, each 55½ × 21in (141 × 54cm), for front and back. Cut out two pieces, each 31½ × 13in (80 × 34cm) for roof ends. On wrong side of one end piece, mark center on one long side. Draw lines joining opposite corners to center point to form diagonal sides. Cut along diagonal lines. Repeat for second roof end.

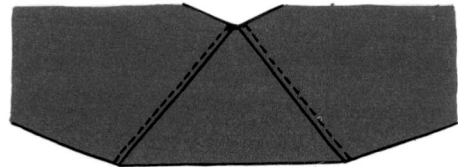

26 Pin, baste and stitch roof end pieces to front and back roof pieces. Pin, baste and stitch center seam of front and back roof.
27 Pin, baste and stitch lower edge of roof to walls, matching corner seams.

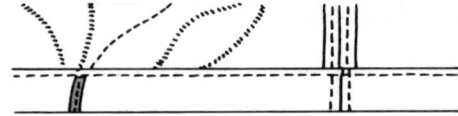

28 Turn up 2in (5cm) at bottom edge; turn under raw edge; pin, baste and hem.

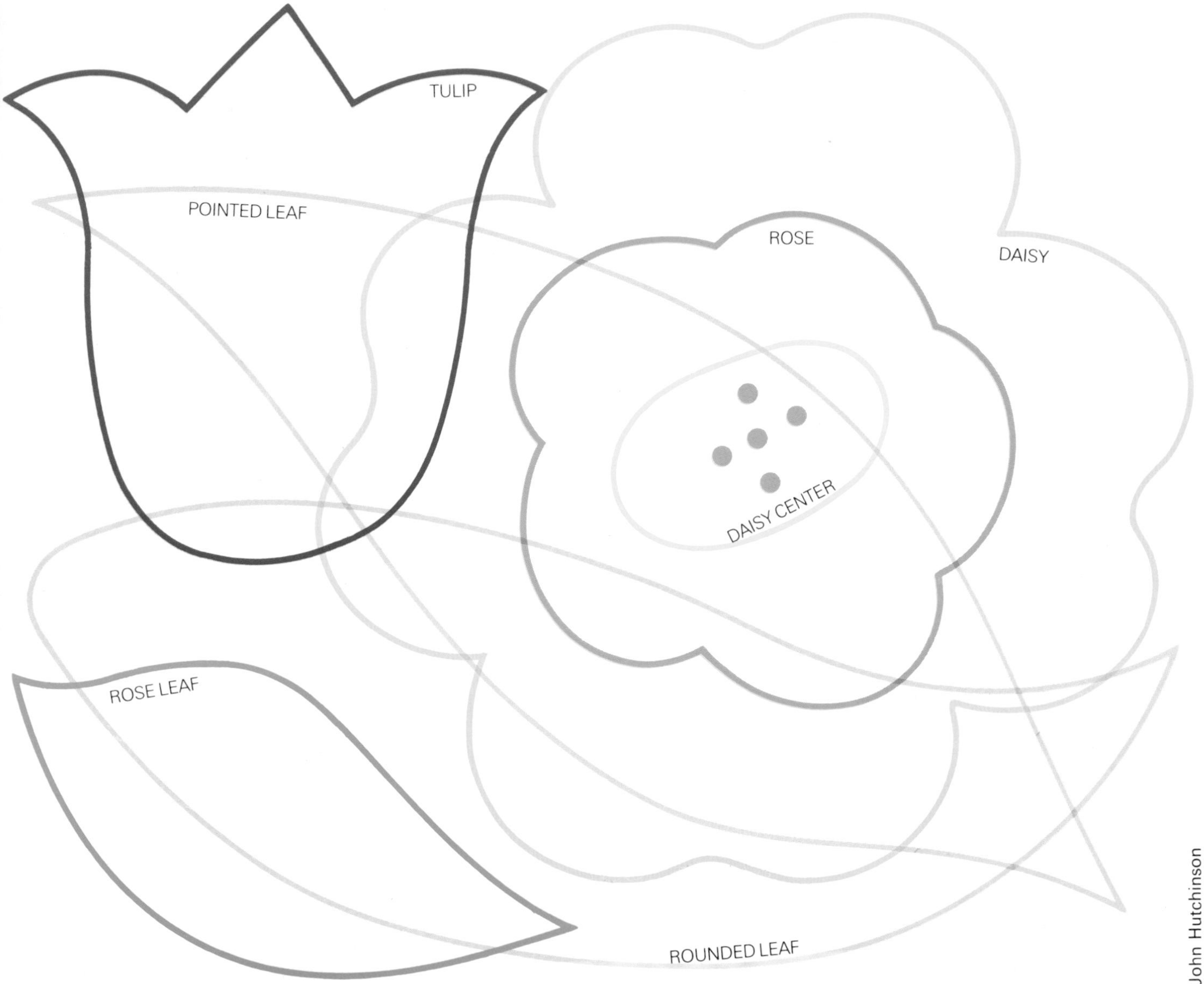

TULIP

POINTED LEAF

ROSE

DAISY

DAISY CENTER

ROSE LEAF

ROUNDED LEAF

John Hutchinson

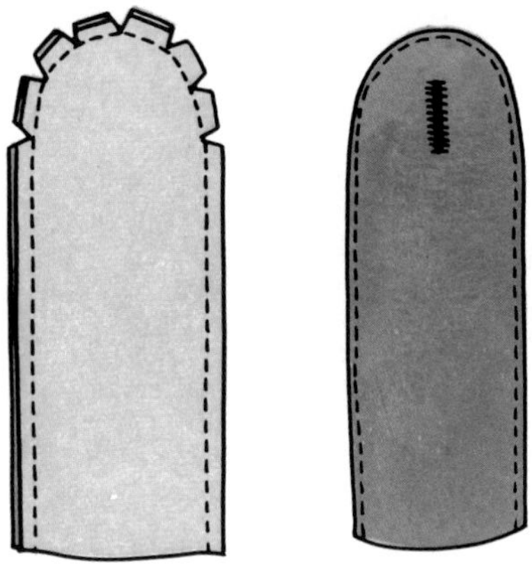

Terry Evans

29 For tabs, cut out four pieces, each 6 × 2¼in (15 × 6cm), from blue fabric. Round off one end of each tab piece. Place tab pieces together in pairs. Pin, baste and stitch all around, leaving straight edges open. Turn tabs right side out. Turn in straight edges; pin and baste. Topstitch around each tab; make buttonhole in the rounded end of tabs.

30 Place each tab behind the top of the door frame, about ⅜in (1cm) from each side edge. Pin, baste and stitch in place.

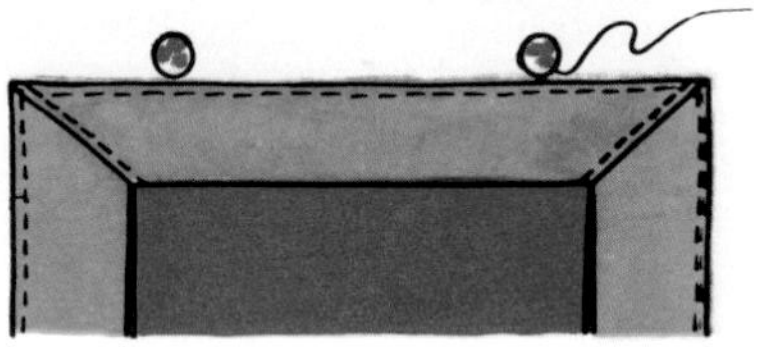

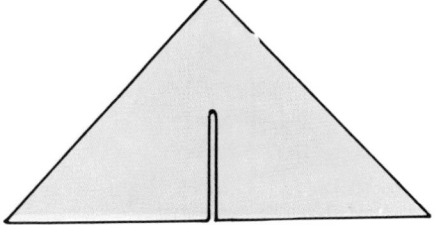

31 Sew buttons to the top front of door frame to correspond with buttonholes on tabs.

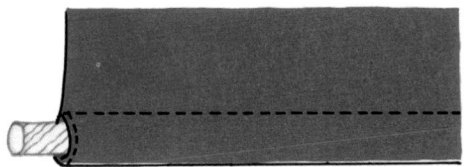

32 Insert dowel into casing at bottom of door.

33 For roof supports, from thick cardboard cut out one piece 54 × 12in (137 × 30cm) for central strut and two pieces 30 × 12in (76 × 30cm) for ends. Mark the center on one side of one end piece. Graduate the opposite corners to center point to form diagonal lines to form a triangle. Repeat for second end piece. Slit up the centers on each end piece for 6in (15cm). Make each slit wide enough to accommodate the thickness of the cardboard. Make a slit in the same way, ¾in (2cm) in from each end of center strut, 6in (15cm) long. Slot the end pieces onto the center strut at each end.

Homemaker

Handsome hankies

Bring your pretty handkerchiefs out and let them see the light of day as a tablecloth or decorative pillow cover.

Tablecloth

Finished size
About 40in (102cm) square.

Materials
Nine 10in (25cm)-square hankies
2½yd (2.2m) 36in- (90cm-) wide cotton
2¼yd (2m) of ¾in- (2cm-) wide double-edged lace
4⅝yd (4.2m) of 1⅛in- (3cm-) wide lace edging
Matching sewing thread

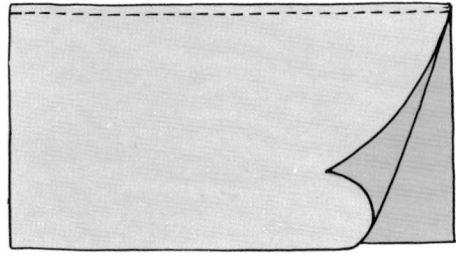

1 Cut the fabric in half widthwise and place the fabric pieces together, wrong sides facing and edges matching. Using a French seam, pin, baste and stitch one long edge together, taking ¾in (2cm) seam.
2 Mark the center point of the fabric, which will be halfway down the seam.
3 Mark the center of first hanky.

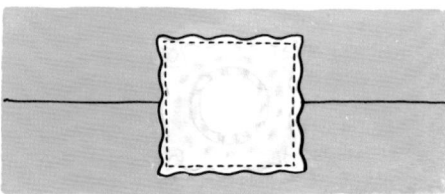

4 Center the first hanky face up on the right side of the fabric. Pin and baste in place ¾in (2cm) from edge.
5 Cut four 2¾in (7cm)-long strips of double-edged lace.
6 Mark the center of each side of the central hanky.

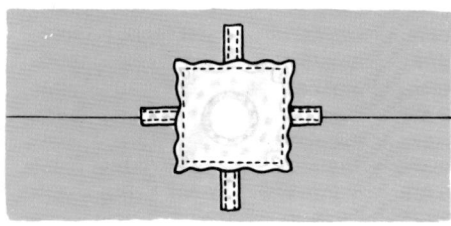

7 Place one 2¾in (7cm)-long lace strip at

each center mark on central hanky, tucking ¼in (5mm) of lace underneath edge of hanky. Pin and baste each strip in place closer to the edge than previous basting. Two of these strips will cover the central French seam.
8 Mark the center of each edge of four more hankies.

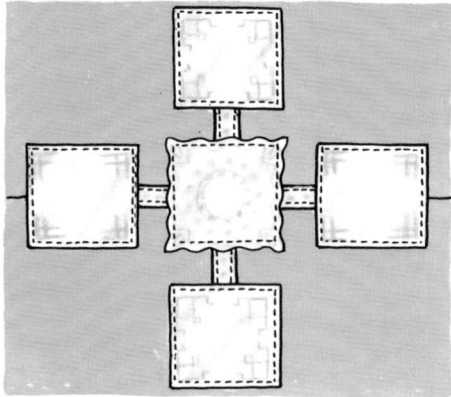

9 Place these four hankies face up on the right side of the fabric, so that they make a cross shape with the central hanky. Place the central mark on one side of each hanky over the projecting lace strips, overlapping lace for ¼in (5mm). Pin and baste hankies and lace strips in place as before.
10 Cut eight more 2¾in (7cm)-long strips of double-edged lace.

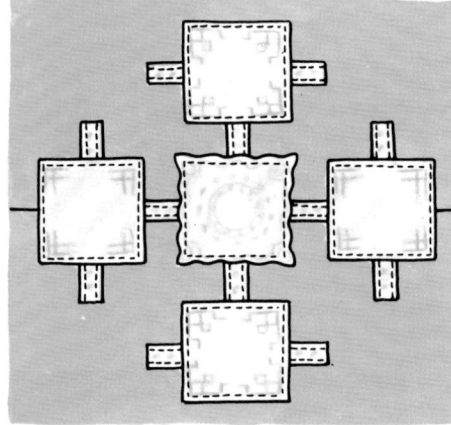

11 Place one 2¾in (7cm)-long lace strip at central mark on each side edge of four outer hankies, tucking ¼in (5mm) under as before. Pin and baste in place.
12 Mark the center of each edge of last four hankies.

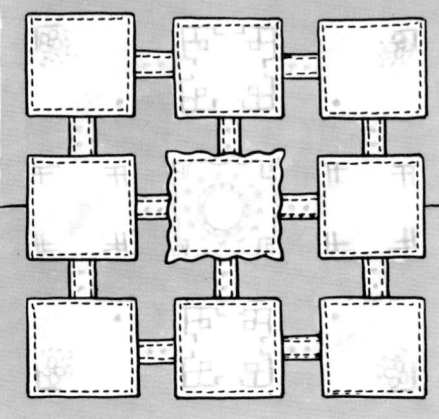

13 Baste the last four hankies in place on the right side of the fabric to complete the square of hankies as shown, tucking ¼in (5mm) of each lace strip under the edges at central marks on two sides and pinning and basting as before.

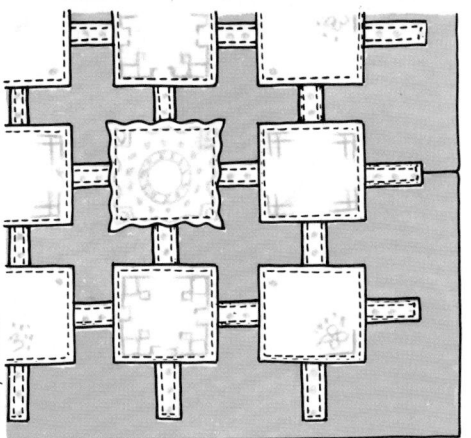

15 Neatly hand sew all hankies and all lace strips in place, so that stitches hardly show on right side. Remove all basting.

16 Trim the base fabric in line with outer edges of outer lace strips.

17 Turn under a double $\frac{3}{8}$in (1cm)-wide hem around outer edge. Pin, baste and stitch.

18 Pin and baste lace edging to wrong side of tablecloth so that outer edge of cloth just overlaps lace. Miter corners and join and finish short edges of lace to fit.

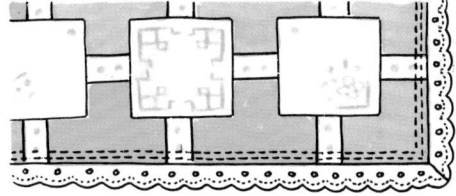

14 Cut twelve $\frac{3}{4}$in (8.5cm)-long strips of double-edged lace. Match each length to marked centers on outside edges of all outer hankies, tucking $\frac{1}{4}$in (5mm) of each strip under center mark on each hanky as before. Pin and baste in place.

19 Topstitch around outer edge of tablecloth, catching in lace edging.

117

Envelope pillow

Finished size
12in (30cm) square.

Materials
   *One 18½in- (47cm-) square white
      hanky with drawn thread motifs
   One 12in (30cm) pillow form
   Matching sewing thread*

1 Fold the handkerchief in half with right sides together, matching motifs.

2 Pin, baste and stitch one side edge, from the fold to opposite long edge, ¾in (2cm) from outer edge.

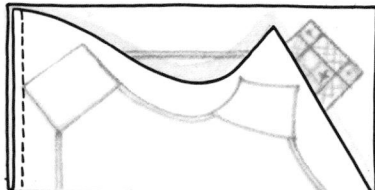

3 With seam at left-hand side, fold top right-hand edge of fabric with motif inward over to the left, so three corners meet. Pin, baste and stitch this newly-formed seam ¾in (2cm) from edges.

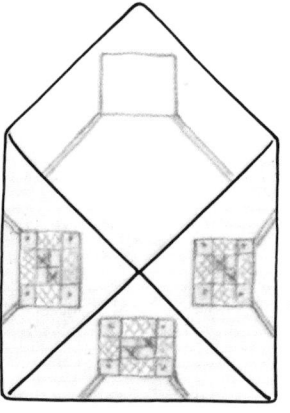

4 Turn pillow cover right side out. Press, so cover forms an envelope shape.

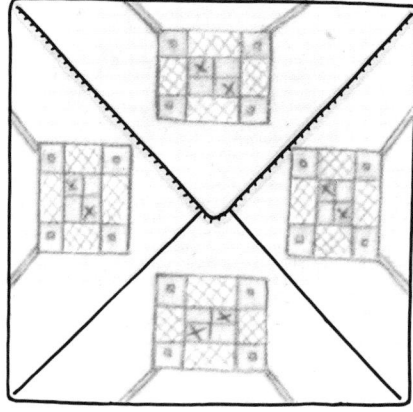

5 Slip pillow form inside cover. Fold over the fourth corner with motif. Turn in ¾in (2cm) on both free edges, pin, baste and slip stitch in place.

Lacy pillow

Finished size
12in (30cm) square.

Materials
   *One 12in- (30cm-) square white
      handkerchief, with wide lace
      border
   One 12in (30cm) pillow form
   ½yd (.4m) of 36in- (90cm-) wide
      beige shiny lining fabric
   Two small fabric flowers
   Matching sewing thread*

1 From lining fabric, cut out two pieces for pillow back and front, each 13½in (34cm) square.

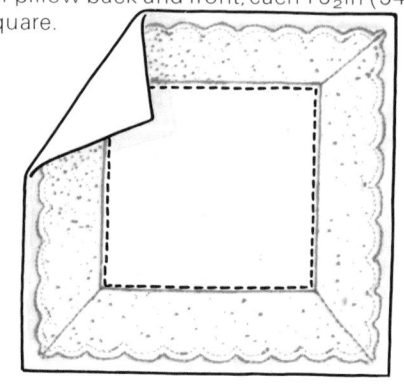

2 Center lace hanky face up on right side of one fabric piece, the pillow front. Pin and baste around the central fabric square on the hanky, leaving the lace edge free. Topstitch in place.

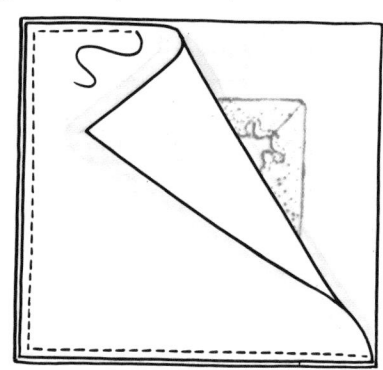

3 Lightly press lace edges toward center

and baste, so that edges are kept free from subsequent stitching. Place second fabric square, the back, on pillow front, right sides facing and all outer edges matching. Pin, baste and stitch all around pillow, $\frac{3}{4}$in (2cm) from outer edges, leaving a 10in (25cm) opening in the seam of one side, for turning.
4 Trim seams and clip across corners. Turn pillow cover right side out. Remove all basting. Press carefully.

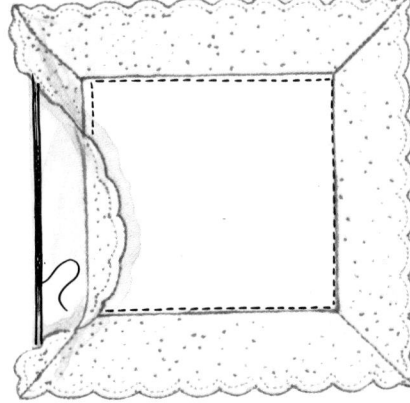

5 Place pillow form inside pillow cover. Turn in open edges and slip stitch edges together to close.

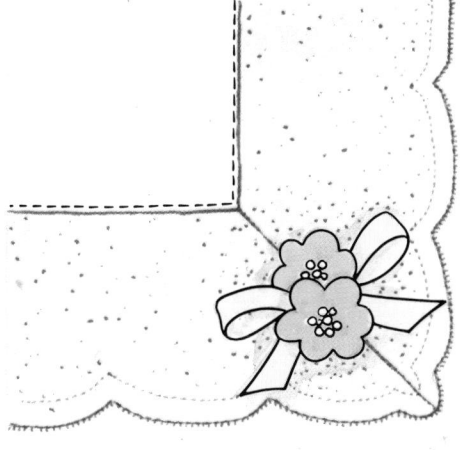

6 Hand sew fabric flowers to one corner of hanky.

Heart-centered pillow
Finished size
15in (38cm) square.

Materials
16$\frac{1}{2}$in (42cm) square of white and beige printed cotton fabric
Two pieces of beige printed cotton fabric, one 16$\frac{1}{2}$in (42cm) square and one 12$\frac{1}{2}$in (31.5cm) square
1$\frac{1}{2}$yd (1.3m) of $\frac{1}{4}$in (5mm)- wide brown velvet ribbon
One 11in (28cm)-square white handkerchief with 1$\frac{1}{8}$in (3cm)- wide lace border
One 12$\frac{1}{2}$in (31.5cm) square of light-weight batting; thread
One 15in (38cm) pillow form
A sheet of drawing paper

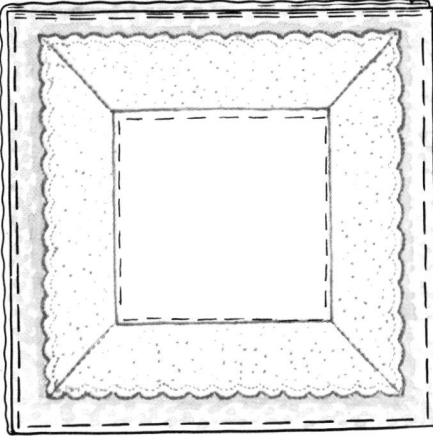

1 Center hanky face up on right side of small beige print square; baste.
2 Place this fabric square, right side up, on batting. Pin and baste.

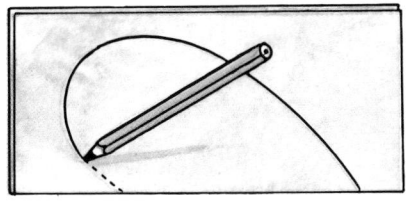

3 On piece of paper draw a heart pattern: fold paper in half, draw half the heart shape 4$\frac{3}{4}$in (12cm) long and 2$\frac{1}{2}$in (6.5cm) wide at widest part, with fold at center. Unfold paper.

4 Center heart pattern on right side of hanky and pin in place. With contrasting sewing thread, work fine running stitch around pattern through all thicknesses of fabric and batting. Remove paper pattern.

5 Work two more rows of running stitch, inside the first, about $\frac{1}{8}$in (3mm) apart.
6 Using contrasting sewing thread, stitch around the edge of the hanky, through all thicknesses of fabric and batting. Stitch a second row, $\frac{3}{8}$in (1cm) inside the first row.

7 Center completed fabric square face up on right side of white and beige print fabric square. Pin, baste and stitch in place, close to edge.

8 Pin, baste and slip stitch velvet ribbon around pillow front over existing stitching line, mitering the corners.

9 Place completed front of pillow cover on the larger of the two beige print fabric squares, right sides together and raw edges matching. Pin, baste and stitch all around, $\frac{3}{4}$in (2cm) from outer edge and leaving a 10in (25cm) opening in the center of one side seam.
10 Trim seams and clip corners. Turn pillow cover right side out.
11 Insert pillow form. Turn in open edges and slip stitch edges together to close.

Terry Evans

119

Homemaker

Cushioned comfort

This stylish patchwork headboard is just two cushions hung from a curtain rod. The traditional patchwork design, called log cabin, can be made on a sewing machine.

Finished size
Each is about 28×21in (72×54cm).

Materials
2¾yd (2.5m) of 45in (115cm)-wide solid dark cotton poplin
¾yd (.6m) of 45in (115cm)-wide cotton print fabric in each of seven different but harmonizing prints— three dark and four light colored
⅜yd (.3m) of 45in (115cm)-wide solid light cotton fabric
1¼yd (1.1m) of 45in (115cm)-wide white cotton fabric for backing
Matching sewing thread
Two pieces of 3in (7.5cm)-thick foam, each 28×21in (72×54cm)

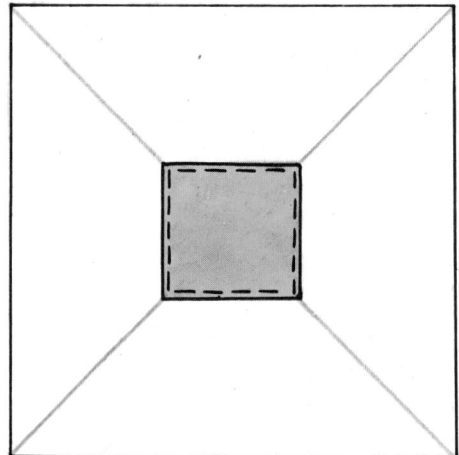

1 Cut out the pieces from solid dark cotton poplin, following the cutting layout. These measurements include ⅜in (1cm) seam allowances.
2 Cut out 48 strips 1½×8in (4×20.5cm) long from each of the eight fabrics, cutting parallel to the grain of the fabric.
3 From solid light cotton fabric cut out 24 pieces 1½in square for the centers.
4 From white cotton backing fabric cut out 24 pieces 8½in (22cm) square. Measure and draw the squares accurately on fabric before cutting them.

5 On the side of each white backing square, using a pencil, lightly draw two diagonal lines from corner to corner to establish the center point.
6 Center one solid light square on one marked backing square, matching center points and the straight grain; baste in place.
7 Choose your arrangement of fabrics so that two adjoining sides are in light colors and the opposite adjoining sides are in a darker or contrasting color; this forms the basis of the design.

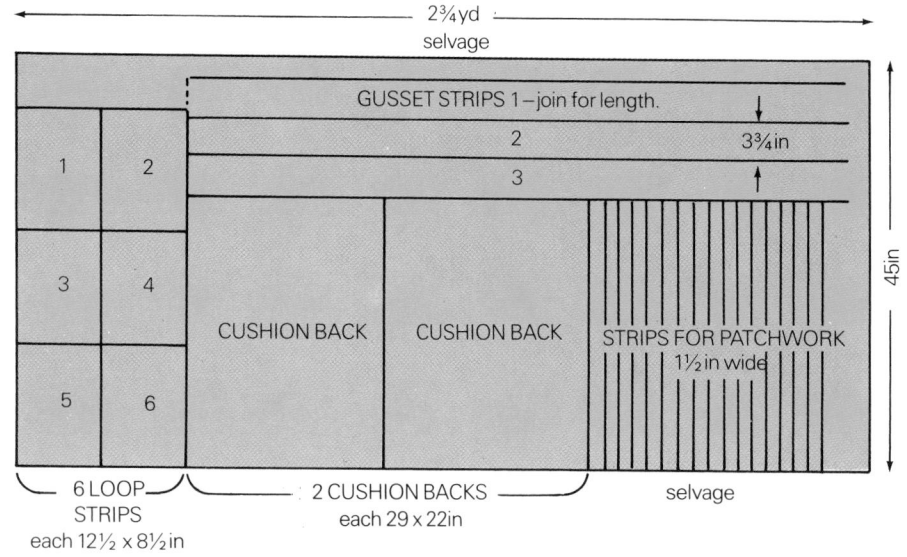

John Hutchinson

120

Terry Evans

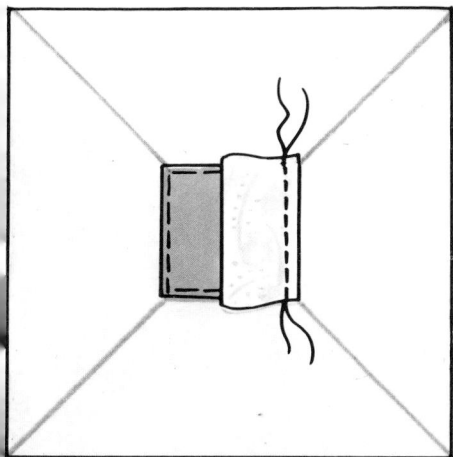

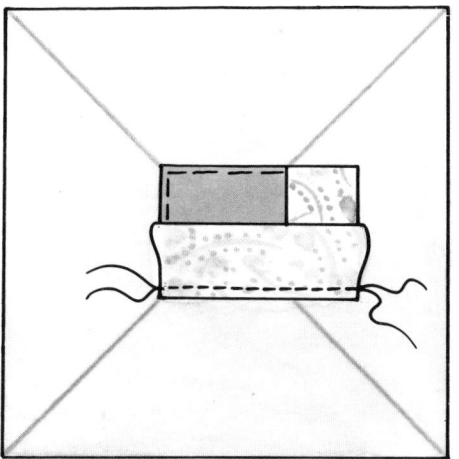

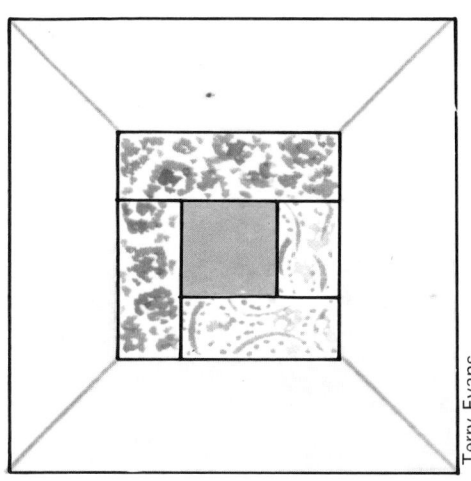

8 Place the first strip face down on center square matching raw edges, trimming off excess strip to fit. Pin, baste and stitch along seamline. Fold strip over to right side.

9 Similarly, working in a clockwise direction, pin, baste and stitch a second strip in the same fabric to the second side of the center square and the end of the first strip.

10 Continue around the square, attaching the next two (darker) strips, again trimming the strips to the correct length. This completes the first round of the patchwork.

Paul Williams

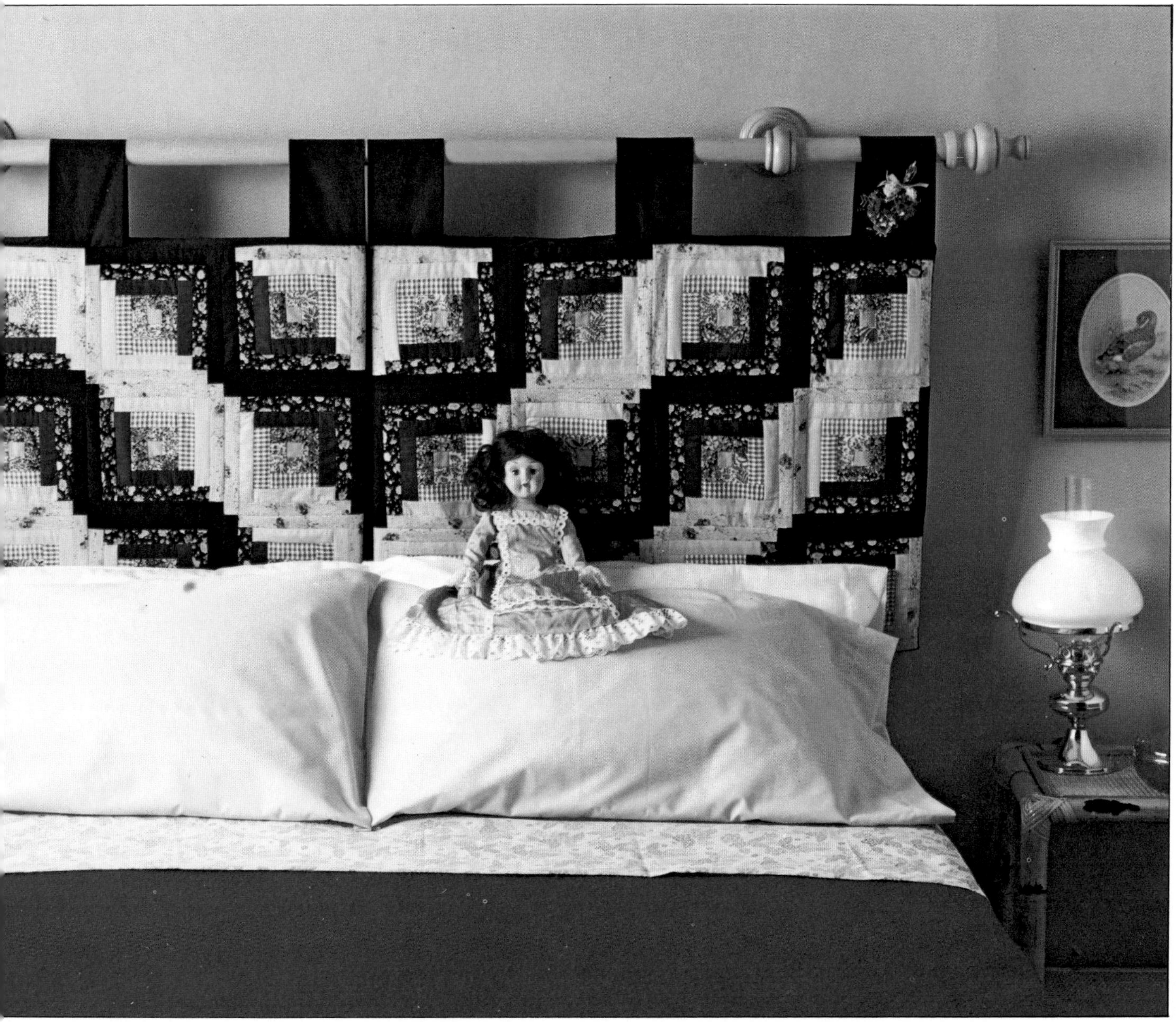

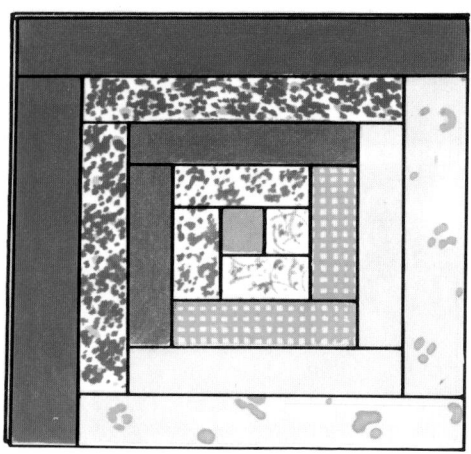

adjoining squares with right sides together, matching edges; pin, baste and stitch together. Repeat to stitch all the 12 patchwork squares together to form the cushion front, which measures about 29 × 22in (74 × 56cm).

15 Repeat step 14 to make the second cushion front in the same way.

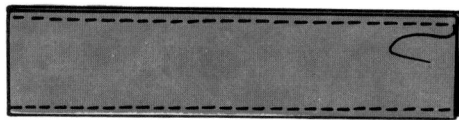

16 Fold one loop piece in half widthwise with right sides together. Pin, baste and stitch long edges. Turn loop strip right side out. Topstitch ⅜in (1cm) from the edge of both long sides.

17 Repeat step 16 to make five more loop strips in the same way.

18 With right sides together, pin and baste one short edge of three loop strips along the top edge of the patchwork

11 Continue this pattern, working around the square clockwise, until you have used all the different fabric strips. Always use light fabrics for the first two sides and the darker or contrasting fabrics for the opposite sides. The finished square is about 8in (20cm).

12 It is important to keep the strips parallel to the sides of the original square in the center to ensure that the final shape is accurate, although you may find each patchwork square varies slightly.

13 Repeat steps 8 to 12 to make 23 more squares in the same way.

14 Arrange 12 of the patchwork squares in an interesting pattern. Place two

cushion front, with the two outer loop strips ⅜in (1cm) from side edges of cushion front and the third loop strip halfway between the two.

19 With right sides together, pin, baste and stitch gusset strip pieces together to form one long strip.

20 With right sides together and leaving a ⅜in (1cm) overlap at the first corner, pin, baste and stitch the gusset strip around the patchwork cushion front. It is easier to stitch one side at a time, then snip the gusset seam allowance at the corner before turning the fabric. Just before the end of the fourth side, cut away excess gusset strip, leaving ⅜in (1cm) for seam. Use the rest of strip for second cushion.

21 Pin, baste and stitch the short edges of gusset strip together to fit cushion front. Finish stitching gusset to cushion front.

22 Fold loop strips up to meet the other

side of the gusset; pin and baste in place. With right sides together, pin, baste and stitch cushion back to gusset, catching in loops and matching corners with corner positions on gusset. Leave a 27in (68cm) opening along the bottom edge.

23 Turn cushion cover right side out. Insert foam. Turn in opening edges and slip stitch together to close.

24 Repeat steps 20 to 23 to complete the second cushion in the same way.

25 Fix a drapery rod to the wall securely, at the correct height for a headboard, and slip the cushions over it.

Paul Williams

Rug in the round

This circular rug in warm harmonious colors is easily made from heavy cord covered with bands of rug yarn.

Finished size
About 37½in (95cm) in diameter.

Materials
- 10½oz (300g) each of six shades of rug yarn
- 68yd (63m) of heavy cord
- Masking tape
- Two large tapestry needles
- Fabric glue
- Sharp craft knife

1 Choose the starting color for the rug center and cut a 2¼yd (2m) piece from the first ball of yarn.

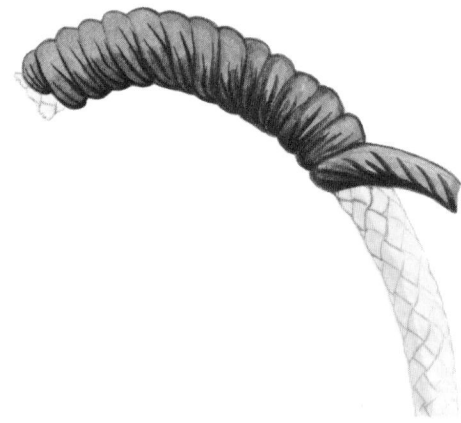

2 Open a package of cord and find the end. Wind one end of the yarn around and around the cord end tightly. Tuck in the end of the yarn and keep winding evenly around the cord, until you have covered a length of about 3in (7.5cm), which is long enough to be coiled.

3 Thread·the other end of the yarn onto one of the needles.

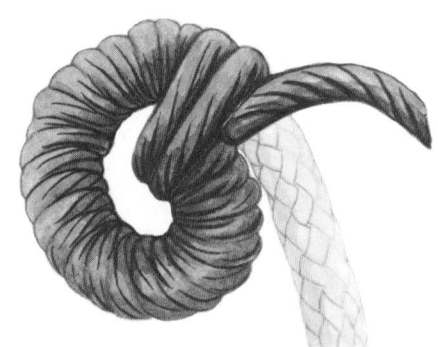

4 Bend the bound end of the cord into a coil. Hold the coil tightly and draw the threaded needle through the center of the coil twice, pulling the yarn taut each time, to hold the coil in place.

5 Lay the uncovered cord against the coil and wind the threaded yarn three times around the cord and then twice through the center of the coil.

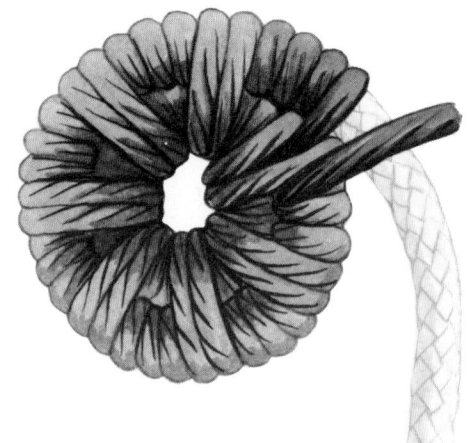

6 Repeat step 5 until you have worked once around the coil. This forms the center on which to work.

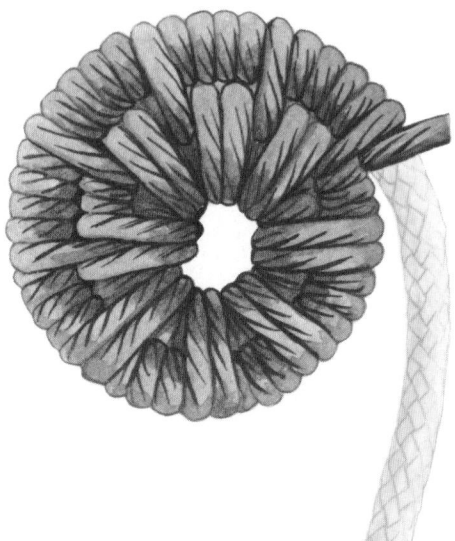

7 Keep laying the uncovered cord against the previously-worked section and wind the yarn four times around the cord and then once into the previous row. This is the pattern and is repeated continuously to make the rug.

8 Alternate bands of different colored yarn to produce the random color scheme.

9 To change to a different color yarn or to add a new piece of the same color, use the following method: The change-over should take place when you still have about an 8in (20cm) length of the working yarn left and at the beginning of the winding pattern.

10 Cut a new piece of yarn. Thread one end of the new piece of yarn onto the second needle.

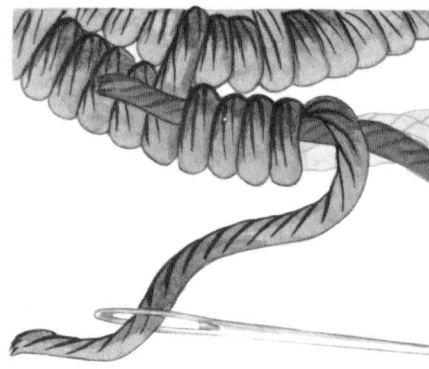

11 Lay the unthreaded end of the new piece of yarn behind the cord and the working piece, at the back of the rug. Work over the cord and the new piece of yarn four times.

12 Then take the new piece and twist it around the old piece at the back of the cord, reversing their places. Take the new piece of yarn and finish the pattern by working a stitch into the previous row in the normal way. Continue working with the new piece.

Spike Powell

124

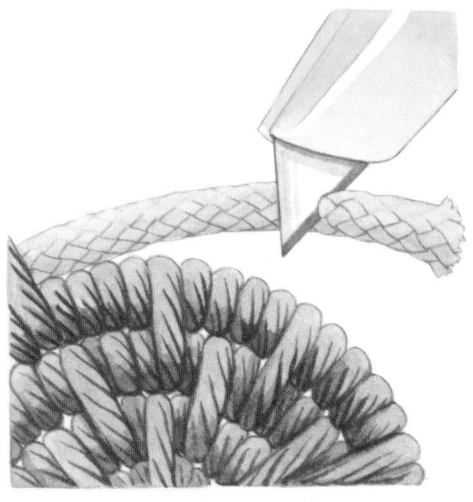

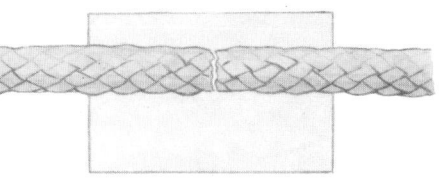

15 Cut a piece of tape 2in (5cm) long. Place both ends of cord in the center of the tape, so they meet in the middle. Put a dab of glue between the two ends and press them together.

16 Roll the tape tightly around the cord ends once. Trim the tape and smooth it in place.

17 When the rug is finished, trim away any extra cord. Place the end neatly against the last round and continue working around until the cord end is covered.

18 Weave the end of the yarn into the back of the rug.

19 Press the rug with a damp cloth and hot iron to smooth it out flat. Brush if necessary.

13 Keep the old end of yarn at the back of the cord and work the next four rounds over it. Cut off the old piece and continue as before with the new length of yarn.

14 To add a new piece of cord, trim off both ends of cord—the old and the new—with a sharp craft knife. Be careful to cut straight across the cord, not at an angle, so they butt together neatly.

Homemaker

Swing high, swing low

Crochet a hammock and spend your days lazing in the shade. We made ours in a strong white cotton yarn and dyed it bright pink.

Size
87in (220cm) by 26in (66cm).

Materials
18 x 4oz (100g) of a medium-
   weight cotton yarn
Size F (4.00mm) crochet hook
Two pieces of bamboo 1¼in (3cm) x
   22in (55cm)
Two fiberglass rings with a diameter
   of 3in (7.5cm)
Packet of colorfast dye

Coral Mula

Gauge
3 patts measure 4¼in (11cm) on size F
(4.00mm) hook with yarn used double.

Note The yarn is used double throughout.
If you want to dye the hammock, dye and
fix the cotton yarn before you start to
crochet. Unfold each skein and follow
the detailed instructions that are
enclosed with the dye.

1 Make a slip knot on the hook and then
1 ch. Work 1 sc into the 1 ch.

2 Extend loop on hook, drawing it out so
that it is approx ¾in (2cm) in length.
Wind yarn over hook and draw it through
this loop.

3 Insert hook from front to back under the
top of the vertical loop, wind yarn over
the hook and draw it through so that
there are 2 loops on the hook and all the

extended strands of yarn are held together at the top.

4 Now wind the yarn over the hook and draw it through the 2 loops on hook to complete the first Solomon's knot st.
5 Repeat steps 2 to 4 36 times more, until you have 37 Solomon's sts in all.

6 Now work the patt row. Begin by working 6 ch, work 1 Solomon's st, sl st into first free knot before the 6 ch, * 1 ch, now work 2 Solomon's sts, skip next knot, sl st into the next knot, rep from * to end.
Turn.

7 Continue to work the patt row, but working last sl st into top of the ch, until work measures 87in (220cm) at side edge. Fasten off.

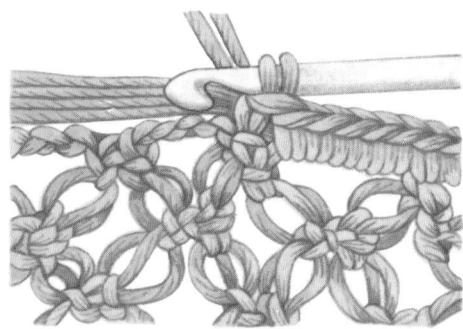

8 Cut 4 pieces of yarn each 100in (250cm) long. Placing pieces of yarn along one side edge and using yarn double, work sc over ch and yarn to reinforce edge working 5 sc over 6 ch and 1 sc into each row end. Fasten off. Leave about 6in (15cm) of reinforcing yarn free at each end. Work other side to match.
9 To attach bamboo, join 2 strands of yarn to first free knot at one end of hammock. Working over bamboo, work 1 sc into each free knot to end. Fasten off. Attach bamboo to other end of hammock in the same way.
10 Using the 6in (15cm) of reinforcing yarn that was left free at each end, bind the ends of the bamboo and fasten with a square knot.

11 Cut 18 pieces of yarn each 55in (140cm) long. Fold pieces in half and fasten to ring as shown (36 strands in all). Divide strands into 3 groups of 12 strands each and braid for 12in (30cm). Tie a knot at the base of each braid. Divide strands in half, wrap ends over bamboo and knot tightly. Trim ends about 4in (10cm) from knot to form tassel.
12 Repeat step 11 and work another braid onto same ring and attach to other end of bamboo.
13 Repeat steps 11 and 12 at the other end of the hammock.